Fort Gibson

Terminal on the
Trail of Tears

Fort Gibson
Terminal on the Trail of Tears

Brad Agnew

University of Oklahoma Press
Norman and London

Library of Congress Cataloging in Publication Data

Agnew, Brad, 1939–
    Fort Gibson, terminal on the trail of tears.

    Bibliography: p.251.
    Includes index.
    1. Indians of North America—Oklahoma—Govern-
ment relations—1789–1869. 2. Indians of North
America—Removal. 3. Fort Gibson, Okla—History.
I. Title.
E78.I5A37   323.1'19'70766   78-21391
ISBN: 0–8061–2207–2 (pbk.)

To Sue and Kelly

Contents

Illustrations

Maps

Acknowledgments

MANY PEOPLE have contributed materially to this study of the first two decades of the history of Fort Gibson. Above all, I wish to express my gratitude to Professor Arrell M. Gibson, George Lynn Cross Research Professor of History at the University of Oklahoma. Throughout a protracted graduate program his support was steadfast, his criticism helpful, and his friendship deeply appreciated. Jack Haley of the University of Oklahoma Western History Collection spent hours of his time suggesting possible avenues of research and assisting in my quest for letters and documents relating to the early history of the post. I also wish to express my gratitude to Mrs. Alice Timmons, former curator of the Phillips Collection of the University of Oklahoma, Mrs. Marie Keene, Gilcrease Museum Library, Mrs. Rella Looney, former Indian Archivist of the Oklahoma Historical Society, and Dr. Elaine Everly of the Old Military Branch of the National Archives. Don Duncan, legislative assistant to Congressman Clem McSpadden, provided significant assistance at several critical junctures by cutting through bureaucratic red tape to help obtain copies of important government documents concerning the history of the post. I also wish to thank Professor David Baird, chairman of the History Department, Oklahoma State University, for making available to me an extensive microfilm file of letters received by the Adjutant General during the 1820's and 1830's. All the members of the staff of the John Vaughan Library of Northeastern Oklahoma State University were helpful, but I wish to express my particular thanks to Mrs. Obera Cude and Mrs. Helen Wheat, whom I called on for assistance repeatedly. My student secretary, Miss Jean Richards, performed yeoman's service in typing notes and rough drafts and transcribing tapes. I am also grateful to Mrs. Madaleine Bauer, who copyread the final draft of the manuscript. Finally, a special word of appreciation to my typist, literary critic, and wife, Sue.

Fort Gibson

Terminal on the
Trail of Tears

Chapter 1

Introduction

THE END OF the War of 1812 was followed by a population surge that brought Americans to the banks of the Mississippi River and beyond in less than a decade. As more land in the east was occupied, the public demanded that the government fulfill promises to remove the Indians from the path of settlement. Although the federal government had advocated removal since the administration of Thomas Jefferson, it was not until public pressure compelled action that federal officials gave removal serious consideration.

James Monroe's Secretary of War, John C. Calhoun, believed that relocation of the Eastern Indians beyond the area of white settlement would allow them time to adjust to the culture and technology of the white man, but like his predecessors Calhoun was not ready to compel the reluctant tribes to vacate their lands. He hoped rather to persuade them of the benefits of removal. That task was made difficult by strife between the Osages and Cherokees in the area where Calhoun planned to settle many of the Eastern tribes. To pacify the region and thus make it more attractive, Calhoun sent a single company of riflemen up the Arkansas River in 1817 to Belle Point, where Fort Smith was established. Although the troops did reduce friction, one company was clearly incapable of stopping it entirely. The garrison was reinforced and in 1824 moved to the Grand River, close to the center of the area contested by the feuding tribes. From that site, eventually named Fort Gibson, the army endeavored to maintain the peace for the next two decades while fifty thousand Eastern aboriginal immigrants reestablished themselves in new homes. The soldiers surveyed boundaries, constructed roads, escorted delegations of Eastern Indians on reconnaissances of the region, established relations with the Plains tribes, mediated intertribal disputes, and attempted to implement the government's removal policy in dozens of other ways.

Charged with executing a policy many Indians bitterly opposed, the army at Fort Gibson became the natural adversary of the tribes residing in the vicinity. Newspapers and letters of the time suggest that conflict was anticipated, and on several occasions war hysteria swept the region. Yet during the emotionally charged years of Indian removal there were no clashes between the Indians and soldiers from Fort Gibson, no Indian was killed by the army, and only one soldier from the post died at the hands of the Indians. The study of army-Indian relations at Fort Gibson during the era of removal indicates considerable restraint on both sides and suggests that sweeping indictments concerning the inhumanity of the army to the Indians during the period of removal must be qualified. During the 1820's and 1830's, the troops at Fort Gibson assisted in the resettlement of the immigrant Indians and cushioned the cultural shock caused by the clash of two divergent cultures.

The history of the first two decades of the post is marked by no dramatic battles or massacres; rather, it is a recital of repeated and frustrating attempts to arrange truces between feuding tribes, to pressure the warlike Plains Indians to abandon their bellicose tendencies, and to resolve intratribal conflicts. Although these mundane peace-keeping activities were not glamorous and received scant attention in most accounts of Indian removal, they restrained the anger and bitterness of fifty thousand immigrant Indians and prevented an uprising that could have set the entire frontier aflame.

The officers and men of Fort Gibson shared the ambitions and prejudices of most civilians. Many of them regarded the Indians who were settling around the post with contempt and suspicion. But unlike civilian pioneers, the soldiers were neither vying with the Indians for land nor attempting to turn a profit by trading with them. Consequently, the army at Fort Gibson usually represented the interests of the Indian more conscientiously than any other frontier institution.

Elected officials at all levels from local through national were frequently confronted with requests from constituents that were difficult to ignore. When popular pressure ran counter to the best interests of the Indian, few politicians could resist the desires of the electorate. Regular army officers were not elected, and their responsibility was to the federal government. Unlike civilian officials in territories or states bordering the Indian frontier, they were better able to resist popular pressure and protect the rights of the Indian.

Matthew Arbuckle, officer who established Fort Gibson and commanded it throughout most of its first two decades.

Since there was relatively little danger to the troops in Indian Territory from hostile Indians, and since the army and tribes lived in close proximity, the soldiers had a better opportunity than most frontier people to know and understand the Indians and their way of life. Because of the cultural gap separating them, few soldiers could appreciate the Indians' traditions and morality, but some of them could understand the problems confronting the tribes as they were forced to accommodate to white society. As a result, military personnel generally were more willing to make allowances for the failures of the Indians to conform to Anglo-Saxon law and Christian morality.

The army of the early nineteenth century was a fairly stable institution. Commanders at all levels retained their positions for years, even decades. Matthew Arbuckle, who founded Fort Gibson, remained at that post until 1841.

During that same period the nation had six presidents and eight secretaries of war. These officials had varying ideas concerning Indian policy and used their high offices to implement these ideas. Although American Indian policy was often erratic, the army tended to minimize the impact of the government's ambivalence and vacillation. During his twenty years in command of the Southwestern frontier, Arbuckle developed a close relationship with the Indians. The tribes of the area knew him and learned to anticipate his reactions. Even though national policy changed, Arbuckle's presence provided an element of stability in government-Indian relations.

Matthew Arbuckle and the soldiers at Fort Gibson, then, served not as the shock troops of white expansion but rather as a cultural buffer between the whites and the Indians. The stereotype that pits the army against the Indian is not confirmed by a study of Fort Gibson during the 1820's and 1830's. Although there are exceptions, military policy was generally designed to ease the clash of cultures, and many of the officers who served at the post showed genuine concern for the welfare of the Native American.

Chapter 2
The Osage-Cherokee Rivalry

GENERAL MATTHEW ARBUCKLE wrote his last report from Fort Gibson on June 21, 1841, with unconcealed pride. For almost two decades he had commanded the turbulent Southwestern frontier and served as a principal agent in implementing the government's policy of Indian removal. Overcoming chronic shortages of personnel and funds, the small garrison commanded by Arbuckle had reduced intertribal strife, opened channels of communication to the Plains tribes, and maintained order as tens of thousands of bitter immigrants established themselves in Indian Territory. Never dashing or heroic, Arbuckle commanded the nation's Southwestern frontier with reason and restraint. His men avoided battle, sought compromise, and endeavored to buffer the accompanying cultural shock to tribes uprooted by the government's policy of Indian removal.

Such service earned the general and his troops no fame and little appreciation, but it enabled Arbuckle to leave Fort Gibson reporting that "at no period have Whites on our border or the Red people of this frontier been in a more perfect state of quiet and Security than they enjoy now."[1] In 1822, when Arbuckle arrived in the Southwest, the American frontier could hardly have been described as quiet and secure. The entire area resounded with the battle cries of Indians forced there by the surge of American settlers filling the interior valleys of the continent.

The Osages were one of the first tribes forced by white pressure to migrate to the area that would eventually be designated Indian Territory. In 1802, the year before the United States acquired Louisiana from France, the governor-general of the province revoked the monopoly to trade with the Osages which had been granted Auguste Chouteau, a St. Louis merchant. Refusing to relinquish this profitable commerce, Chouteau sent his half brother, Pierre, to persuade a number of influential chiefs, including Cler-

7

mont and Pawhuska, to move their bands to the southwest near the confluence of the Arkansas, Grand, and Verdigris rivers. In this Three Forks region, Chouteau could maintain his commercial relations with the Osages without violating the terms of the monopoly which had been transferred to one of his rivals.[2]

When the United States acquired Louisiana, efforts were made to persuade the Osages living near the Three Forks to rejoin the tribe in Missouri. Pierre Chouteau, who had been appointed Agent of Indian Affairs for Upper Louisiana, promised his superiors that he would strive to effect such a reunion. By 1806, however, it was apparent that he would be unable to convince the Osages to abandon the region. The same year, Captain Zebulon M. Pike, who visited the Osage villages in Missouri, recommended that the government alter its policy and encourage the entire tribe to move to the Arkansas River to promote white settlement of Upper Louisiana. Eventually, Pike's recommendation was accepted, and by the mid-1820's, the majority of the tribe resided in villages along the Grand and Verdigris.[3]

The Osages' claim to their new home did not go unchallenged; the Cherokees were also interested in the region beyond the Mississippi. They asked the Quapaws' permission to settle along the Arkansas River in the mid-1790's, and the first significant movement of the Cherokees across the Mississippi was stimulated by an incident that occurred in 1794. An anti-white faction of Cherokees led by Chief Bowles quarreled with a party of white immigrants on their way down the Tennessee River. A number of whites were killed, and Chief Bowles, fearful of reprisals, led his followers across the Mississippi to the St. Francis River valley, outside the jurisdiction of the United States.[4]

During the administration of Thomas Jefferson, federal officials actively encouraged Cherokee removal. In 1808, Jefferson's Secretary of War suggested that the tribe exchange Eastern lands for a tract in Arkansas. That same year, in an effort to facilitate removal, the government induced the Osages to cede to the United States their claim to much of their land in what is now Missouri and Arkansas. Jefferson notified the Cherokees that they were free to exchange their eastern lands for a tract beyond the Mississippi. Cherokee reconnaissance parties were dispatched and returned with favorable reports on the region. Although no formal agreement was negotiated, many Cherokees relocated on lands ceded by the Osages.[5]

Chief Bowles, sometimes called "The Bowl," was one of the first Cherokee chiefs to settle west of the Mississippi River. From a sketch by William A. Berry.

In December, 1811, violent earthquakes rocked the St. Francis River region where most of the Western Cherokees had settled. Secondary tremors continued for many years, convincing the Cherokees that the Great Spirit disapproved of the region. The Indians abandoned the area and moved westward, resettling between the Arkansas and White Rivers. The migration of so many Cherokees made it difficult for their agent in Tennessee to supervise the entire tribe. In June, 1813, William L. Lovely, who had been assistant agent in Tennessee, established an agency for the Western Cherokees on the Arkansas River. Within a few months after his arrival, Lovely was reporting conflict between the Cherokees and Osages.[6]

The Osage-Cherokee rivalry was of long standing; as early as 1777, a Spanish official reported that the Osages were hostile to the tribes residing east of the Mississippi in the "English district." The antagonism between the two tribes increased as their relocations brought them closer together. By 1808, the Osages were protesting against Cherokee hunting parties on the White River which "crept into [the area] without there promission."[7]

The American government expressed little concern over the conflict which existed in the Indian country beyond the frontier until whites began settling along the Arkansas River. Intertribal warfare often produced white victims. With the tide of westward settlement moving across the Mississippi, the danger to American citizens could no longer be ignored. Agent Lovely's major concern after his arrival in the country being settled by the Arkansas Cherokees was to protect whites by ending hostilities among the tribes. Accordingly, in the fall of 1813, Lovely persuaded the Cherokees to send a chief and eight men to the Osage villages to propose an end to the strife. About the same time, a deputation of Osages reached the Cherokee agency bearing letters of peace. Lovely suceeded in negotiating a shaky truce between the feuding tribes.[8]

The frontier's problems were not exclusively Indian in origin. Lovely described some of the whites living in the Arkansas valley as having "the Worst Character" and as being dangerous to the peace of the area. The presence of these people, as well as the eventual collapse of the Osage-Cherokee truce, led the agent to conclude that two companies of troops were "absolutely necessary" to maintain peace. Territorial Governor William Clark concurred with Lovely's evaluation and predicted inaccurately that a corps of troops would probably be stationed on the Arkansas in the summer of 1815.[9] In reality, two more years would elapse before the War Department established a garrison on the river.

While Clark's recommendation was being considered in Washington, Lovely arranged another council between the Osages and Cherokees at the Three Forks in the summer of 1816. There he suggested that tension between the tribes might be eased if the Osages allowed the Cherokees access to the western hunting grounds. In return for Lovely's promise that the government would reimburse the Cherokees and whites who had claims against them, the Osages ceded a seven-million-acre tract to the Cherokees as a hunting outlet. This cession, known as Lovely's Purchase, encompassed the region north of the Arkansas River extending from the Western Cherokees' settlements to the Verdigris River.[10]

The Osages regarded their agreement with Agent Lovely as something less than a total commitment. The Indian concept of land proprietorship was summarized subsequently by Clermont, who asserted that the sale of Lovely's Purchase "did not give to the Cherokees all the Beaver, Bear, Buffaloe and Deer on our Lands—we Sold. . .Land but not the game on our Land."[11] The Osages' resentment of Cherokee encroachment into their hunting territory provoked renewed conflict. By August, 1817, Governor Clark had received complaints of Osage outrages which were turning the rivers "red with the blood of Cherokees." The enraged leaders of the Arkansas Cherokees informed the governor that they intended to march against the Osages to recover stolen horses. The Cherokees promised to try to avoid bloodshed, but the bitterness of their complaints suggested that recovery of stolen horses was a secondary objective. The Cherokees seemed determined to exact revenge. A St. Louis newspaper of August 23, 1817, reported that a formidable coalition of tribes hostile to the Osages was assembling at the Cherokee villages on the Arkansas River.[12]

In October, 1817, this multi-tribal force marched west. The Osages, who had been lulled into a feeling of security by Cherokee messages of friendship, had departed on their fall hunt little concerned for the safety of the women, children, and old men left behind. The six-hundred-man invading force stopped short of Clermont's village and sent forward a few messengers who invited the Osages to attend a peace council. In Clermont's absence an old man was designated to meet and negotiate with the Cherokees. He became their first victim. Now aware of the defenseless state of the Osage village, the invaders rushed forward to exact retribution for the wrongs their people had endured. The villagers offered little resistance as the Cherokees and their allies plundered and burned the settlement and killed or enslaved those not fortunate enough to escape. Some eighty Osages died in the attack, and over a hundred were taken prisoner. Several of the attackers were wounded, but only one, a Delaware, was killed.[13]

This engagement, generally called the Battle of Claremore Mound, resolved nothing. Its melancholy consequences appear even more tragic in view of the War Department's approval of Lovely's three-year-old request to locate troops on the Arkansas River. The troops that might have prevented the massacre were en route the day the Cherokees struck. In late July, the War Department had ordered General Andrew Jackson, commander of the army's Southern Department, to establish a garrison on the Arkansas near the Osage-Cherokee border to restore peace. Major Stephen H. Long, a member of the army's Corps of Topographical Engineers, made a hasty reconnaissance and selected a site where the Poteau River joined the Arkansas. The actual work of constructing and commanding the post, designated Fort Smith, was left to another major, William Bradford, a veteran of the War of 1812. He reached the site selected by Long on Christmas Day, 1817.[14]

Although fewer than a hundred men were assigned to the garrison, the presence of the military temporarily restrained the warring tribes. Leaders of the Cherokees, accompanied by their new agent, Reuben Lewis, enlisted Major Bradford's assistance in terminating hostilities. Bradford informed the Osages of the Cherokees' desire for peace and proposed a meeting of the belligerents. In September, 1818, both tribes sent delegations to St. Louis, where they affixed their marks to a document which obligated them to keep the peace. At the same time, another treaty was negotiated by which the Osages ceded to the United States the land purchased unofficially by William Lovely in 1816. They also agreed not to restrict the free passage of the Cherokees to the hunting grounds.[15]

The truce negotiated at St. Louis was of short duration. By winter each tribe was accusing the other's hunting parties of stealing horses or furs. The Cherokees refused to honor the provisions of the St. Louis treaty obligating them to return prisoners. The Osages considered war, but were reluctant to renew large-scale hostilities with their better-armed adversaries. Nathaniel Pryor, a trader residing among the Osages, hurried to Fort Smith to seek the army's assistance in forcing the Cherokees to honor the treaty. At the insistence of Major Bradford, both tribes met at the post in September, 1819, where the Cherokees returned most of the Osage prisoners. Their refusal to restore all the captives insured that intertribal animosity would continue.[16]

Before the spring of 1820, the Cherokees accused Osage hunting parties of stealing horses and killing at least three of their men. Arkansas' first territorial governor, James Miller, warned the Secretary of War that "The Cherokees are very strongly inclined to make war on the Osages." The observation was accurate. In February, 1820, a Cherokee war party surprised a number of Osages at Pryor's trading post on the Verdigris River. Pryor diverted the Cherokees long enough to enable the Osages to escape. The enraged Cherokees retaliated by stealing 150 pounds of beaver pelts from Pryor.[17] In this charged atmosphere, a full-scale resumption of hostilities seemed certain.

The energetic response of Arkansas' newly appointed governor served to delay the inevitable. Shortly after reaching the territorial capital at Arkansas Post, Governor Miller traveled to the Cherokee settlements, where his discussion with tribal leaders convinced him that their claims against the Osages were exaggerated. The Cherokees seemed to be attempting to create a justification for plans to seize Osage lands, which they considered superior to their own holdings between the Arkansas and White Rivers.[18]

Despite doubts concerning the accuracy of the Cherokee accusations, Miller traveled to the Osage country, where tribal leaders confessed that some of their men were guilty of robbing and killing three Cherokees. While expressing their willingness to surrender the assailants, the Osages protested that the Cherokees' demands for justice appeared contrived in view of their refusal to honor the St. Louis treaty of 1818, which called for a restoration of all captives. When four young Cherokee warriors who had accompanied the governor confirmed that their tribe still held Osage captives, Miller decided to defer action until both sides were willing to comply fully with their promises. Representatives of the two tribes agreed to meet in October at Fort Smith, where both pledged to fulfill their commitments.[19]

The meeting planned for Fort Smith had to be postponed because Governor Miller was unable to leave Arkansas Post while the territorial legislature was in session. By the time he reached the fort in November, prospects for reconcilation between the two tribes had been shattered by an Osage attack on a Cherokee party hunting on the Canadian River earlier in the month. Miller, who had spent almost a year trying to bring the tribes to terms, held out little hope for "settling the difficulties." The governor's pessimistic evaluation was confirmed by the Osage refusal to attend the conference at Fort Smith.[20]

Not ready to admit failure, Miller journeyed up the Arkansas River to negotiate directly with the Osages. Apparently, they promised to refrain from immediate offensive action until the governor informed them of Cherokee intentions. The Cherokees were in no mood to compromise; they had already determined on retaliation. By December, Shawnee and Delaware warriors were reported en route from Indiana to join the Cherokees in a campaign against the Osages. The *Arkansas Gazette* reported that "Miller was reluctantly obliged to let them [the Cherokees] settle their dispute in their own way."[21]

Immediate conflict was averted by the intercession of Matthew Lyon, the government agent at the United States Factory at Spadre Bayou, who persuaded the Cherokees to delay their planned counterattack. Lyon's efforts to restrain the Cherokees suffered a setback, however, when the chiefs received a letter from Governor Miller reiterating his decision to free the Cherokees to resolve their problems with the Osages in their own way. Lyon grumbled that Miller's letter had left the Cherokees "at liberty to let loose the Dogs of War," but still the chiefs did not send their war parties against the Osages.[22]

Not everyone learned that the Cherokees had been restrained. The Osages, who had kept their promise not to renew the conflict until they heard from Governor Miller, were informed by messengers from Major Bradford that the Cherokees had decided on war. This breakdown in communication was a reflection of conflicting instructions from Washington. The War Department directed the governor to endeavor by "prudent exertion of your influence and authority" to preserve peace. If the tribes persisted in their hostilities, Miller was instructed not to intervene except to protect American lives and property. But about six weeks earlier, Secretary of War John C. Calhoun, the author of Miller's instructions, had advised Major Bradford that the Cherokees "must not go to war to obtain" redress even if they had been injured by the Osages.[23]

In effect, then, the Secretary of War sent two of his agents contradictory instructions. Miller was following his orders when he sanctioned the resumption of hostilities. Not surprisingly, Bradford wrote his superiors, "I felt some delicacy in interfering while Gov. Miller was here inasmuch as his and my views on Indian Subjects differ." However, when Miller left Arkansas Territory to spend the summer in New Hampshire, Bradford resorted to threats to prevent conflict. He sent warnings to both parties that refusal to allow government authorities to resolve their differences would result in a termination of government "favours."[24] Although Bradford and Lyon were successful in their endeavor to restrain the Cherokees, news of their success apparently failed to reach the Osages.

In early April, 1821, the Osages, assuming that war had begun, assembled a force of about four hundred men and marched down the Arkansas valley to strike the Cherokees on their own ground. En route the Osages requested gunpowder at Fort Smith. Had Major Bradford been there, he might have turned the Osages back by informing them that the Cherokees had been restrained. Unfortunately, at that time the major was visiting his family in St. Louis, and the officer left in command, fearing the garrison was about to be attacked, refused to allow the Osages to cross the river. Within sight of the fort the war party killed three Quapaws and then continued downriver. Advance parties reached the outskirts of the Cherokee settlements, where they killed three Delawares before being forced to retreat by Cherokee defenders. This incursion left the Cherokees determined to carry the war to the heart of the Osage Nation. Seeking the assistance of the Eastern Cherokees and neighboring tribes, the Arkansas Cherokees planned to counterattack in late May. Pleas of government agents for moderation were ignored.[25]

Sensing the danger to his people, Clermont, who apparently had consented to the attack on the Cherokees, announced that he deplored the killing of the Quapaws and Delawares and the looting of the property of American citizens. Many of the Osage chiefs were "sick of the war, and sorry for the misconduct of their people." Hoping to avoid more conflict, Clermont sent word to Cherokee chief Walter Webber offering to restrain his warriors for three months to give the Cherokees time to decide whether they would retaliate or seek peace. The chief warned that he was not begging for peace; if the Cherokees rejected his offer, he threatened to "send an army of 1500 warriors" who would continue the war "with vigor."[26]

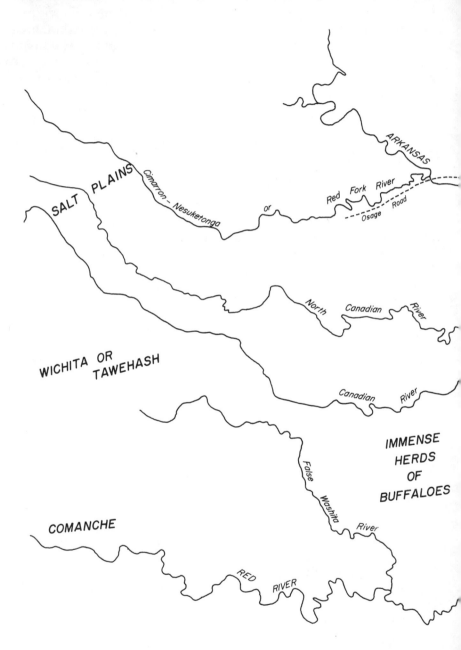

THE AMERICAN SOUTHWEST BEFORE 1830
INDIAN AND WHITE SETTLEMENTS, SURVEYS, TRAILS, AND ROADS

ARKANSAS

SALT PLAINS

Cimarron - Nesuketonga

or

Red Fork River

Osage Road

North Canadian River

WICHITA OR TAWEHASH

Canadian River

IMMENSE
HERDS
OF
BUFFALOES

False Washita River

COMANCHE

RED RIVER

Compiled by Grant Foreman

The American Southwest before 1830.

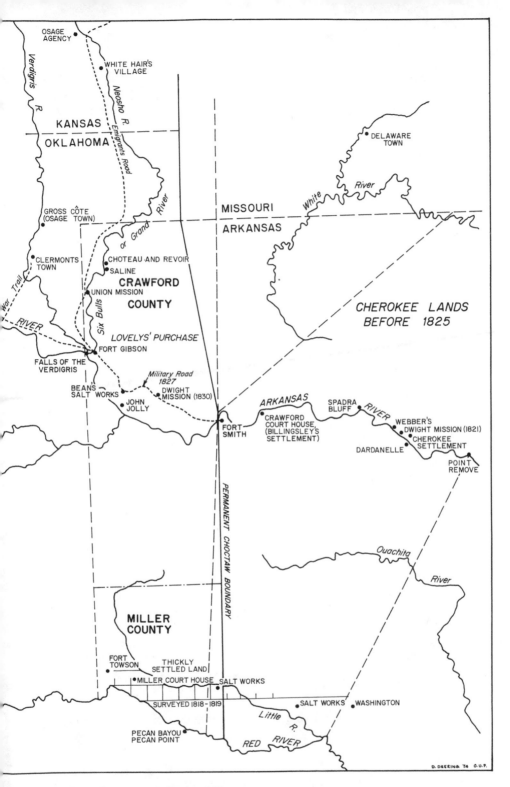

OSAGE
AGENCY

WHITE HAIR'S
VILLAGE

Verdigris R.

KANSAS

OKLAHOMA

Neosho R.

Emigrants Road

DELAWARE
TOWN

White River

GROSS CÔTE
(OSAGE TOWN)

MISSOURI

ARKANSAS

or Grand River

CLERMONTS
TOWN

CHOTEAU AND REVOIR
SALINE

CRAWFORD
COUNTY

CHEROKEE LANDS
BEFORE 1825

War Trail

UNION MISSION

Six Bulls

RIVER

LOVELYS' PURCHASE

FORT GIBSON

FALLS OF THE
VERDIGRIS

Military Road 1827

BEANS
SALT WORKS

DWIGHT
MISSION (1830)

JOHN
JOLLY

ARKANSAS

SPADRA
BLUFF

RIVER

WEBBER'S

FORT
SMITH

CRAWFORD
COURT HOUSE,
(BILLINGSLEY'S
SETTLEMENT)

DWIGHT MISSION (1821)

CHEROKEE
SETTLEMENT

DARDANELLE

POINT
REMOVE

PERMANENT CHOCTAW BOUNDARY

Ouachita River

MILLER
COUNTY

FORT
TOWSON

THICKLY
SETTLED LAND

MILLER COURT HOUSE

SALT WORKS

SURVEYED 1818-1819

Little R.

SALT WORKS

WASHINGTON

PECAN BAYOU
PECAN POINT

RED RIVER

D. DEERING 74 O.U.P.

From Grant Foreman, *Indians and Pioneers*.

Anticipating further violence in the Southwest, the War Department ordered the Seventh Infantry from Georgia to posts on the Arkansas and Red rivers. Before the regiment arrived, the Cherokees rejected Clermont's offer of peace and sent a war party under the command of Walter Webber to invade the Osage country. On June 23, 1821, this force attacked the trading post of Joseph Revoir, a French-Osage business associate of Auguste Pierre Chouteau. After killing Revoir and looting his trading post, the Cherokees retired without further acts of violence.[27]

The attack left the frontier alive with rumors during the summer. White settlers were advised to evacuate their homes because of Cherokee plans to resume offensive operations. The Osages were reported to be gathering a fifteen-hundred-man force on the White River. Their agent asserted that the Arkansas band was "decidely in favour" of war. Major Bradford worked vigorously to avert a renewed confrontation. In early September he visited Clermont, who again indicated a willingness to restrain his warriors until negotiations could be arranged. Bradford immediately notified the Cherokees, who refused to consider the new peace proposal. They did, however, agree to confer with him on their way to attack the Osages. At the meeting the major explained the Osage proposal and assured the Cherokees that the "President would see Justice done them in every respect." The Cherokees rejected the offer, explaining that "they had started for war and they was determined to have satisfaction in their own way." Neither reason nor threats dissuaded the Cherokees. The three-hundred-man party continued on its mission of revenge.[28]

As in 1817, the Cherokees had picked a time to attack when most of the Osage warriors had marched west to the Plains. The fall campaign of 1821 was in some respects similar to the 1817 attack that resulted in the massacre at Claremore Mound. About November 1, the Cherokees stormed an Osage village. Although a few warriors in the village were able to hold the Cherokees at bay until some of the women and children escaped, Osage losses were estimated at about one hundred killed or captured.[29]

In the months following the Cherokee attack, a number of efforts were made to restore peace. Governor Miller sent the Osage sub-agent, Nathaniel Philbrook, to confer with Clermont, who was bitter about duplicity on the part of government agents who had restrained his warriors while allowing the Cherokees to attack. Tally, the second chief of Clermont's village, proved more receptive. He and Philbrook eventually convinced Clermont and his warriors of the desirability of peace. Weary of the constant strife, Tally told his people, "I do not want to live always with *my thumb on the lock of a gun.*"[30]

Philbrook carried the Osage appeal for peace to Governor Miller, who decided to relay the offer to the Cherokees in person. When he arrived at their settlements, he learned that war parties were already out. The principal Cherokee chiefs refused to discuss peace until their return. The governor sent Philbrook to the Osages to urge continued restraint. Over two months had elapsed when Philbrook returned to the Three Forks. It had been a difficult time for the Osages, who were apprehensive about renewed Cherokee incursions. The threat of imminent attack kept Osage hunters close to their villages, and by March their provisions were almost exhausted. Osage anxiety was heightened by Cherokee war parties which roamed the country. The plight of the Osages convinced at least one group of people, the residents at Union Mission,[31] that "the chief's and all the people want peace." Philbrook told the Osages that the governor was attempting to persuade the Cherokees to end the fighting. He also promised to urge the new commander of Fort Smith to prevent the Cherokees from further incursions against the Osages.

The arrival of Colonel Arbuckle and half the companies of the Seventh Infantry at Fort Smith on February 16, 1822, significantly augmented the government's power on the Southwestern frontier. With 250 soldiers between the Osages and the Cherokees, the colonel was optimistic that a treaty could be worked out, but he believed, too, that neither side would honor it unless "they are induced to comply from a fear of the Military force at this post."[32]

The resolute stand taken by Philbrook and Arbuckle apparently influenced Cherokee chief John Jolly to call the other chiefs together to consider an armistice. Without the usual delays, the Cherokees agreed to suspend hostilities until a general peace council could be convened at Fort Smith. Philbrook carried the news to the Osages, who readily affixed their marks to the preliminary treaty.[33] The armistice reassured the destitute Osages, who could now turn their attention to hunting.

From his headquarters at Louisville, Kentucky, General Edmund P. Gaines, commander of the army's Western Department which included Fort Smith, wrote the chiefs of both tribes urging them to observe the armistice. When Tick-e-Toke, a revered

Cherokee leader known as the Beloved Man, received the letter he scoffed at the proposal of peace and hurled the letter down, ground it to shreds with his foot, and spit on it. Tick-e-Toke was convinced that "the treachery, faithlessness, and deceit of the Osages" would prevent them from honoring any treaty. His solution to the Osage problem was extermination.[34]

As the date of the meeting approached, Tally, considered by the missionaries at Union as the most progressive of the Osage chiefs, initially refused to participate in the conference at the fort. This refusal boded ill for peace, since the absence of a leader of his stature would have lessened the chances of reaching an agreement. His oppostion probably stemmed from a difference in opinion with Clermont rather than an objection to the meeting. He eventually relented and joined the other chiefs on their journey to Fort Smith. En route Clermont sounded a note of optimism. "Our heads. . .have been under a cloud, and we could not see. But now the darkness was to be dispersed."[35]

Despite misgivings on both sides, the conference convened on schedule. A delegation of 150 warriors led by Clermont and Tally represented the Osages. Most of the Cherokee chiefs, with the conspicuous exception of Tick-e-Toke, participated. The government delegation was headed by Governor Miller and included Colonel Arbuckle, Cherokee agent David Brearley, and Osage subagent Philbrook.[36]

The negotiations were acrimonious. The Osages were disturbed by Tick-e-Toke's refusal to participate, and the Cherokees considered the Osage demands for the return of all captives unreasonable. It required over a week of negotiation, but on August 9, members of both tribes affixed their marks to a treaty which formally ended hostilities, required the return of Osage captives, granted mutual concessions concerning access to the hunting grounds, and limited redress to legal channels rather than retaliatory raids.[37]

A faction of the Cherokees led by Tick-e-Toke refused to honor the treaty and elected voluntary exile rather than accept the peace. With his followers the old chief migrated to the Kiamichi valley north of the Red River. From its inception this new settlement operated as an irritant to Osage-Cherokee relations.[38]

The first threat to the new peace, however, came not from the dissident Cherokees of Tick-e-Toke's village but rather from the Choctaws. This tribe, like the Cherokees, had a history of conflict

A sketch of Clermont, Osage chief who led his people in their struggle against the Cherokees. From George Catlin, *Letters and Notes on the Manners, Customs, and Condition of the North American Indians*, 1857.

with the Osages. In mid-September, 1822, wounded Osages sought medical assistance at Union Mission. They told the missionaries they had been attacked by Indians from the Red River. A skirmish had occurred on September 12 near the mouth of the Canadian River while the Osages were going to Fort Smith to receive captives the Cherokees had agreed to return. Initial reports reaching Arbuckle implicated the Cherokees in the attack, diminishing hopes that the Fort Smith treaty would be honored. When the colonel learned that only Choctaws were involved in the skirmish, he rushed this information to the Osages and dispatched an express to advise the culprits that the President of the United States "Will not longer permit them to Continue the War with the Osages."[39]

Representatives of the Arkansas Cherokees who were at Fort Smith for the prisoner exchange also hurried to the Osages to assure them they had no role in the attack. Chiefs Walter Webber and John Rogers emphasized that the Cherokees still intended to carry out the treaty's promises by returning the prisoners. Their assurances and Arbuckle's prompt action helped maintain the peace. In fact, the *Arkansas Gazette* reported that after the prisoner exchange at Fort Smith, the Cherokees and Osages "took leave of each other in good friendship."[40]

Prospects for further stabilization of the Osage frontier improved when Auguste P. Chouteau decided to reestablish the Revoir trading center. Located on the site of the old Revoir settlement, the new post increased the Chouteaus' influence over the Arkansas Osages at a time when they were about to be joined by the remainder of the tribe from Missouri. Reports of the impending migration caused Arbuckle to urge officials in Washington to station an agent in permanent residence with the Arkansas Osages.[41]

The colonel also proposed that the garrison he commanded at Fort Smith be relocated higher up the Arkansas near the mouth of the Verdigris. Located there, Arbuckle reported, his command could provide greater security for the territory and encourage white settlement of the area. The commanding general of the army and the secretary of war considered the proposal to relocate Fort Smith but rejected it.[42]

The decision reflected Calhoun's conviction that the Indians should be segregated from the white population in a western territory of their own. The secretary apparently believed that the establishment of a fort at the Three Forks would encourage white settlement of an area he wanted reserved for the Indians. Land-hungry whites needed no such encouragement; by early 1823, Arbuckle informed the War Department that white settlement above the fort was well underway and that many more families were "coming from the Missouri and other places, to settle on the Arkansas between the Poteau & Canadian." Their homes extended forty to fifty miles beyond the garrison and, the colonel warned, "Should their be further difficulties between the Osages and Cherokees . . . the Settlers will be much exposed to the depredations of both parties." If the colonel believed the danger to the settlers would cause Calhoun to reconsider his decision against moving the garrison farther up the Arkansas, he was incorrect. The secretary's response to Arbuckle's report was an order to remove all whites settled beyond the Poteau just as soon as the harvest was completed.[43]

Despite the explicit nature of Calhoun's order to evict white squatters, Arkansas' acting territorial governor, Robert Crittenden, authorized the settlement of four white families in the area and forwarded a persuasive appeal to the Secretary of War. Describing Lovely's Purchase as "the garden spot, of our Territory, its boast and its pride," the acting governor urged that the prohibition on white settlement be lifted. He informed Calhoun that the people of the territory refused to believe that the tract would be turned into an Indian hunting ground. It would be far better, according to Crittenden, to open the territory for white settlement, thus converting it into a barrier between the feuding Osages and Cherokees. Within a month the territorial legislature seconded Crittenden's recommendation, requesting that Congress extend the territory's western boundary to include Lovely's Purchase. The territorial delegate to Congress urged the Secretary of War to move the garrisons on the Red and Arkansas rivers farther west, where they could provide better protection for the frontier.[44]

The disintegration of the peace established by the treaty of 1822 reinforced the recommendations of Arkansas' territorial delegate and Colonel Arbuckle that the troops at Fort Smith be relocated higher up the Arkansas River. By December, 1822, there were clear indications that the treaty of August was no guarantee of peace on the frontier. In Miller County a party of twenty Osages attacked and wounded a white man. Less than a month later, Cherokee hunters reported that one of their companions had been shot and mutilated by an Osage party while he was hunting on the North Fork of the Canadian. The victim was Red Hawk, a nephew of respected Cherokee chief Thomas Graves. The Osages acknowl-

Tally, distinguished Osage warrior of Clermont's village. From George Catlin, *Letters and Notes on the Manners, Customs, and Conditions of the North American Indians,* 1857.

edged that one of their warriors had killed a Cherokee, but they were reluctant to turn the man over to the military for punishment.[45]

In September, after months of futile negotiations, Arbuckle personally visited the Osages, whom he found unreceptive to his suggestions concerning the punishment of the individual accused of killing Red Hawk. Their attitude was not a gesture of defiance; Clermont and many of the leaders of the tribe sincerely desired peace. Hoping to avoid a renewal of fighting, they proposed a compromise which Arbuckle conveyed to the Cherokees. As an indemnity for the death of Red Hawk, the Osages offered to transfer to the Cherokees a part of their annuity. The Cherokees refused, insisting that the letter of the treaty be enforced, which required the surrender of the accused Osage.[46]

Later in September, Arbuckle again met with the Osages and discussed Red Hawk's murder and a recent skirmish with the Cherokees of Tick-e-Toke's band. These discussions bolstered the colonel's confidence that his diplomacy would keep the antagonists apart at least through the hunting season. He was not so optimistic about the following spring. If no solution had been reached by March or April, Arbuckle predicted that the Cherokees and their allies would attempt to administer justice themselves. By then military strength on the Arkansas frontier would be critically low. Accordingly, Arbuckle repeatedly warned the War Department of his dwindling manpower. Other than a stinging rebuke from his immediate superior, General Winfield Scott, for departing from the chain of command by appealing directly to Washington for replacements, Arbuckle accomplished very little.[47] Officials in the War Department moved slowly in response to the colonel's pleas for replacements until an Osage war party spurred them into action.

The Osages were showing the strain of a decade of intermittent warfare in which they suffered heavy casualties and endured great hardship. In November, 1823, in an act of impetuous vengeance, Mad Buffalo, an Osage chief, led his warriors in an attack that produced reverberations all the way to Washington. Two parties of hunters had established camp on the Blue River, a tributary of the Red, about 170 miles southwest of Fort Smith. One party of about a dozen mixed-blood Quapaws was led by Antoine Barraque, a French trader who lived among the Quapaws. They were joined by nine white hunters led by Major Curtis Welborn. Mad Buffalo and about eighty warriors were passing through the same area on their return from an unsuccessful raid against the Caddoes. Osage custom required that lives of warriors lost to an enemy be revenged. The Osages discovered the camp of the Barraque-Welborn party and reconnoitered it for a day. Deciding to attack, the Osages quickly overpowered the hunters, who could offer little resistance against the larger force. It was every man for himself as the hunters fled, leaving four or more of their comrades, including Welborn, dead or dying at the hands of the Osages. A captured Quapaw pleaded with the Osages to spare him because he too was an Indian. Exulting over their victory and anxious that word of it travel rapidly, the Osages spared the Quapaw, ordering him to spread the news that "all were dead." To insure that they received the credit due them, the Osages took care to identify themselves as belonging to Clermont's band.[48]

Reaction to the attack was varied. In its account of the episode, the *Arkansas Gazette* suggested that relations with the Indians had reached a crisis. The editor recommended prompt government action to insure the safety of American hunters and traders. Colonel Arbuckle asserted that the Osage action "leaves but little doubt of their being disposed to go to war with the United States." Further forbearance on the part of the government, Arbuckle believed, would only lead to more aggression. The missionaries at Union disagreed with Arbuckle's conclusion that the massacre was an act of "national hostility." They insisted that "the chiefs of the Nation wholly disapprove of the act and regret it[s] occurrence." The Reverend William F. Vaill, superintendent of Union Mission, hurried to Chouteau's settlement to discuss the attack with Clermont, who was attempting to recover the horses and plunder stolen by his warriors. Vaill noted that while the attack could not be condoned, the Barraque and Welborn parties had been hunting on Indian land without a license.[49]

Arbuckle's position mellowed somewhat when he learned that Clermont had disavowed the act and offered to surrender the offenders, two of whom were his own sons. To test the cooperation pledged by Clermont, the colonel sent Major Alexander Cummings to demand the surrender of the murderers of the white hunters. The Osage chiefs, including Mad Buffalo, returned some of the horses and fur that had been stolen. They again expressed sorrow over the episode and explained that their warriors had not realized they were attacking white men. But when asked to surrender the leaders of the attack, the Osages were evasive. Arbuckle advised

General Gaines that the Osages would probably not surrender the culprits without a show of force and urged that the military garrison on the Arkansas be reinforced and that a small fort be established on the Red River near the mouth of the Kiamichi.[50]

Arbuckle's superiors ordered him to demand the surrender of those responsible both for the attack on the white hunters and for the death of Red Hawk. He thus sent Major Cummings to the Osage villages again to relay a "final demand." Even before he learned the results of the meeting, the colonel predicted that Cummings would "have but little if any prospect for Success." His prediction proved correct. Of the principal chiefs, only Clermont was present; the others were reported to be "scattered on their hunts." Despite Clermont's promise to endeavor to send the culprits to the garrison within fifteen days, Cummings was certain that the Osages had no intention of surrendering them. The missionaries, who had observed the tribe's inability to honor similar commitments, also doubted that the chief would be able to make good on his promise. Despite the seeming finality of Cummings' demand, the army was not prepared to risk a full-fledged Indian war. The major told the missionaries that Arbuckle would do nothing to force the issue until he received specific instructions from Washington. The War Department meanwhile moved cautiously, waiting to see how the Osages would respond to the demands for the surrender of Mad Buffalo and his principal subordinates.[51]

Convinced that the Osages would commit further acts of violence if they were not punished for their earlier offenses, Arbuckle began increasing the pressure on them to surrender the accused warriors. The colonel summoned Subagent Philbrook and instructed him to repeat Cummings' demand to the tribe. Philbrook more than any other man was responsible for the negotiation of the 1822 treaty. If anyone could persuade the Osages to surrender the accused warriors, it was he. The subagent left Fort Smith in late March for the Three Forks. En route, probably while attempting to cross the swollen Grand River, Philbrook was fatally shot by an assailant whose identity was never discovered.[52]

The death of Nathaniel Philbrook was dramatic proof of the inadequacy of the War Department's response to the Osage-Cherokee rivalry. By reacting to the conflict instead of anticipating the predictable consequences of encouraging the tribes to relocate in the west, the department made it difficult for Major Bradford and Colonel Arbuckle to adopt effective measures to resolve the feud. The attack on the Barraque-Welborn party and its aftermath underscored the inability of the military to police the Indian frontier from Fort Smith. In the years since its founding, the tide of white settlement had swept past the garrison. Matthew Arbuckle realized that Fort Smith's location had lost its strategic importance within six months of his arrival. As early as September, 1822, he had suggested that the fort could provide greater security for the territory if it were located higher up the Arkansas a few miles above the mouth of the Verdigris. By 1824, developments on the Southwestern frontier compelled the War Department to accept Colonel Arbuckle's recommendation.

Chapter 3

Garrison on the Grand

IN JANUARY, 1824, two recommendations for bolstering the defenses of the Southwestern frontier were sent to the War Department. Arkansas' Congressional delegate urged Secretary of War John C. Calhoun to relocate the troops on the Red and Arkansas rivers, and General Winfield Scott, commander of the Western Department, recommended the establishment of a post on the Red River near the mouth of the Kiamichi to check the "evils existing, on the Spanish border." About the same time, Scott received a report from Colonel Arbuckle recommending the movement of his command up the Arkansas River. On February 7, 1824, Jacob Brown, the General-in-Chief of the Army, authorized an extension of the military frontier in the Southwest. A month later, General Scott ordered Arbuckle to move his garrison to the mouth of the Verdigris. Scott also ordered two companies of the Seventh Infantry stationed on the Red River to establish an outpost at the mouth of the Kiamichi. The decision to abandon Fort Smith was also influenced by the post's unhealthy condition. In August, 1823, Arbuckle had reported that his "loss by deaths had been considerable," and Scott characterized the post as "an extremely sickly position."[1]

When Scott's directive reached Fort Smith on April 2, 1824, Arbuckle lost little time in executing the orders he had long recommended. Within a week the colonel had completed plans for moving his five companies and essential military supplies to the Three Forks. On April 9, the Seventh Infantry abandoned Fort Smith. Two keelboats carried supplies and a few troops upriver. Most of the soldiers accompanied the regiment's wagons west along a trail already well marked by the Indians, white traders, and missionaries. The supplies that could not be taken and the abandoned facilities at Fort Smith were left in the custody of a fourteen-man caretaker force under the command of Lieutenant Benjamin L. E.

Bonneville. Although the relocation of the garrison was hampered by a "great scarcity of officers and men," operating under strength was the rule in the peacetime army of the nineteenth century and seems to have presented no serious problems in the movement of men and equipment. By April 22, Arbuckle had selected a site and named the new post after the army's commissary general, Colonel George Gibson. Apparently the danger of Indian uprisings on the Arkansas frontier was sufficient to prompt the War Department to respond to Arbuckle's repeated requests for replacements for his depleted companies. Within a mouth of the establishment of Cantonment Gibson, two steamboats carried 102 replacements up the Arkansas.[2]

At the same time Arbuckle was establishing Cantonment Gibson, Major Alexander Cummings proceeded from Fort Smith to the mouth of the Kiamichi, where he rendezvoused with troops from Cantonment Jesup and established a garrison to guard the upper Red River frontier. The post was named Cantonment Towson in honor of General Nathan Towson, Paymaster General of the Army and a hero of the War of 1812.[3] Since both of the companies that garrisoned Cantonment Towson as well as those that remained at Cantonment Jesup belonged to the Seventh Infantry Regiment, those posts were under the operational jurisdiction of the regimental commander, Colonel Arbuckle. Cantonment Gibson was actually the headquarters for all American troops on the Southwestern frontier, although it would be ten years before the War Department would give it that official designation.

Arbuckle's orders instructed him to establish his post at the mouth of the Verdigris River. Since the landing sites for several miles from the mouth of the Verdigris were already occupied by small settlements of Indian traders and fur trappers, the colonel decided that the best place to locate the new post would be three miles up the Grand River on its eastern bank, where a rock ledge extending into the river formed a natural landing. In the vicinity of the post, an extensive canebrake bordered the river and formed an almost impenetrable barrier two miles wide in some places. Beyond the canebrake was a prairie drained by Bayou Menard, which ran to the northeast. The valley was densely timbered with oak, ash, and hackberry and heavily overgrown with nettles and tall weeds. The location was described as a commanding and healthy place "admirable calculated to give security to our western frontiers." An excellent spring was located within two hundred yards of the post.[4]

The men, temporarily housed in tents, set to work hacking back the cane and undergrowth, felling trees, and sawing and hewing logs for buildings for the new garrison. Work continued steadily throughout the post's first year. The health of the men was excellent. No one suspected that malarial fevers and gastro-intestinal maladies endemic to the area would soon give the post the distinction of being the "Charnel House" of the army. By May, 1824, Arbuckle could report that work was nearing completion. Three sides of the garrison's breastworks and barracks for the enlisted personnel were completed. The remaining wall and officers' quarters were scheduled for completion by June. Arbuckle's timetable was optimistic, for in January, 1826, the fourth side of the cantonment remained incomplete and a number of rooms were still under construction. The slow progress on the post prompted General Edmund P. Gaines, the new commander of the Western Department, to express his concern for the defense of the installation in the event of Indian hostilities. Gaines' apprehensions proved groundless; no Indians had threatened the post by April, 1827, when Arbuckle reported the breastworks completed.[5]

The accommodations at Cantonment Gibson were serviceable but not luxurious. Milled lumber and pine for window sashes had to be brought up the Arkansas and consequently were in short supply. Most of the building materials used in the construction of the garrison were fabricated by the troops from the plentiful oaks. Logs for buildings and pickets for the breastwork were hewed by the soldiers, planks were hand sawed, and shingles were split from oak logs. Mud was used to chink cracks. Unfortunately, the green logs did not prove to be a durable building material. Within ten years the post would be "fast going into decay."[6]

The residents at Union Mission did not mind the cantonment's crude appearance. Its location, approximately half a day's ride down the Grand, provided more protection than the missionaries had enjoyed since their arrival in 1820. One of the ministers wrote, "the presence of an adequate military force to awe the uncivilized Indians whose passions are so easily excited, and whose hands are so frequently stained with blood is a consideration which calms and cheers the mind."[7] The prospect of more frequent and faster mail service provided by Colonel Arbuckle's bimonthly military courier was an added advantage of having the post close by.

Improving the lines of communication and transportation to the new outpost was essential. The trail from Fort Smith to the Three

Forks had been adequate for the early traders but could not serve an army post. In March, 1825, Congress authorized the survey of a road between Little Rock and Cantonment Gibson. Because of stringent budgetary limitations, the Secretary of War directed the commander of Cantonment Gibson to employ his troops in building the road. Arbuckle, whose men were still constructing the buildings and fortifications, informed the War Department that "Want of Money, Tents & Tools," made it impossible to begin work immediately. If his troops were scattered on road building parties, the colonel warned, the possibility of a full-fledged Indian war would be increased. Construction of a road to Little Rock would require a force of at least a hundred men for six to eight months. Arbuckle wanted his troops available for immediate assignment, not miles from the post performing common labor on a road.[8]

Apparently Arbuckle's reluctance prompted the adjutant general to appoint a quartermaster officer to superintend the construction of the road. By November, 1825, the Indian danger had subsided and work on the post had advanced enough that Arbuckle agreed to provide a detail of men to open the road. Yet despite the colonel's promise, no troops had been detailed for road work eighteen months after Congress had authorized the survey of the route. In December, 1826, the House of Representatives asked the President to inform it of the status of the project. The War Department explained that the survey had been completed but that Colonel Arbuckle had not been able to spare the men to begin work on the road. Obviously irritated by Arbuckle's dilatory tactics, the Adjutant General ordered him to provide the troops to begin work. Arbuckle assigned Captain Pierce Butler and a detachment of fifty-five soldiers to the task of constructing the section between Cantonment Gibson and Fort Smith. By late August, 1827, Butler had completed the road as far as Fort Smith, and civilian contractors had been hired to construct most of the remainder of the route to Little Rock.[9]

Before construction began on the Cantonment Gibson–Little Rock road, the Adjutant General reported that a road connecting Cantonment Jesup to Cantonments Towson and Gibson was necessary for the defense of the frontier against Indians and potential foreign powers beyond the Red River. In June, 1826, Congress authorized construction with one modification; Arkansas delegate

Henry Conway amended the War Department's proposal to make Fort Smith rather than Cantonment Gibson the northern terminus of the road. Once again the War Department was called upon to provide troops for the project. Arbuckle advised the War Department that a direct route between Cantonment Gibson and Cantonment Towson would provide better protection for the frontier. The colonel was informed that the route had been designated by Congress and could not be changed. Construction on this road did not advance rapidly. Cantonment Towson was permanently short of troops, and in 1828, acute Indian problems along the Red River and poor weather forced the commander of the garrison to discontinue work. Construction on a road running from Fort Smith toward Cantonment Towson would not be resumed until 1832, when the Choctaw agent pressed the War Department to open the route to facilitate the Choctaw migration.[10]

Despite the efforts of the military to improve overland routes, the Arkansas River continued to be the primary link connecting Cantonment Gibson to the rest of the nation. When the post was established, its heavy equipment and supplies were poled upstream in keelboats. Poles soon gave way to steampower, and the river remained the post's principal avenue of resupply for personnel as well as material. Until 1824, Fort Smith had been considered the head of steamboat navigation on the Arkansas; beyond there the river could be treacherous. But the stimulus of army contracts to supply the new post spurred enterprising steamboat captains to extend service to the Three Forks. Cantonment Gibson was not yet a month old when the *Florence* left Little Rock carrying recruits for the Seventh Infantry and thirty tons of freight for the post store. The next spring the steamboats *Spartan* and *Louisville* delivered contractors' supplies and more merchandise for the sutler's store to Cantonment Gibson.[11] Traffic on the river grew steadily, serving not only the army but also civilian merchants and traders residing in the area. In 1827, the steamers began carrying a new cargo to the frontier: the displaced Indians from the East.

The presence of Cantonment Gibson did more than stimulate steamboat navigation above Fort Smith; it also provided justification for a request by Arkansas' territorial delegate for federal funds to improve the river. The delegate argued that "it should not be forgotten that the troops of the garrison are stationed on this river which are designed for the protection of the frontier and that through this channel they are annually supplied." He urged that $15,000 be appropriated to "improve the navigation of the Arkansas river" which "is filled with snags and renders the danger of navigation verry great." In 1832, Congress approved the project. The following year Captain Henry M. Shreve, who developed the army's river clearance program on the Ohio and Mississippi, was ordered to begin work on the Arkansas as soon as his current project was concluded. Shreve's crews worked steadily, but the river was never completely cleared. Seasonal flooding furnished newly uprooted trees to replace those cleared by Shreve's snagboats. But the effectiveness of his work was reflected in the declining insurance premiums paid by riverboat owners.[12]

Congressmen could be generous in their appropriations to the military if it served the interests of their constituents, but few military activities had as much popular support as the army's river clearance project. Throughout most of the nineteenth century the peacetime military operated on an austerity budget, and army posts had to be as self-sufficient as possible. Not only were the troops at Cantonment Gibson expected to build their own fort and construct roads through the frontier, they were also encouraged to grow as much of their own food as possible. In 1818, the War Department had issued a General Order which required military commanders to assign troops to cultivate vegetable gardens. Although no funds were provided for seeds, farm implements, or fencing materials, the department thoughtfully sent commanders copies of *The American Gardener*.[13]

The men required to tend the garden plots outside the walls of Cantonment Gibson, like those erecting buildings and constructing roads, were often excused from military drill, which probably explains the observation of the army's Inspector General, George Croghan, that soldiers of the post knew nothing "about the manual of Artillery or of Lt Infty exercises." Such criticism was valid, but in an army which provided only pork, flour, beans, vinegar, salt, and whisky for its troops, the post vegetable garden added variety and nutrition that were as essential to the army's well-being as military proficiency. Cantonment Gibson's garden in the fertile bottom of the Grand River usually produced bumper crops. In 1827, it was reported that the troops at the post "have raised . . . a sufficiency of vegetables and other products of the soil, to render them as comfortable as their *isolated* situation will admit of." Even in 1830, a year of drought, the post gardens provided "sufficient to supply the wants of the Post, and leave a considerable surplus."[14]

The criticism of Croghan and others concerning the employment of soldiers as farmers prompted the War Department to modify its policy in 1833 by greatly restricting the scope of post gardens and limiting the employment of troops as farm hands. The new directive did allow gardening on a limited scale by individuals or companies. Arbuckle complained that the new policy could not be implemented at once "without great inconvenience to the whole of my Regiment." He observed that company or individual gardens will "produce difficulties" and asked that Cantonment Gibson be allowed to continue "in the usual way." In reply the Adjutant General stressed that the new policy encouraged gardening for "the personal use and comfort of the garrison," but added that in the future cultivation should not "be permitted to interfere with the regular instruction, regular military duties and regular drill of *Companies*, and of the *Regiment*."[15] It is difficult to determine how faithfully Arbuckle followed the new guidelines concerning gardening, but maps of Fort Gibson dated after 1833 still indicated large post gardens.

Even if no troops had been detailed for gardening, road building, or construction, the five companies at Cantonment Gibson could not have adequately patrolled the vast frontier beyond the post. Throughout most of the area, the absence of an effective military presence produced little complaint, since few whites had yet penetrated the region. One group of traders, however, was vociferous in its demand for more adequate military protection on the Southwestern frontier. Since the overthrow of the Spanish regime in Mexico in 1821, the Santa Fe traders had repeatedly asked for army protection against the Southern Plains tribes which roamed the region beyond Missouri and frequently attacked stragglers. Responding to their demands in 1826, the governor of Missouri advocated the establishment of a military post where the Santa Fe Trail crossed the Arkansas River. A company of mounted soldiers stationed there, the governor said, could escort the caravans and could keep "in check the savages who infest that road." Senator Thomas Hart Benton pushed a resolution through Congress recommending the establishment of such a post.[16]

Anticipating the action of the Missouri Congressional delegation, General Winfield Scott advised his superiors to reject any plan to move the troops stationed at Cantonment Gibson higher up the Arkansas to protect the Santa Fe road. He stressed that the isolated position of the proposed post would render supply and communication difficult. At such a great distance beyond the frontier, it could give little protection to American settlers. Rather, Scott advocated reinforcing Cantonment Gibson with the two companies stationed at Cantonment Towson and sending annual or biennial expeditions from Cantonment Gibson to protect the Santa Fe Trail. Arbuckle also objected strenuously to the relocation of his garrison higher up the Arkansas. He believed that the proposed location would not provide the security desired by the Santa Fe traders and that the cost of establishing a new garrison could not be justified by the volume of the trade. The reduction of force or abandonment of Cantonment Gibson, Arbuckle pointed out, would diminish the prospects for maintaining peace on the frontier of Arkansas Territory.[17]

The objections of the military were not ignored. Cantonment Gibson was not relocated, and over the next decade patrols from the post were ordered west to escort and protect the caravans en route to New Mexico. Congress also responded to the pressure from Senator Benton and his colleagues. In 1827, it acknowledged the increasing difficulties with the Plains tribes by establishing Fort Leavenworth to provide security for the Santa Fe traders.[18]

Commerce of a different kind, the illegal sale of whisky near Cantonment Gibson, constituted another major problem for Colonel Arbuckle. The Indian Intercourse Act of 1802 as amended in 1822 prohibited the sale of ardent spirits to Indians and directed military commanders to confiscate all unauthorized whisky in the possession of Indian traders. General Edmund P. Gaines informed Arbuckle of the new law in June, 1822, and ordered him to search the stores of any Indian traders suspected of possessing ardent spirits. The colonel was apparently less than vigorous in implementing the new law. By January, 1825, residents at Dwight Mission were complaining of the effect on the Cherokees of "ardent spirits, introduced by white men into the Indian country in open defiance of the laws and authority of the United States."[19] Although the influx of white and Indian settlers along the Arkansas frontier was accompanied by growth in the illicit liquor trade, it was not until 1829 that Colonel Arbuckle mounted a determined effort against whisky vendors. By then they had developed considerable political influence. Policing the traffic was complicated by a presidential directive which allowed Indian traders to transport whiskey into Indian country for their personal use.[20]

In the spring of 1829, the Creek agent informed Colonel Arbuckle that Indians in the Cherokee Nation were frequently drunk and disorderly on liquor obtained from the store of Peter A. Carnes and William DuVal. On May 5, the colonel dispatched Captain Nathaniel G. Wilkinson and Lieutenant Gabriel J. Rains to the nearby trading house to investigate the charge and to determine whether Carnes and DuVal possessed a license permitting them to engage in trade with the Indians. The officers not only discovered five barrels of brandy, rum, and wine, but also noted that the firm's agent was unable to produce a license. Accordingly, Captain Wilkinson seized the store's merchandise and transported it to the post for safe-keeping. Arbuckle learned that Carnes and DuVal originally had about two wagon loads of whisky, but most of that supply had already been sold to the Indians. Several weeks after the seizure, Carnes visited Cantonment Gibson and produced a license authorizing the firm to engage in the Indian trade. Colonel Arbuckle referred the matter to the United States Attorney at Little Rock for prosecution. Since this was the first time traders had been charged with violating the Intercourse Act by introducing whisky in Arkansas Territory, civil authorities were timid and uncertain in their prosecution of the case.[21]

Carnes and DuVal acted more energetically. They protested to Secretary of War John Eaton the seizure of their goods, arguing that the few barrels of liquor found at their store did not constitute a violation of the Intercourse Act. The secretary directed Arbuckle to return the confiscated property, and Carnes and DuVal agreed to release Arbuckle and his subordinates from any liability except for confiscated merchandise actually lost or damaged. Colonel Arbuckle, who disagreed with the decision, informed the Secretary of War that the firm's boat had come up the Arkansas River carrying "at least Eighteen barrels of whiskey, independent of Gin, and other ardent spirits; that they sold to Indians, and Indian Country men in ascending the River . . . nearly half the whiskey, and that they sold the residue of the whiskey to Indians, Indian-Country men, & soldiers in this vicinity." Arbuckle further charged "that scarcely a day passed, after the arrival of DuVal & Carnes Store in this vicinity until it was seized, without a number of Indians being drunk at it." Had the case come to trial, the colonel predicted that he would have been able to prove the guilt of the firm in selling liquor to the Indians.[22]

The colonel's assertion was supported by the accusations of several prominent residents of the frontier. The Reverend Mr. Cephas Washburn of Dwight Mission informed the Commissioner of Indian Affairs that within a ten-day period in 1830, five Indians died as a result "of the intemperate use of whiskey." Not wishing to be classed as an informer, Washburn declined to name the specific merchant who had provided the Indians with whisky. He did assert that "Nearly every one engaged in the Indian trade is guilty." Cherokee agent George Vashon was more specific; he charged Carnes and DuVal of being "without any doubt . . . in the constant habit [of] selling large quantities of Whiskey to the Indians."[23] Colonel Arbuckle was correct; Carnes and DuVal were involved in the whisky trade, and he had caught them with the evidence. Nonetheless, the matter was settled. The political influence of the firm was sufficient to allow it to violate the intercourse laws with impunity. The Carnes and DuVal case was the first test of these laws on the Arkansas frontier. Its outcome multiplied the enforcement problem of the army in Indian country.

Cephas Washburn, who understood the difficulty of enforcing the intercourse laws from Cantonment Gibson, recommended that a government official be stationed at Fort Smith to interrupt the flow of whisky into Indian Territory. Arbuckle concurred; in May, 1830, he told his superiors that he could not carry out the laws prohibiting the sale of whisky to the Indians "unless a Military force is established at Fort Smith." Stressing the magnitude of the trade, the colonel reported "that the Indians are furnished with whiskey by almost every . . . Boat of any description which passes up the Arkansas, above Fort Smith." The War Department deferred action, informing Arbuckle that the "reoccupation of Fort Smith will be a matter of future consideration." Ignoring the problems Arbuckle had encountered attempting to enforce the intercourse laws against Carnes and DuVal, the Acting Secretary of War naively informed the colonel that rigid enforcement would put an "effectual stop" to the trade.[24] Such enforcement was of course a practical impossibility under the circumstances.

The whiskey traffic became a major business on the Arkansas frontier. From Van Buren, Arkansas, the center of the trade, one hundred traders peddled their wares to the Indians across the territorial border. Many of the traders were married to Indian women and claimed tribal citizenship and exemption from the intercourse laws. In 1832, Congress moved to stop this nefarious trade by enacting a stronger intercourse law which decreed that "no ardent spirits shall be hereafter introduced under any pretense, into the Indian country." When Arbuckle learned of the law, he informed his superiors in Washington that Cantonment Gibson had been "much annoyed by the sale of Liquor by Cherokee Indians" and asked if he were authorized "to seize Liquor in Indian Country, without regard to the owner."[25]

Before Arbuckle received further instructions, George Vashon, the Cherokee agent, attempted unsuccessfully to confiscate the stock of Cherokee merchant John Drew. In view of the determined opposition of the Cherokees to his efforts, Vashon predicted enforcement of the ban on the introduction of ardent spirits "will require the application of Military force." He explained:

> The ruling party here, have no respect for the views of the Government. . . .Whiskey is the agent employed to accomplish the purpose of intrigue, and it yields the largest profit in trade—and it is expected that the Government will have greater difficulties in effecting its benevolent purposes amongst the Cherokees than with any others.[26]

Vashon was correct. The Rogerses, one of the leading Western Cherokee families, were deeply involved in the trade. John Rogers, the partner of John Nicks, sutler at Cantonment Gibson, had frequently been accused of selling liquor to the Indians. At the time of the passage of the 1832 Intercourse Act, his son Charles was constructing a distillery on Spavinaw Creek north of Cantonment Gibson. Business was excellent, and even the flood of 1833, which severely damaged the works, could not stop production for long. Ironically, the troops at Cantonment Gibson, who were supposed to enforce the ban on the introduction of whisky, were among Charles Rogers' best customers.

By late 1832, Arbuckle had assigned men to patrol duty on the Arkansas River to stop the flow of illicit whisky. The distinctive red color of the patrol's vessel did not make their task easy. The impossibility of controlling the Arkansas River from Cantonment Gibson quickly became apparent, and in 1833 the War Department ordered a company from Cantonment Gibson to reoccupy Fort Smith, where it could better observe and control the traffic. On May 10, 1834, at the suggestion of its commander, Captain John Stuart, this company was relocated ten miles higher up the Arkansas at Swallow Rock. From this site, named Fort Coffee, the company continued its effort to stem the flow of illegal liquor into Indian Territory.[27] This mission proved even more difficult than concluding the Osage-Cherokee feud.

Chapter 4

A Troubled Truce

THE ESTABLISHMENT OF Cantonment Gibson on the Grand River in 1824 did not bring the warring Cherokees and Osages to terms immediately. It did, however, alarm the Osages, whose village was located within fifty miles of the new garrison. Colonel Matthew Arbuckle's first action after selecting the site of the post was to send word to Union Mission that he considered it "indispensable that the bad men among the Osages should come to trial."[1] For some time the tribe had been considering the surrender of the murderers of Major Curtis Welborn and his fellow hunters. The proximity of the troops spurred the tribe to action.

On June 7, 1824, Clermont's entire village of some 4,000 Indians camped at the falls of the Verdigris about four miles from the post. Arbuckle, uncertain as to the Osages' intentions, ordered hasty fortifications erected to enclose his encampment and stores. The Reverend William Vaill from Union Mission noted that the colonel was apprehensive that the Indians "might become turbulent if not terrific." Tension mounted in the early afternoon, when four hundred heavily-armed warriors stopped outside the breast works of Cantonment Gibson. Arbuckle invited Clermont and a few other chiefs to discuss the surrender of the warriors accused of the murders. The invitation was accepted by the principal chief, who was elegantly dressed for the occasion in a style more white than Indian. Clermont wore a ruffled linen shirt, blue pants, a sash, and a hat surmounted by a towering pink plume. Instead of a sword he carried a "magnificent pipe." Vaill was reassured by Clermont's appearance.[2]

The colonel opened the discussions by announcing that he was ready to receive the men responsible for killing the hunters. The chief agreed, provided that his men would be tried at the post by Arbuckle. The colonel explained that he lacked the power to hear the case but promised that the warriors would be transported safely to Little Rock and given a fair trial. Clermont appeared satisfied. Eventually six warriors, including Mad Buffalo and one of Clermont's sons, surrendered themselves. Mad Buffalo told Arbuckle that the killing of the white hunters had been an accident and that he was willing to comply with white man's justice. The other warriors also protested their innocence of intentional wrong-doing and proclaimed their friendship. The forthrightness of the Osages and their willingness to submit to American justice impressed Colonel Arbuckle, who told the Osages that he believed the accused warriors were innocent and that "he never entertained so high an opinion of the nation before."[3]

Nevertheless, the Indians were placed in irons and sent down the Arkansas River to Little Rock for trial, guarded by a detachment commanded by Captain John Philbrick. Despite the presence of the guards, one of the Osages managed to escape during the first night. The five remaining prisoners arrived safely at Little Rock on June 25.[4]

Arbuckle's belief in the innocence of the Osages was not shared by the civil authorities in Little Rock. Acting Governor Robert Crittenden was convinced at their guilt" and believed that their execution would serve as an example to others. The five warriors were indicted and tried for murder in October, 1824. Mad Buffalo based his defense on the premise that he had believed the victims of the attack were Caddoes and that he and other leaders of the attack had remained in the rear where they "employed themselves smoking their pipes, and envoking the Great Spirits to give success to their warriors." The court rejected this defense and found Mad Buffalo and another warrior named Little Eagle guilty. They were sentenced to be hanged on Tuesday, December 21. Both men received the sentence with composure and no display of emotion. Mad Buffalo did express his distaste for the method of execution and a few days later attempted to take his own life with a small pen knife. The blade was too short to reach his heart, and he succeeded only in inflicting a number of deep wounds which were not considered dangerous.[5]

On learning of the court's decision, Colonel Arbuckle at Cantonment Gibson informed officials in Washington that he had talked to almost everyone present at the massacre and that he was "firmly of the opinion that the Osages under Sentence Merit the clemency of the President of the United States, and that their pardon . . . Would be productive of the best Effects." Arbuckle also wrote to the acting governor of the territory requesting that the date of execution be postponed.[6]

Before news of the verdict reached Washington, President James Monroe had taken a personal interest in the case and directed that further legal action be stayed. A week later, Secretary of War John C. Calhoun personally requested that the acting governor forward "a minute and detailed statement of all the facts attending the case" to Washington. Apparently the stay arrived none too soon, for the December 14 issue of the *Arkansas Gazette* reminded its subscribers that the execution was just a week away.[7]

Replying to the request for information, Crittenden assured the Secretary of War concerning the justness of the sentence. He observed, "there can be no doubt . . . that they [Mad Buffalo and other chiefs] Sanctioned if they did not order and direct the attack." Crittenden reported that the Indians were following the case with great interest and would "consider the release of these men as guaranteing for the future impunity for the perpetration of the worst crimes." Alexander McNair, the newly appointed Osage agent, disagreed with Crittenden's evaluation. Based not only on his discussions with the Osages but also on the opinions of the officers stationed at Cantonment Gibson, white traders in the area, and the residents of Union Mission, the agent concluded that "much good would result from these men being pardoned."[8]

On March 21, 1825, President John Q. Adams pardoned Mad Buffalo and Little Eagle. The pardon was a reflection of the President's compassion for "his Red Children," not a lack of indignation concerning the "enormity of their crime." Adams hoped his act of clemency would promote "peace and harmony" and encourage good conduct among the Osages.[9] Relations with the Osages did improve, but the explanation is more likely to be found in the proximity of Cantonment Gibson rather than the magnanimous gesture of the President.

Two days after the surrender of Mad Buffalo and his companions, Colonel Arbuckle and the new subagent for the Osages, David Barber, attempted to restructure the tribal organization. The Osages' lack of centralized authority had frustrated government efforts to compel them to obey the laws. To correct this situation, Arbuckle and Barber met with the Osages at their camp at the falls of the Verdigris. There they encouraged the chiefs to adopt a civil government patterned on the American model. The tribe established a thirteen-member National Council headed by Clermont as President and Tally as Vice President. A national guard of forty warriors was appointed to carry out the laws and decisions of the government. Observers at Union Mission were enthusiastic about these arrangements, writing that it was "the first step towards civil Govt. in a Nation hitherto law less to an extreme." John Joseph Mathews, in a recent study of the Osages, was less optimistic about the new government established for the tribe. He concluded that it "lasted about as long as it took Barber and Arbuckle to arrive home."[10]

The failure of constitutional government to take root among the Osages was offset by several positive gains. A meeting between the Osages and Cherokees was arranged at which most of the existing areas of conflict between the two tribes were resolved. Not one incident of Osage depredation against whites or Cherokees was reported in the year following the establishment of Cantonment Gibson. The presence of the garrison also stimulated Osage enterprise. In early August, an Osage sold a canoeload of watermelons and green corn to the soldiers at the post. The missionaries at Union, with obvious pleasure, recorded that it was the first time to their knowledge of "an Osage going to market and selling his produce for cash."[11]

The garrison was a market place for ideas as well as produce. Among the visitors at the post were several Cherokee chiefs who were making arrangements to meet with the Osages to discuss an exchange of stolen horses. During their negotiations the Cherokees extolled the virtues of accepting change and acquiring property. The Osages were invited to come to the Cherokee settlements to observe how far the Cherokees had advanced from their "former poverty and wretchedness." One of the Cherokee chiefs attributed their progress to " the good advice of the whites for the acquisition of his present property by which he could live comfortable." Most Osages were not yet ready to settle down to a life of agriculture, but such advice was beginning to win converts. In 1823, the Union missionaries had persuaded a few Osages to adopt the agricultural lifestyle of white pioneers. About four miles above Union Mission, a small Osage agricultural community named Hopefield Station was built. The number of Osage families who built cabins and cleared and tilled the fields grew steadily. "The preserverance and success, and the general improvement... surpassed [the] expectation" of the missionaries.[12]

The presence of Cantonment Gibson and the influence of the missionaries had restrained but not eliminated the martial propensities of the Osages. Rather, the Osages had learned to channel their natural inclinations into activities less objectionable to the whites. In mid-August, Osage warriors marched west to engage their traditional enemy, the Pawnees. The missionaries protested, but Clermont defended the tribe's decision with shrewdness, accusing the Pawnees of faithless behavior and atrocities against the Osages. The objections of the missionaries went unheeded, and according to the missionaries, the war party marched off in search of plunder, horses, glory and blood.[13] No strenuous efforts were made to halt the expedition by the military because a Pawnee-Osage war did not immediately endanger Union Mission or the white frontier.

Although relations between the Osages and Cherokees had improved, the unresolved murder of Red Hawk in 1823 remained a major irritant to relations between the tribes. In early January, 1825, Thomas Graves called on Colonel Arbuckle seeking redress for the murder of his nephew by the Osages. Arbuckle promised to investigate the incident thoroughly and assured Graves that the Osages would be compelled to make restitution in accordance with the treaty of 1822.[14] Before this matter could be resolved, reports of horse stealing on both sides exacerbated feelings between the tribes. Peace broke down completely in the winter of 1825–26, when a party of Cherokees, Delawares, and perhaps some Shawnees attacked an Osage party on the Red River and killed five warriors. Although the Cherokees participated in the attack, it appears to have been organized by the Delawares.

In 1825, William Anderson, a Delaware chief, ordered a campaign against the Osages in revenge for the death of his son. Delaware and Cherokee bands on the Red River were quickly drawn into the conflict. Reports from Cantonment Towson suggested that a confederation of tribes hostile to the Osages might be conspiring to exterminate them. Arkansas governor George Izard warned that such an alliance, if successful, would assuredly be turned against the white settlers on the frontier. Responding to the renewed threats of border warfare, General Edmund P. Gaines, commander of the Western Department, increased Arbuckle's authority and promised him more troops if hostilities began. The colonel was ordered to "keep the peace—quietly if you can, but *forcibly* if force is ... employed against the peaceable and unoffending frontier inhabitents ... whether of the red skin or the white."[15]

Before Gaines's order reached Arbuckle, the conflict had spread. In late April, 1826, reports that the Delawares had killed an Osage on the Illinois River led the colonel to suspect that the Delawares were on their way to a rendezvous with the Cherokees and other tribes planning to move against the Osages. Arbuckle speculated that an attack might not come before early May, after the Cherokees had fulfilled a promise to meet with the Osages at Cantonment Gibson to discuss grievances. "I do not believe," Arbuckle wrote, "that the proposed Council will have the desired effect; or that any thing short of force, can maintain peace between the Tribes ... much longer." The colonel again advised his superiors that the troops at his disposal were inadequate to prevent the impending hostilities.[16]

The chance that peace could be restored by the council at Cantonment Gibson was diminished when the Osage agent, Colonel Alexander McNair, died in St. Louis six weeks before the meeting was to begin. One of the first duties assigned to McNair after his appointment as Osage agent in 1824 had been the settlement of the Red Hawk case. It is doubtful that the differences between the tribes could have been compromised by McNair or any government agent at Cantonment Gibson, but no one was given an opportunity to try. Although the Cherokee delegation assembled at the post, the Osages refused to participate, claiming that negotiations could not take place before a new agent was appointed to represent them.[17]

The Osages, ever skillful at procrastination, had again deferred the question of handing over Red Hawk's murderer, but their dilatory tactics infuriated the Cherokees and pushed them to the brink of open warfare. In fact, the *Arkansas Gazette* announced that the Osage refusal to negotiate led to "an immediate declaration of war" by the Cherokees. This announcement was premature, for Colonel Arbuckle secured the Cherokees' promise that they would restrain their warriors for at least three months to give the government additional time to try to arrange a solution. The colonel assured the Cherokees that if they honored their pledge to keep the peace, the government would employ force if necessary to secure justice. The tribe's agent advised his superiors that nothing less than the prompt "Surrender and Execution of the Murderers will satisfy the Cherokees." Agent Edward DuVal warned that should the three months' truce agreed to by the Cherokees expire without results, the tribe was determined to go to war.[18]

General Gaines authorized Arbuckle to arrest and hold the Osages accused of the murder of Red Hawk while all relevant facts pertaining to the case were assembled and presented to the President, who would decide his fate. The deteriorating relations among the tribes led Gaines to warn the Secretary of War that "war... cannot be much longer prevented." To strengthen Arbuckle's ability to respond to the expected outbreak, General Gaines alerted eight companies from the First and Sixth Infantry to prepare for service in the Southwest in case of hostilities. In the event of war, Arbuckle was ordered "to protect the frontier inhabitants and to require the Indians to abstain from hostile operations against each other at any place eastward or southward of your post."[19]

The Delaware Indians had also refused to send delegates to the council at Cantonment Gibson. Arbuckle, apprehensive that they might ignite the entire frontier, sent an express to the tribe to dissuade them from sending war parties against the Osages. The tribe informed the colonel that they would not take action until they had heard from General William Clark, the Superintendent of Indian Affairs in St. Louis.[20]

Along the frontier, events seemed to confirm the prediction of imminent conflict. In early June, 1826, a band of unidentified Indians stole about a dozen horses within four or five miles of Cantonment Towson. A little later the residents of Union Mission reported a Delaware war party in search of Osages had killed some of their livestock and damaged other mission property. On several occasions Delaware incursions forced mission Indians living at Hopefield and Frenchmen who had married Osage women to abandon their farms to seek protection at Union Mission and the trading houses near the Three Forks. Even there the refugees were not safe. A blind Osage man, sitting in the yard of one of the trading houses, was shot. Eventually, Colonel Arbuckle allowed the Osage refugees to settle at the post.[21]

On July 18, 1826, Auguste P. Chouteau reported that "some strange Indians had been discovered lurking in the woods near his trading house, and that it was probable their object was to commit some outrage." He was correct, for the same evening an Osage was "killed & scalped ... within a few paces of the trading house." The culprits also stole some of Chouteau's livestock. By mid-summer of 1826, it appeared that the frontier was on the verge of war. The

Tahchee, or "Dutch," famed Cherokee warrior and leader of the Old Settlers. From a painting by George Catlin, courtesy the Thomas Gilcrease Institute of American History and Art.

commanding general of the Western Military Department compared the situation in the Southwest to the disastrous reversals suffered by Governor Arthur St. Clair in 1791 at the hands of the Indians.[22] The comparison was overdrawn; there appears to have been little real danger of a wide-scale Indian uprising against whites. The coalition led by the Cherokees and Delawares was directed against the Osages, who were both outmanned and out-gunned.

As the three-month truce elapsed, the Osages, probably realizing the superiority of their enemy, made several concessions. On August 24, 1826, the new Osage agent, John Hamtramck, surrendered the warrior accused of killing Red Hawk in 1823. Colonel Arbuckle placed the prisoner in the Cantonment Gibson stockade while awaiting instructions from Washington. At about the same time, the Osages asked the Delawares to meet with them to resolve their differences. Superintendent Clark arranged a meeting in the fall at St. Louis. Most of the tribes residing near the White River were represented except the Cherokees, who received notification of the meeting too late to send a delegation. At first the Delawares were reluctant to accept the Osage offer to end hostilities, but on October 7, a treaty of amity was accepted by all the participants. The treaty prohibited all parties from hunting in the territory of the others and imposed a $1,000 penalty on any tribe whose warriors took the lives of members of other tribes.[23]

But neither the St. Louis treaty nor the surrender of the Osage warrior resolved the Cherokee-Osage feud. The Cherokees were angered by Colonel Arbuckle's refusal to hand Red Hawk's murderer over to them or to execute him, and the Osages were outraged by the murder and scalping of one of their men near Chouteau's trading post on July 18. Any doubt concerning the identity of the assailants of the Osage was removed when his scalp was displayed in the Cherokee settlement amid "dancing & rejoicing." The man who claimed credit for the act was a well-known chief named Dutch, who lived south of the Red River in the Mexican province of Texas.[24]

Agent DuVal denied the guilt of the Arkansas Cherokees by repeatedly stressing that Dutch had been disenfranchised by them the year before and that the display of the Osage scalp had not really produced widescale dancing and rejoicing. While attempting to absolve the Arkansas Cherokees of responsibility, DuVal again urged the government to expedite the punishment of Red Hawk's murderer.[25]

The Osages had borne the stigma of having violated the treaty of 1822 for four years. During that time they were constantly pressured by their agents and the government to accept the consequences stipulated by the treaty. Now they had an opportunity to make similar demands of the Cherokees, and they apparently relished it. Clermont informed the Cherokees:

> When we herd this [that Dutch had killed one of their warriors] we called on Colonel Arbuckle and requested that he would have Dutch confined, and report his offence to the President, . . . and whatever his decision may require of the Osage Nation, it will be cheerfully complied with, and we hope your Nation [the Cherokee] will do the same.[26]

Disclaiming the actions of Dutch, Cherokee chiefs Captian James Rogers and Thomas Graves traveled to St. Louis, where they asked William Clark to punish the Osage held at Cantonment Gibson for the murder of Red Hawk. Although Clark believed that the public execution "would be a valuable example to the Indians," the treaty of 1822 did not give the government the authority to impose such punishment. The Cherokees were not receptive to the superintendent's proposal concerning an exchange of Dutch for Red Hawk's murderer. Nor would they accept his suggestion that the action of Dutch had evened the score. Graves countered by arguing that Dutch, if guilty, should also die. Unable to satisfy the Cherokees, Clark promised to refer the case to the President. In return, the Cherokees pledged to keep the peace until the President's decision was known. However, Graves made it clear that if that decision called for anything less than death for the murderer of his nephew, he would "take satisfaction on the Osages." By the time the Cherokee delegation returned home, the debate over the surrender of the Osage prisoner had become moot, for during the night of January 13, 1827, he escaped from a sentinel who was accompanying him to the privy outside Cantonment Gibson.[27]

The Cherokees did not wait to learn the President's decision. A tribal council early in February decided that there had already been sufficient "unavailing negotiation" and authorized a war party composed primarily of Red Hawk's relatives to settle the score with the Osages. Tribal leaders assured Agent DuVal that they had no desire for a general war with the Osages. All they wanted was "a life for the life they had lost."[28]

There is no indication that DuVal attempted to restrain the Cherokees, even though their promise to Superintendent Clark and their respect for federal military power indicate that pressure against such an attack from their agent might have been effective. DuVal's earlier scathing indictments of the Osages and his reaction to the decision of the Cherokees to seek justice themselves suggest that he supported or at least condoned the attack. In advising Colonel Arbuckle of the Cherokees' intentions, he warned that the Osages should be advised not to retaliate if they desired peace. Although DuVal did not attempt to deter the Cherokees, he was careful to instruct them to respect the property of white settlers, trading post operators, and missionaries.

Some of the tribal leaders may have had second thoughts about violating their promise to Superintendent Clark, because about a week after deciding to send the war party against the Osages, two of the principal chiefs of the Cherokees, John Rogers and Walter Webber, drafted a letter to the Osage chiefs in which they expressed their desire "to bury the Tomahawk, and become neighbours & friends." But this profession of friendship may have been a strategy to lure the Osages off guard. On March 7, a sixteen-man Cherokee war party was reported en route to the Osage country. Arbuckle responded immediately by sending a patrol up the Grand River to intercept it. The force did not encounter the Cherokees, who had apparently turned back not long after crossing into Osage country.[29]

Meanwhile, President John Quincy Adams reviewed the developments on the frontier and concluded that the death of the Osage at the hands of Dutch balanced the murder of Red Hawk. He declared that neither tribe was entitled to retribution and both were to refrain from further hostile acts. Adams also directed that a council be held to work out a "permanent & amicable understanding."[30]

News of the President's decision was not received enthusiastically by the Cherokees. In July, another Cherokee war party was sent to secure satisfaction, but it returned before contacting the enemy. The Osages on the other hand, never as well armed as the Cherokees, were willing to accept Adams' decisions. Led by Agent Hamtramck, a delegation of twenty-five Osage chiefs arrived on September 15 at Cantonment Gibson, where the President had directed that they should negotiate with the Cherokees. There they received word from Agent DuVal that the Cherokees demanded as a precondition to negotiations the surrender or punishment of Red Hawk's murderer. The Osage agent reported that this demand, which ignored the President's decision, "gave a chilling blast to the warm feelings" of the Osage delegation.[31]

Hamtramck rejected the Cherokee demand and reminded their

agent of the President's decision. The refusal of the Cherokees to negotiate provoked apprehension among the Osages, who remembered the Cherokee duplicity preceding the massacre at Claremore's Mound. Hamtramck feared that the Cherokees' obstinacy had created an atmosphere in which "a slight altercation may lead to bloodshed." While still at Cantonment Gibson awaiting news from the Cherokees, the Osage agent learned that a Cherokee hunting party had stopped at Chouteau's trading house. Hoping that they might be there to negotiate, Hamtramck assembled the tribal leaders and led them to the trading house, where they gave "the Cherokees a kind & hospitable reception." The Cherokee hunters carried Chief Jolly's assurance they had come as friends, but they were not empowered to negotiate.[32]

In November, 1827, William Clark reported to the War Department that "the Cherokees are yet obstanate." The Osages remained apprehensive; their agent told DuVal that "no lasting feeling of mutual forgiveness... can be reasonably expected" until the tribes met in council. While the old antagonists could not be persuaded to meet formally to work out their differences, they did refrain from further aggressive acts. In late February, William Clark could report that he had "heard of no difficulties between the Cherokees & Osages since... the 1st of Novr last; and think it probable the Cherokees will abide by the decision made by the President."[33]

In an effort to secure a reversal of President Adams' decision, the Cherokees sent a delegation to Washington. The tribal representatives were instructed to seek solutions to a number of problems, including their long-standing rivalry with the Osages. In the capital the Cherokee delegation, including Sequoyah and Thomas Graves, capitulated to government pressure and signed a treaty in May, 1828. Article Five of the treaty, which dealt with the Osage-Cherokee feud, ignored the Cherokee demand for the punishment of Red Hawk's murderer. Instead, it awarded the Cherokees $8,760 to satisfy tribal claims against the Osages and American citizens. Thomas Graves, the Cherokee most adamant in demanding the punishment of Red Hawk's murderer, was placated by the grant of $1,200 for "personal sufferings."[34]

After two decades of intermittent warfare, the Osage-Cherokee feud was officially ended, but the treaty could not end the animosities that had developed over the years, nor could it prevent occasional hostility. By mid-July, 1829, Arbuckle advised the War Department that the Cherokees were "unusually dissatisfied" with the terms of the truce between themselves and the Osages. In the autumn a party of fifteen Cherokees killed eight Osages. Although the attackers were probably Cherokees from the Red River, and their actions were disclaimed by the Arkansas Cherokees, Colonel Arbuckle feared the incident might disrupt the peace.[35]

Secretary of War John Eaton was particularly upset when he learned of the disturbance. The Jackson administration was vigorously pressing the Eastern Indians to move west, and violence in the area assigned to those tribes increased their resistance to removal. The secretary advised the army's General-in-Chief Alexander Macomb, "At a time like this when an anxious solicitude is felt to induce the Indians living within the U.S. to remove it is extremely desirous to avoid all contests between them." The general was ordered to "direct the commanding officer at Cantonment Gibson to use his best exertions to restore tranquility." The secretary suggested that Arbuckle consider marching "with all his disposable force....to produce a moral effort and influence on the Indians." Eaton believed that "by persuasion and threats and more especially by means of presents," peace could be restored to the frontier. Specifically, the secretary suggested that Arbuckle offer presents to the families of the victims of the Cherokee attack, provided they promised to refrain from retaliation. As a last resort the colonel was authorized to employ force to constrain refractory warriors.[36]

On receipt of these instructions, Colonel Arbuckle informed the Osage subagent, Nathaniel Pryor, that war parties would no longer be allowed to attack tribes under the protection of the United States. He also asked the subagent to escort Tally and other warriors who had lost relatives to Cantonment Gibson. Pryor found the Osages receptive to the plans of the government and secured their promise not to molest Cherokees or Creeks encountered on the spring hunts. The principal chiefs and warriors of Clermont's band met with Arbuckle and Pryor at Cantonment Gibson. The colonel assured the delegation that he would try to apprehend the assailants and that he had already informed the various tribes along the Red River that the government would punish those who attacked their neighbors. He also distributed $800 in presents in exchange for an Osage promise not to seek satisfaction for the deaths of the eight warriors killed the past November.[37]

Osage assurances that their warriors would not attack tribes under the protection of the United States did not prevent impoverished Osage warriors, driven by hunger during the winter of 1830–31, from stealing livestock from the nearby Cherokees and Creeks. But Paul L. Chouteau, the Osage agent, was quick to assure his superiors that the tribe was embarrassed by the depredations of its hunters and eager to restore good relations by compensating the Creeks and Cherokees for their losses. He explained that the severity of the winter and the shortage of provisions had prompted the Osages to steal their neighbors' livestock. Chouteau arranged a council between the tribes at Cantonment Gibson to restore harmony. On May 5, 1831, negotiations began with the Creeks, who seemed more sympathetic concerning the plight of the Osages than angry about their depredations. Discussions continued without rancor, and on May 10, a treaty of amity and friendship between the two tribes was signed.[38]

The Osages then entered into discussions with the Cherokees, who still harbored bitter feelings against them and at first resisted efforts at compromise. On several occasions discussions almost disintegrated into violence, but eventually the Cherokees agreed to a treaty which established orderly legal procedures for resolving future differences. In Article Four of the treaty, the Cherokees on the Arkansas disavowed responsibility for the conduct of Cherokees residing along the Red River. This provision did not reduce the threat to the Osages from Indians residing along the Red River, but it did diminish the chance that the incursions of those bands would lead to a general renewal of hostilities between the Osages and Arkansas River Cherokees. The *Arkansas Gazette* credited Colonel Arbuckle, A. P. Chouteau, Nathaniel Pryor, and several others for their "zeal and industry" in reconciling the differences between the tribes.[39]

Chapter 5

Arrival of the Immigrants

THE REDUCTION OF tension between the Os-
ages and Cherokees facilitated the efforts of the government to
persuade the Eastern tribes to accept new homes beyond the Mississippi. Removal of Eastern Indians had long been viewed as a
means of resolving the Indian problems in the eastern states and
territories, but the resulting concentration of immigrant tribes in
the west compounded problems there. Cantonment Gibson, established on the eve of an accelerated campaign to remove the remaining Eastern Indians, stood at a strategic crossroads in one of the
primary areas reserved for them.

In 1824, when Colonel Matthew Arbuckle led his men up the
Arkansas River to the Three Forks, the Osages were the only tribe
that had permanent villages in the area. Before Eastern tribes could
be relocated near Cantonment Gibson, the government had to persuade the Osages to relinquish their claim to the area. In 1825, a
delegation of Osage chiefs and warriors met with Indian Commissioner William Clark in St. Louis and ceded all their lands except a
reservation in what is now southern Kansas. Although many Osages refused to leave their old villages, the government began sub-
dividing the area among Eastern tribes who were persuaded to
negotiate removal treaties.

The Choctaws were the first; in 1825 they negotiated a treaty by
which the western branch of the tribe accepted a tract south of the
Arkansas and Canadian Rivers beyond Arkansas Territory. The
legislature of Arkansas objected strenuously to the terms of this
treaty, claiming that its frontier citizens would be surrounded by
four times their number of Indians and dismissing Cantonments
Gibson and Towson as too remote and inadequately manned to
provide protection from the "inroades and depredations from those
Savages." The objections were to no avail. The treaty stood, and in
1827 the Choctaw agent established his headquarters about fifteen

miles above Fort Smith on the Arkansas River, where the troops from Cantonment Gibson could be "quite handy" in the event they should be required to maintain order. Although the agent encouraged immigrants to settle in the area, the Choctaw population grew slowly during the 1820's.[1]

In Georgia, meanwhile, disagreement among the Creeks over the unauthorized signing of a removal treaty antagonized long-standing differences and culminated in the "execution" of Chief William McIntosh and several of his associates. Disregarding this expression of Creek opposition to removal, the John Q. Adams administration renewed negotiations and in 1826 persuaded the Creeks to accept a treaty that authorized a five-man delegation to travel beyond the Mississippi to select land for members of their tribe who wished to emigrate. In early May, 1827, the agent for the McIntosh Creeks, Colonel David Brearley, and a small delegation of Creeks stopped at Cantonment Gibson on their way to survey available land.[2]

Colonel Arbuckle received the deputation cordially and offered them assistance. After obtaining guides, interpreters, additional horses, and a physician to accompany them, the party explored the Arkansas and Canadian valleys before returning to Cantonment Gibson. The Creeks were pleased with the country, and Colonel Brearley was convinced that their report would produce a large and immediate emigration. The agent decided to locate the initial Creek settlement just beyond Arkansas' territorial boundary, about eight miles from Cantonment Gibson. Brearley, apprehensive about the proximity of the Little Osage towns to the site he had selected, asked the secretary of war to direct the commanding officer of Cantonment Gibson to provide military protection to the Creeks during the "infant State" of settlement. The secretary, who was anxious to promote Creek removal, complied immediately. Creek emigration began that fall, when some seven to nine hundred Creeks of the McIntosh party left Georgia for the long trip to their new homes. Another 3,000 planned to remove the next spring.[3]

The first Creeks reached their new settlement on the Verdigris early in 1828. Although the Osages had already ceded the area to the federal government, some members of the tribe would remain for another ten years. If they opposed the Creek immigration, another prolonged period of strife might result. Colonel Arbuckle thus worked to avoid that possibility. Upon the arrival of the Creeks, he and Agent Brearley arranged a meeting of the tribes at which the government's plans relating to Creek immigration were explained to the Osages. They not only proved willing to allow the Creeks to settle there, but also proposed a union of the two tribes. To prove his sincerity the Osage chief, Clermont, suggested that his daughter marry a Creek.[4]

By the spring of 1828, seven hundred Creeks were located in the Lower Verdigris valley. While inspecting Cantonment Gibson, Arkansas Governor George Izard and General Winfield Scott, accompanied by Colonel Arbuckle, visited the new settlement, witnessed the progress of the immigrants, and discussed their problems. To avoid the possibility that the Creeks would be drawn into the rivalry between the Osages and Pawnees, General Scott directed Arbuckle to advise the Pawnees that their old enemy, the Osages, no longer resided along the Lower Verdigris and that the new residents were under the protection of the army. The army's protection, however, did not restrain the Plains tribes from raiding the Creek settlements.[5]

Government persuasion proved ineffective in another area; it failed to weaken the arguments of the opponents of removal. When Brearley returned to Georgia to escort another party, he encountered determined opposition. There were only five hundred in the second emigrating party of McIntosh Creeks who reached the Verdigris in the fall of 1828. Washington officials had hoped for a larger voluntary emigration of Creeks. To spur removal government agents persuaded the Eastern Choctaws, Chickasaws, and Creeks to send representatives to inspect Western lands. An exploring party assembled in St. Louis in 1827 and marched west accompanied by a small military detachment and the Reverend Isaac McCoy, a Baptist minister employed by the government. In late November they reached Cantonment Gibson. From there the party conducted a reconnaissance of the land to the south and west. The delegation remained noncommittal about the region they surveyed. McCoy was certain that the Indian leaders were not impressed by the country north of Cantonment Gibson, and he was unable to learn their estimate of the region between the Arkansas and Canadian Rivers. In reply to McCoy's inquiries, the Chickasaw delegation explained that they were unable to give an evaluation of the land they had seen until "the situation of affairs at home" had been settled. Their situation was but one example of the bitter internal disagreement among the Eastern tribes over the question of removal. Such intratribal dissension delayed but did not prevent removal.[6]

Despite opposition, the government was committed to removal

as the solution to the Eastern Indian problem. The Cherokees, like other tribes, experienced increasing federal pressure. The residents of Arkansas Territory not only wanted the Cherokees moved beyond their western border, they also wanted Lovely's Purchase, the fertile tract promised by the government to the tribe as a hunting outlet. The Cherokees had no desire to leave Arkansas; they had been promised freedom from white pressure there by a succession of presidents who believed that relocation to Arkansas would remove the tribe from the path of Anglo-American settlement. Unfortunately, the advocates of removal had failed to guage correctly the speed of Western expansion. By 1819, when Arkansas Territory was created, white pioneers were already streaming into the region. These settlers threatened to engulf the Cherokees. Tribal leaders reminded government officials of a written commitment from President James Monroe that the Cherokees would "have no limits to the west" so that they would "not be surrounded by white people." This pledge had later been reaffirmed by Secretary of War John C. Calhoun, who specifically acknowledged the Cherokees' right to Lovely's Purchase as a hunting outlet. These promises and subsequent orders from Calhoun to halt white settlement in Lovely's Purchase hindered but did not stop the flow of settlers. In 1823, Calhoun was compelled to reissue his order banning settlement and to direct that unauthorized whites be removed from the area.[7]

Arkansas officials maintained steady pressure on the federal government to open Lovely's Purchase to white settlement. In an attempt to resolve the dispute, Secretary Calhoun ordered surveyors to determine a western boundary for the Cherokee Nation based on an estimate that the tribe was entitled to 3,285,710 acres. Presumably, the land west of that line could then be opened to white settlement. The plan collapsed when white surveyors assigned to the tribe land described by the Cherokees as "a mountaneous broken, barren country fit for nothing." Antagonism mounted in both white and Indian communities. Arbuckle, recognizing the explosive character of the unresolved status of Lovely's Purchase, urged Calhoun to reach a decision concerning final disposition of the region as soon as possible. When the secretary of war learned that Arkansas officials had not followed his instructions in conducting the survey, he reaffirmed the ban on white settlement of Lovely's Purchase until another could be conducted. The new survey was completed by January, 1825, and to the distress of many whites it incorporated a large tract of Lovely's Purchase into the Cherokee Nation.[8]

Not everyone was willing to concede so much prime land to the Cherokees. Shortly after the inauguration of John Q. Adams, his Secretary of War, James Barbour, developed a plan which would have given whites not only all of Lovely's Purchase but also all Cherokee land in Arkansas. The secretary directed the territorial governor of Arkansas to propose an exchange of land that would relocate the Arkansas Cherokees west of Lovely's Purchase. The governor was skeptical that the Cherokees would accept the proposal, for the lands offered were inferior to Lovely's Purchase and the tribe's holdings in Arkansas.[9]

As predicted, the chief of the Western Cherokees, John Jolly, rejected the plan and called on the government to honor its pledges to his tribe. The Arkansas legislature for its part, petitioned the federal government to open the unassigned portion of Lovely's Purchase to white settlement and thus free their western border "from the nuisance of an Indian population."[10]

Colonel Arbuckle was again drawn into the controversy in the fall of 1825, when he reported that many of the tribes on the Southwestern frontier were dissatisfied. The opening of lands to the west of the Cherokees, the colonel believed, would diminish the prospects for peace unless the government's military force in the area was strengthened considerably. The War Department apparently agreed, for it issued explicit instructions that no one should be allowed to settle on the tract until specific orders were issued.[11]

Ignoring the agitated state of the Cherokees, the governor of Arkansas urged the Secretary of War to grant government authorization of white settlement west of the Cherokees. Izard suggested that such action might dispose the tribe to accept the government's proposal that they relinquish their Arkansas lands. "Indigenes themselves," the governor maintained, "are fast migrating to the upper waters of the Arkansas & Red Rivers." Those who opposed the plan were the "Whites & half-Casts of the Tribe" who do not share the "Views of the U. States for the Improvement & Civilization of the Indians."[12]

The territorial delegate from Arkansas was striving for the same objective. Since the establishment of Cantonment Gibson, he had been urging Congress to open the purchase to settlement. In support of his proposal, the delegate argued that the establishment of

Cantonment Gibson and the relocation of the territorial boundary had removed "substantial objection on the part of the government" to white settlement of Lovely's Purchase. Ultimately Congress agreed; on April 5, 1826, that body authorized the survey and sale of the unassigned portion of Lovely's Purchase. Little time was lost in implementing the decision. By mid-June, instructions were issued to the surveyors concerning the subdivision of Lovely's Purchase, but white settlers did not wait until the survey was completed. By the end of July, a number of families had taken up residence in the area, prompting Colonel Arbuckle to recommend that his orders to remove settlers be revoked. The Adjutant General accordingly informed Arbuckle that the prohibition on settlement was suspended until further notice. Within a year, the *Arkansas Gazette* reported that "Lovely's Purchase is settling rapidly," and soon thereafter the region was designated as Lovely's County by the Arkansas legislature.[13]

These developments evoked angry objections from the Cherokees, who considered white settlement of Lovely's Purchase a breach of faith on the part of the government. Tribal leaders protested that Secretary of War Calhoun had promised that the purchase would be kept free of white settlers to give the tribe a hunting outlet to the Western Plains. They viewed with apprehension not only the encirclement of their lands by white settlements, but also the ease with which the promises of the "Great Father and the Secretary had been broken." The Cherokees did more than protest. They also enacted a law requiring the death penalty for any tribal member who advocated the sale or exchange of their lands.[14]

Responding to Cherokee opposition, President Adams ordered a suspension of the survey. Neither side was satisfied. Settlers continued to enter Lovely's Purchase, but their hopes of obtaining title to land had been dimmed by the suspension of the survey. The Cherokees, seeing their hunting outlet claimed by others, were frustrated. The Arkansas legislature drafted another memorial seeking to persuade the federal government to open the purchase, and the Cherokees decided to send another delegation to Washington to secure the area for the tribe.[15] Although neither side appeared willing to compromise, federal officials were prepared to compel mutual concession.

In the winter of 1827-28, a group of the Western Cherokees' most prominent men, including Sequoyah, Thomas Graves, and John Rogers, accompanied by their agent, Edward W. DuVal, arrived in

Washington to express the tribe's concern over the violation of government promises, particularly those regarding Lovely's Purchase. The delegation had no authority to cede or exchange any Cherokee territory. In fact, any Cherokee who negotiated such a transaction faced the death penalty. Secretary Barbour reiterated his proposal to exchange Cherokee lands in Arkansas for an area beyond the western boundary of the territory, and to make the offer more attractive, he proposed to move the western boundary of Arkansas approximately forty miles to the east. Such an arrangement, the secretary suggested, "looks in its consequence to the present and future happiness and prosperity of the Cherokee."[16]

When tribal representatives rejected the offer, President Adams railed that the tribe "had already more than they have any right to claim." The promise by his predecessor of a western outlet, Adams recorded, "is very embarrassing, and it is scarcely imaginable that within so recent a period the President and Secretary of War should have assumed so unwarranted an authority and have given so inconsiderate a pledge." Adams decided promises made to the Indians must give way before the "just and reasonable demands of our own people."[17]

To make the Cherokee delegation more receptive to Barbour's proposal, the President announced that the tribe was entitled to 3,194,784 acres in Arkansas—several million acres less than the Cherokees claimed. Adams's strategy forced the Cherokee delegates to reconsider. If the tribe refused to move from Arkansas, the government might actually reclaim land already given the tribe. The strategy was successful; the Cherokee delegation did not long resist Presidential pressure and other inducements. Acceding to the wishes of President Adams, the delegates on May 6, 1828, concluded a treaty by which the Western Cherokees agreed to give up their Arkansas lands and accept a tract beyond the western boundary of that territory. This boundary was moved eastward approximately forty miles to a line running from Fort Smith to the southwestern corner of Missouri.[18] Although the treaty required that the Arkansas Cherokees again abandon their homes and improvements, it did give them seven million acres including several million acres of choice land in Lovely's Purchase.

The Cherokees reacted with anger to the news of the treaty provisions. Meetings were called to discuss the enforcement of the law decreeing death to anyone who ceded tribal lands. Poles were erected in front of houses to receive the heads of the delegates who had betrayed the tribe. The National Council found the delegates guilty of fraud and denounced the treaty, proclaiming it void.[19] Although the death penalty was not levied against the delegates, Cherokee opposition to the treaty persisted—but to no avail. The United States Senate had ratified the document, leaving the Cherokees no alternative. Reluctantly, they abandoned the farms they had cleared a decade earlier and moved west once again.

Chapter 6

New Dangers from the West and South

THE CHEROKEE TREATY of 1828 not only resolved the controversy over Lovely's Purchase, it also formally ended the Osage-Cherokee feud. For over a decade the army had labored on the Arkansas frontier to resolve that intertribal clash. Now, while there was still little affection between the tribes, both respected the power of the United States sufficiently to insure there would be no resumption of large-scale conflict. The winding down of the Osage-Cherokee rivalry was paralleled by the growth of new threats to the security of the frontier which demanded the attention of the army at Cantonment Gibson. To the south, in the Red River valley and Texas, dissident elements of several tribes had sought refuge from the advance of American pioneers. To the west the Plains Indians were just beginning to react to the same pressure. From both directions Colonel Matthew Arbuckle could anticipate problems.

Arbuckle's command extended south to the Red River, the international boundary. Warriors of half a dozen tribes who were dissatisfied with their treatment at the hands of the American government had congregated on both sides of the Red River and had become a menace to the peace and security of that region. Cherokees living in the Red River valley, not subject to the authority of the Arkansas branch of the tribe, had been harrassing the Osages since 1823, but it was not until early 1826 that their feud posed a serious danger to the growing white community in the region.

On January 13, a party of Cherokees and Delawares killed five Osage warriors near Red River. Retaliating indiscriminately, an Osage party headed by Mad Buffalo attacked a group of American citizens hunting in the Caddo Hills. Four escaped, but two were captured, stripped, and abused before they were released far from the nearest outpost. A few days later Mad Buffalo raided white settlements in the vicinity of Cantonment Towson in search of horses. Hostilities continued in the fall, when a band of Indians, probably Kickapoos and Delawares from the Red River, killed one Osage and wounded three others near the Arkansas River. Osage war parties apparently more than evened the score, for warriors from Clermont's village boasted of killing nine Kickapoos and taking three more prisoners.[1]

Colonel Arbuckle viewed the disturbances along the Red River as a serious threat to the progress he had made in pacifying the Arkansas valley. While the Cherokees, Kickapoos, Shawnees, and other tribes residing south of the Red River continued at war with the Osages, there was a distinct possibility of intertribal war along the entire Southwestern frontier. In March and April, 1827, reports from Major Alexander Cummings, commander of Cantonment Towson, reinforced Arbuckle's apprehensions concerning the situation on the Red River. Texas Cherokees had started to settle on the Little River in the region recently assigned to the Choctaws. Cummings described these Cherokees as "the most troublesome part of the Indian population in our neighbourhood." He also suggested that his inability to communicate with the tribes of his region prevented the gathering of "information as to their designs or intentions." Arbuckle authorized Cummings to employ an interpreter and sent Captain Benjamin L. E. Bonneville and his company to reconnoiter the troubled area just above the Red River.[2]

Before Bonneville arrived, information reached Cantonment Towson that a large body of Indians assembling along the Sabine planned to attack the settlements near the Red River. Major Cummings was informed of the plan by a Shawnee who did not speak English, and there may have been a breakdown in communications, for the anticipated attack did not materialize. But unfortunately there were many unanticipated problems which kept the Red River frontier in a state of turmoil. Two white men, John Bowman and James Roberts, tied and whipped one Cherokee, and a few days later someone, probably Roberts, killed another member of the tribe. Cummings feared that these incidents would "lead to serious results."[3]

Less than a week later, news of more violence reached Cantonment Towson. Osage Indians crossed the Red River, killed a farmer, and created a panic which sent white settlers fleeing north to safety. A detachment was ordered into the field, but Major Cummings recalled the patrol because of the futility of pursuing mounted Indians with infantrymen. Cummings appealed to Arbuckle for assistance, writing that "the pursuit of Marauders and murderers" had "nearly worn out" the small force available to him. Before he dispatched the letter, a messenger from settlers south of the Red River arrived with a request that the army supply "a Guard to protect them from the Pawnee Indians." Another message stressed the "weakness and nakedness" of the white settlements against "the heathens skulking about us, taking off our Stock & Killing our Neighbours."[4]

The calls for help were justified. Just three days later a large party of Osages crossed the Red River and plundered farms, killed cattle, and forced many of the remaining families to leave their homes. Major Cummings did not even bother to dispatch a patrol to challenge the invaders, who were mounted and could easily outdistance his troops. Thoroughly frustrated, Cummings warned Arbuckle that "the time is not far distant when we may expect trouble from the Savages on our borders." The colonel was not as pessimistic as Cummings; while admitting that a large proportion of the Indians living in the vicinity of Cantonment Towson "have unfriendly feelings toward the people of the U.S.," Arbuckle did not believe they would resort to war. To relax Indian-white relations, he advocated removal of white settlers living in the area and suggested forcing the dissident bands residing near Cantonment Towson to rejoin their parent tribes. The colonel expected the arrival of Bonneville and his company to restore calm along the Red River, and to further bolster military power in that area, he ordered Lieutenant William S. Colquhoun and his company to reinforce Cantonment Towson.[5]

The increased violence along the international border was a result of developments in the Mexican province of Texas. In December, 1826, Benjamin Edwards, outraged by the cancellation of his brother's land grant by the Mexican government, proclaimed the land from the Sabine to the Río Grande independent. He named the area the Republic of Fredonia and enlisted the aid of many of the Texas Indians. The rebellion was quickly crushed, but Mexican authorities were disturbed by the disloyalty of the Indian population. The Mexican military launched a campaign to drive hostile tribes from Texas. Many sought safety to the north, where they encroached on bands already established near the American border. There an American official predicted that "want & poverty will exasperate and drive them to desperation."[6]

Another unstable element was added to the already turbulent Red River frontier in late June, 1827, when a company of armed men was organized ostensibly to chastise the Comanches. The agent at the Red River agency advised Major Cummings at Cantonment Towson that the company was composed of a number of men "of the worst description" whose "object is plunder & robbery." The leaders of this undertaking were Charles Burkman and Nathaniel Robbins, both former residents of Miller County, Arkansas, who claimed to have been commissioned officers in the Mexican army. Robbins and a Dr. Lewis B. Dayton had complained to Mexican authorities about being taxed by the United States even though they resided south of the Red River at Pecan Point. The commander of the Department of Texas suggested that the residents of Pecan Point establish a provisional government and recognized Robbins and Dayton as its official representatives to the Mexican Republic. Two months later Burkman issued a proclamation promising pay and plunder for those who would enlist in a campaign against the Indians in Texas. American officials took a dim view of representatives of a foreign power recruiting American citizens.[7]

Governor George Izard of Arkansas Territory pledged to employ the militia, if necessary, to block the Burkman and Robbins expedition, and Major Cummings dispatched Lieutenant Colquhoun to Pecan Point to warn Burkman that his force would be treated as a public enemy. The lieutenant reported that he "discovered no disposition on the part of the inhabitants to join any party." The vigorous display of opposition by American officials quashed the plans of Robbins and Burkman. Their followers "dispersed to their own Accord before they had marched far into the Interior of Texas."[8]

The collapse of the plans of Burkman and Robbins did not restore tranquillity. Colonel A. P. Chouteau warned Arbuckle that four hundred Osage warriors divided into two bands had gone to war and that one force was moving in the direction of the Red River. Arbuckle, believing that his earlier efforts to maintain peace along the Red River had been counterproductive, decided to make no further efforts to mediate between the Osages and the tribes living in that region. His candid opinion was that "there is no hope of a permanent peace being effected between the several Indian Bands on the Red River and the Osages." In any case, the Indians constituted only part of the problem. The region had attracted settlers Arbuckle called "the worse description of our Citizens." He suggested that the disorders were "as often produced by the improper conduct of our people as by a similar conduct on the part of the Indians."[9]

Reports from the Southwestern frontier prompted the commander of the Western Department to recommend an increase in troop strength along the upper Red River in order to insure protection for the growing "heterogeneous mass of white and Red population." About the same time, the War Department received a similar recommendation from the commander of Cantonment Towson. Obviously disgruntled by the lack of manpower, Major Cummings inferred it would be better to have no post at all than one so inadequately manned that it could not fulfill its mission. More troops were desperately needed, not only to keep the Indians in check, but also to police the whites, most of whom Cummings described as "no better than the savages." Cummings suggested that his investigations revealed that the Indians "are more sinn'd against than sinning."[10]

In spite of these pleas, however, no substantial reinforcements were authorized by the War Department, and the frontier situation did not improve. As a result forty-five citizens of Miller County signed a petition addressed to the territorial governor complaining about the Indians, particularly the Shawnees, who were squatting on their fields, pilfering their homes, and stealing their cattle. They requested that the governor remove the Indians and save their homes and fields. The forty soldiers stationed at Cantonment Towson were obviously inadequate to dislodge the Shawnees. Therefore, Governor Izard ordered the Adjutant General of the state militia, Colonel Wharton Rector, to employ force if necessary to evict the Indians.[11] Upon reaching the principal Shawnee and Delaware villages on the Red River, Rector ordered the Indians to get off lands claimed by the white settlers. The Delawares readily agreed, but the Shawnees refused, vowing to retaliate if force were employed against them.

Colonel Rector, undeterred by the Shawnee threat, called upon Captain Russell B. Hyde, the new commander of Cantonment Towson, for assistance. Hyde, however, viewed Rector as a frontier adventurer "who wishes to Immortalize himself by plundering an Indian town & killing a few Women and Children." Since the Shawnee village was clearly in Mexican territory and Hyde's command numbered only thirty-four privates, the captain rejected Rector's request. Rector responded by raising a force of sixty-three men in Miller County and marching on the Shawnee village. Six miles short of his objective he was intercepted by the Shawnee chief, who agreed to leave the territory within twenty days.[12] Nevertheless, the show of force brought no permanent security to the Red River frontier. The stiffening resistance of the Plains Indians to encroachment spelled new difficulties throughout the Southwestern frontier.

For generations the Osages had engaged in regular campaigns against the Pawnees and other Plains tribes. Government pressure on the Osages to end their war with the Cherokees had turned the tribe's warriors to the west, where their superior arms usually enabled them to emerge victorious in their clashes with the Plains Indians. The opening of the Sante Fe trade in 1821 brought Americans into contention with the Plains tribes, and near the end of the 1820's, the immigrating Eastern Indians also came into conflict with them. At Cantonment Gibson, the threat posed by the Plains Indians became one of the major concerns of the garrison.

The army's interest in the Plains Indians predated the establishment of Cantonment Gibson. In March, 1819, Major William Bradford, then commander of Fort Smith, learned of a large intertribal council on the Salt Plains about three hundred miles west of Fort Smith. The Osages, Pawnees, Arapahos, Comanches, and several other tribes were represented. Bradford was unable to ascertain the purpose of their council, but he was apprehensive about a possible alliance between these tribes and the Spanish. American-Spanish relations were strained, and the major had heard that Spaniards were on the Upper Canadian in American territory. Bradford recommended that the chiefs of the Comanches, Kiowas, and Arapahos be invited to Washington to see the power of the United States and to negotiate a treaty.[13] The handful of soldiers on the Arkansas frontier could not control the Osages and Cherokees. An expedition to contact the Plains tribes was out of the question.

Bradford's apprehensions were well founded. In April 1820, the citizens of Hempstead County in southwestern Arkansas Territory warned of a Caddo confederation under the leadership of a chief who reputedly held a colonel's commission in the Spanish army.

The estimated strength of the confederation was over fifteen hundred warriors. Reports from Texas indicated that several Plains tribes had joined the Caddoes, greatly increasing their strength.[14] The Spanish ratification of the Adams-Onis Treaty relaxed tension between the two countries, and the Mexican Revolution ended forever the threat of a Spanish-Indian alliance against the United States, but the Plains tribes would be an obstacle to the pacification of the Southwestern frontier for the next half-century.

When Cantonment Gibson was established, hundreds of miles separated the hunting grounds of the Plains tribes and the nearest American or immigrant Indian settlements, and this separation minimized friction. By 1826, dissident elements of the Cherokees, Delawares, and Shawnees had taken up residence on the Red River beyond Cantonment Towson. Their presence antagonized the Plains tribes, who vented their disapproval on the immigrant Indians and white settlers.[15]

In mid-spring, 1826, about a dozen men from Miller County in southwestern Arkansas were hunting wild horses on the Washita, a tributary of the Red River. The party had broken into small groups which were surprised by Indians who killed three hunters, all members of the Lawrence family. The others, abandoning their equipment and about twenty-five mustangs, escaped. The assailants were at first believed to be Osages, but a subsequent report identified them as Pawnees. Apparently the Lawrences were not their only victims, for one observer reported that the Pawnees claimed credit for the deaths of eight white men. Angry whites called a meeting at which it was decided to send a force against the Pawnees. The commander of Cantonment Towson opposed the plan and predicted it would plunge the frontier into an Indian war. His opposition apparently dissuaded the settlers, for newspapers and reports do not indicate a settlers' campaign against the Pawnees in the summer of 1826.[16]

It was more difficult to restrain the Osages. A band from Pawhuska's village on its fall hunt took eighteen to twenty Pawnee scalps, and warriors from the Little Osage village returned with Pawnee horses.[17] But such clashes were not of immediate concern to the government as long as they did not involve whites or impede the immigration of Eastern Indians.

The Indian incursions of the winter and spring of 1827 were a different matter. In January news of another clash between white traders and Plains Indians alarmed the frontier. Some twenty men from southern Arkansas were attacked in Texas by 250 to 300 Comanches. In April, Indians entered the settlements across the Red River from Cantonment Towson and killed one resident. There was some confusion concerning the identity of the Indians, but the commander of the post believed they were Pawnees. These attacks prompted the settlers in the Red River valley to renew their request to the commander of Cantonment Towson for protection against the Pawnees. The cause of the Indian unrest along the Red River was the Mexican campaign to push the Indians beyond the borders of Texas in the months following the collapse of the Fredonian rebellion. Colonel Arbuckle reported to his superiors that American citizens in the Red River area would be "liable to considerable interruption from the wandering and disaffected Indians in that quarter." His recommendation was to shift a company from the Seventh Infantry to the troubled area.[18]

The citizens of the region did not give the government time to respond to their call for army assistance; they began raising a force to be employed against the Comanches. The organizers of the expedition, claiming authority from the Mexican government, encountered substantial opposition from American officials and were forced to abandon the campaign before it was well under way. The abortive expedition resolved nothing; the governor of Arkansas Territory reported that "some Hundreds of Indians of various northern Tribes are now assembling in the Mexican Territory adjoining ours." Warning that "there are considerable Bands of these Savages at no great Distance from our Posts," he advised reinforcing these garrisons immediately.[19]

Conflict was not restricted to the Red River area. Osages from the Three Forks region raided a Pawnee town during their 1827 summer expedition. With the aid of two Frenchmen, the Pawnees offered a spirited defense, inflicting almost as many casualties as they suffered. For years Washington had tolerated the Osage-Pawnee conflict, but their warfare was increasingly impeding government plans. The reports of Osage–Plains Indian hostilities frightened government surveyors, who refused to continue running the boundary line for the new Osage reservation.[20]

The growing menace of the Plains tribes was one of the topics of discussion when the army's Inspector General, George Croghan, visited Cantonment Gibson in August, 1827. Croghan acknowledged that the Plains Indians would be more troublesome as the frontier expanded westward. He recommended the creation of an additional garrison on the frontier between Cantonments Gibson and Leavenworth to hold the Pawnees at bay.[21]

Until the late summer of 1827, Plains Indians had not been reported in the immediate vicinity of Cantonment Gibson. That situation changed when Pawnee war parties invaded the area. One band in search of horses sneaked into an Osage village under the cover of darkness. The next morning, the Pawnee warriors were discovered and pursued by the Osages, who returned with three scalps. In another encounter the Pawnees fared better. They killed a Frenchman named Ols Swiss near Chouteau's trading house within three miles of the post. Another man, wounded by the Indians, escaped and was pursued to the Grand River within musket range of the garrison. Arbuckle dispatched a detachment in pursuit of the assailants, but it was unable to overtake them. The arrows recovered from the victims confirmed that the attackers were Pawnees. Inspector General Croghan, who was visiting the post about the time of the attack, urged that one or two companies of cavalry be stationed at Cantonments Gibson and Leavenworth. The mobility provided by mounted troops, Croghan predicted, would secure "the peace of the whole frontier from Prairie du Chein to Cantonment Jesup."[22] Again, an economy-conscious Congress proved reluctant.

The hostilities of the summer and fall caused the Osages to anticipate a retaliatory raid by the Pawnees. The Osage agent urged the government to arrange a meeting between his tribe and the Plains Indians to secure a cessation of hostilities. He also advocated the establishment of a military post at the Osage agency to "strengthen the chain [of frontier posts] & security, render communications certain & rappid & give an efficient support to our traders & protection to our Citizens, independent of insuring peace among the different tribes."[23] This recommendation, like Croghan's, produced no immediate results, but the continued strife on the Southwestern frontier would soon compel federal officials to take action.

The Osages were not the only tribe in conflict with the Plains Indians. In 1827 and 1828, Cherokee hunting parties clashed with the Pawnees. Although the better-armed Cherokees inflicted more casualties than they received, the desire for revenge was strong among most of the thirty-five Cherokees who traveled onto the Plains to hunt during the winter of 1828. The party encountered four Plains Indians, rejected their friendly overtures, and killed two of them. The two survivors alerted their tribe, which overtook the assailants and attacked them. The superior arms of the Cherokees enabled them to withstand the attack while losing only two of their warriors.

Although they had provoked the Plains Indians, the Cherokees vowed revenge. A seven-man party located a Plains Indian village where they planned to redeem their pledge. As they surveyed the camp from the hill above, a member of the party discovered a beehive within a tree. Disregarding the warnings of his companions, he began hacking at the tree to obtain honey. Not surprisingly, he aroused not only the bees but also the Indians from the village. Caught in the open, the seven Cherokees' one hope was flight. Five of them escaped. The Plains Indians celebrated their victory at a dance during which the corpse of one of their victims was mutilated. An account of this victory celebration was eventually reported to the Cherokees. A continuation of the conflict was inevitable.[24]

In the summer of 1828, the Plains Indians again threatened the frontier settlements close to Cantonments Gibson and Towson. In August two soldiers from Cantonment Towson on their way to the Kiamichi to fish were murdered and scalped by Pawnee Indians. A party of soldiers, white settlers, and friendly Delawares tracked the attackers to the Blue River, about ninety miles from the garrison. In the ensuing skirmish, seven Pawnees were killed and the scalps of the murdered soldiers recovered. The pursuers suffered only one casualty, a Delaware chief who was wounded by a poisoned arrow in the leg. Colonel Arbuckle felt certain that prompt retaliation against the Pawnees would prevent their early return to the vicinity of Cantonment Towson. In reporting the episode to his superiors, the colonel called attention to the need for strengthening the frontier garrison not only by increasing the number of men, but also by providing enough horses to enable the troops to pursue the marauding bands. Arbuckle's recommendations for reinforcing Cantonment Towson were supported by the territorial governor of Arkansas who warned that the Pawnees' ally, the Comanches, could "muster some Thousands of armed Men" and that "the utter Uselessness of the Military Post at Fort Towson," was obvious.[25] Neither additional troops nor horses were forthcoming, however, and the Cantonment Towson area remained turbulent.

Even though the garrison at Cantonment Gibson was many times the size of Cantonment Towson's, the summer of 1828 was an uneasy time for the people living in the region. Reports of Plains Indian activity prompted Arbuckle to send an express to warn Union Mission of the approach of fifteen hundred Comanches. Although the war party never reached the Three Forks, one of the missionaries noted, "We have had two seasons of alarm on account of these people [the Plains Indians] fearing they were coming in upon us like a flood."[26] Both Indians and whites looked to Cantonment Gibson to stem the Plains Indian flood.

Despite the obvious dangers, the prospects of high profits lured traders beyond the frontier. Disregarding warnings, a five-man trading party from Hempstead County, Arkansas, entered the Comanche country in October, 1828, to trade with the Plains tribes. At first the Indians appeared friendly, and trading commenced, but the mood suddenly changed, and the Indians fell upon the white traders, all of whom were killed except one who escaped by leaping from a high bluff and concealing himself until dark in a thicket. Unarmed and with little food, the survivor fled from the Comanche country and reached the settlements fifteen days later. His report fueled the belief that the Plains tribes intended to ravage the exposed frontier in the spring.[27]

The episode prompted the editor of the *Arkansas Gazette* to urge the government to provide better military protection from the "numerous hordes of Indians who inhabit the country bordered on the south-western part of this Territory." He also recommended replacing infantry units stationed at the frontier posts with mounted troops. "A *single* company of Mounted Gun-men," the editor claimed, "composed of experienced woodsman, could do more towards repressing the aggressions of the Indians, than *three* or *four* companies of Infantry." The War Department had already recognized the desirability of mounted troops for service on the Southwestern frontier. The commanding general of the army, Alexander Macomb, had recommended to the President that some of the companies in each regiment serving on "the plains towards the Mexican frontier, and towards the Rocky Mountains," be mounted. This organization, Macomb said, "would enable the commandants of the garrisons in that quarter to overtake and punish promptly any of those mounted tribes, which inhabit the plains, that may venture to commit depredations on the frontier inhabitants."[28] The need for mounted troops was obvious; but the wheels of government moved slowly; it would require three years for Congress to respond to the general's recommendation.

Plains Indian attacks on the Santa Fe caravans underlined the need for the mounted force requested by Arbuckle and Izard. The Comanches and Pawnees not only plundered the traders but also broadcast the news of the success to the other Plains tribes to incite them to join in future attacks. Lack of manpower at Cantonments Gibson and Leavenworth forced the government to accept an Osage offer to provide between eight hundred and a thousand warriors to engage the Indians harrassing the Santa Fe Trail.[29] Such measures did not satisfy the American traders, who demanded military escorts. In 1829, the government finally acceded to their demands and sent a command under Major Bennett Riley to guard the caravan.

News of Plains Indian attacks to the west produced fears that the white settlements near Cantonment Towson would be paid another visit in the spring or summer of 1829. The beleaguered commander of the post informed his superiors of "the great *necessity*, of an increase of force at this place." Arbuckle concurred and had already recommended that an entire regiment be stationed on the Arkansas River and a similar force on the Red to police the increasing Indian population. In Washington, Arkansas congressional delegate Ambrose H. Sevier urged the Secretary of War to bolster the garrison on the Arkansas to save his people from an Indian war in the spring.[30]

Ignoring the recommendations of its commanders in the field, the War Department directed that Cantonment Towson be abandoned. When the troops left the post on the Kiamichi River in June, 1829, Cantonment Gibson remained the only military outpost on the frontier of Arkansas Territory. Colonel Arbuckle stretched his meager resources to show the flag in the Red River area. In September, he sent Captain John Stuart and his company to reconnoiter the region between the Arkansas and Red Rivers. Of course, an understrength infantry company conducting an occasional reconnaissance in this vast area could not restrain the Indians or calm the agitated white settlers. One resident warned that the removal of Cantonment Towson exposed the frontier to not less than thirty thousand Comanche, Pawnee, and Waco Indians. He reported, "All is hurry and confusion here, to get off from this neglected region & out of the reach of the devastation & ruin which is anticipated from the hostile Indians on the withdrawal of the troops."[31]

The Arkansas territorial assembly emphasized the same theme in a memorial addressed to the United States Congress in which the legislators directed the attention of Congress to the "danger from the Indian population, which stretches across their whole western frontier." Two months after the memorial was drafted, on January 22, 1830, the Pawnees proved the assembly's point by killing a settler within three miles of Miller Court House. The assailants were pursued to the Cross Timbers but escaped. The pursuers returned with the alarming news that there were signs of numerous bands of Indians within twelve miles of their settlements.[32]

The situation on Arkansas's southwestern frontier had deteriorated to the point that the acting governor ordered Colonel John Clark of the territorial militia to hold his command "in readiness . . . to take the field at a moments warning," and to send four men beyond the frontier to "spy" on the Indians. These measures were recommended to the acting governor by Colonel Arbuckle, who was apprehensive about the safety of the American citizens on the Red River frontier and realized that Cantonment Gibson was "too remote to give them timely support, against the usual attacks of the Indians." In a letter to the Secretary of War, Arbuckle repeated his belief that a full regiment was required on the Arkansas River and another on the Red River to insure the security of the frontier.[33]

The commander of Cantonment Gibson was not the only person directing the attention of his government to the problems of frontier defense. The territorial delegate from Arkansas was urging Congress to establish a mounted force to police the Indians of the frontier. To support his proposal, Sevier introduced a letter from the Quartermaster General of the Army, who wrote that it was impossible to control the Plains Indians by infantry alone and stressed that mounted troops "are indispensable to the complete security" of the frontier.[34]

If the federal government was slow to respond to the threat posed by the Plains Indians, the Cherokees were not. Smarting from the treatment their comrades had received at the hands of the Pawnees, the tribe was determined upon revenge. John Smith, a Cherokee who lived in the vicinity of Cantonment Gibson, led a party of Cherokee and Creek warriors to the settlements of the Texas Cherokees in the early spring of 1830. Volunteers from the southern branch of the tribe swelled Smith's force to a total of sixty-three warriors, who marched west onto the prairie to meet the Pawnees. After a journey of ten days, the force located a Pawnee village which they attacked at dawn. Displaying no compassion, the attackers ignored pleas for mercy and killed warriors, women, and infants. Surviving Pawnee warriors withdrew to a large fortified lodge and withstood repeated assaults until the arrival of other Plains Indians forced the Cherokees to abandon the attack. The Cherokees, who lost only five men, departed with sixty scalps. The success of the expedition inspired the victors to plan another.[35]

The Cherokees were not the only tribe that sought revenge against the Pawnees. Some months before, a three-hundred-man Osage war party surprised a band of Pawnees in their village on the Arkansas River. Outnumbered and surrounded, the Pawnees abandoned the village and retreated to the shore of a lake, where they were trapped between the Osages and the water. The attackers discarded their guns and fell upon the Pawnees with knives and tomahawks, killing all except a few who were taken prisoner. The victorious Osages returned to their village with eighty to ninety scalps, five women prisoners, and eighty-four horses. The missionaries at Union observed that the Osages "have never carried on their war so briskly, and slaughtered so many, as during the last year."[36]

Colonel Arbuckle did not intervene in the conflict between the Osages and Plains tribes. In fact the colonel believed that continued strife had some value. He explained that "there are many restless spirits among the different Tribes on this Frontier, who must and will be Employed in war or mischief of some kind." The arrival of large numbers of Eastern Indians, Arbuckle believed, would eventually compel the Plains tribes to seek peace.[37] This seemingly callous policy was not a sinister plan to encourage the Indians in a war of mutual self-destruction but rather a reflection of the primary objective of the government to protect white settlers and encourage Indian removal with a minimum outlay for military expenses. However, the conflict with the Plains Indians and disaffected bands along the Red River became increasingly troublesome as the government succeeded in persuading more Eastern tribes to relocate in the newly established Indian Territory. The policy of the 1820's which tolerated intertribal conflict beyond the frontier gave way in the 1830's to an active effort to establish peace among the Western tribes.

Chapter 7

Houston: an Indian Interlude

A PLAN TO pacify the Plains Indians was proposed in 1829 by one of the most colorful of Cantonment Gibson's many visitors. On his arrival in the early summer, General Sam Houston offered to undertake an expedition to the Pawnees to end their conflict with the Osages. Colonel Matthew Arbuckle was not receptive to the idea, but the general was not a man who could be ignored. Houston repeated his offer until 1832, when the War Department finally accepted. Actually, Houston was more than a visitor at Cantonment Gibson; from 1829 to 1833 he played an important role in the relations between the post and the tribes of Indian Territory. Equally welcome at Cantonment Gibson or in the lodges of the Indians, Houston became an intermediary who conveyed the requests of Colonel Arbuckle and the government to the neighboring tribes and transmitted the Indian point of view to the post and Washington.

Matrimonial problems had dashed Houston's promising political career in Tennessee and, according to his own description, left him "the most unhappy man now living." Resigning as governor of Tennessee in 1829, Houston decided to return to the Cherokees with whom he had lived for several years as a boy. On his journey to Indian Territory, the general considered a number of schemes to revive his shattered career, including the formation of a "Rocky Mountain Empire" and the conquest of Mexico and Texas. The latter, Houston hoped, would make him "worth two million in two years." It was even rumored in Tennessee that Houston had resigned to capitalize on Andrew Jackson's plans for the removal of the Cherokees.[1] What the general hoped to accomplish is now unclear, but there is little doubt that the Indians with whom Houston planned to live figured prominently in his schemes.

In the Cherokee country the former governor was warmly received by John Jolly, the principal chief of the tribe. Jolly had taken

Sam Houston as he appeared in Washington serving as the ambassador from the Cherokees. From a photograph of a miniature painted in 1830, courtesy Mrs. F. T. Baldwin.

Houston into his family about twenty years earlier, when the monotony of farming and clerking had driven the youthful Houston from the family store to the Cherokees for the first time. The aging chief believed that the Great Spirit had prompted the return of his adopted white son to counsel and aid the tribe. The general's words seemed to confirm Jolly's belief; plunging into the politics of Indian Territory, Houston zealously protested the machinations of the agents and government officials charged with the administration of Indian affairs. His pleas were eloquent, but his sincerity was open to question. Marquis James, a sympathetic biographer of Houston, concluded that the general regarded the Indian as a means of achieving power.[2] Behind the public Houston, the ardent advocate of Indian causes, there seems to have existed a clever opportunist whose real concern was personal, economic, and political aggrandizement.

Houston first saw Cantonment Gibson in June, 1829, about a month after his arrival in Indian Territory. For the next three years, he was a frequent visitor at the post, yet nowhere in his writings is there a description of the fort or its inhabitants. Most visitors recorded their impressions of the post and its personnel in considerable detail; Houston seldom mentioned it. While the general may have been oblivious to Cantonment Gibson, he must have been a major topic of conversation among the soldiers and civilians there. Nor was interest in the former governor restricted to the post. Even before Houston arrived, President Jackson had passed the word to Arkansas officials to keep him under surveillance and to report his actions to Washington. The President apparently had heard the rumors circulating in Washington that Houston was considering adventures in Mexico that might jeopardize diplomatic negotiations with that nation. Houston wrote the President from Little Rock in May, 1829, to assure him that the charges were rumors started by individuals who hope "to complete my ruin." The former governor also offered his services to the administration in keeping "peace among the Indians, & between them & the *whites.*"[3]

Houston reached Cantonment Gibson about the same time a large delegation of Creeks headed by Roley McIntosh called upon Colonel Arbuckle to protest the government's failure to honor fully its commitments to Creeks settling in Indian Territory. The delegation presented its grievances to the colonel in a memorial addressed to President Jackson. Houston witnessed the document and was given a copy by McIntosh to forward to Washington in order to insure that Creek views were reported to the President himself. In his letter transmitting the Creek memorial, Houston urged the President to order an investigation of the Creek charges.[4]

In his first weeks in the Cherokee country, Houston met with leaders of the Cherokees, Osages, Creeks, and Choctaws, the major Indian tribes in the Cantonment Gibson area. These discussions convinced Houston that he could with "little difficulty" pacify the Indian country. From Cantonment Gibson he wrote Secretary of War John Eaton, proposing a plan to end the conflict between the Osages and Pawnees. Termination of this long-standing dispute, he predicted, would pave the way for bringing the Plains Indians to terms. Asserting that "Peace would cost a mere trifle to our Government," the general recommended A. P. Chouteau as the logical man for the delicate job of persuading the Pawnees. He offered to accompany and assist Chouteau should the government approve the project. Houston's concern for the Indians was no doubt genuine, but it does not strain credulity to suggest that he and Chouteau may have discussed the lucrative trade that awaited those who won the friendship of the Pawnees and the other Plains tribes. If Chouteau and Houston could pacify the Southern Plains, profits from trade with the less sophisticated tribes would be enormous. In his letter to the Secretary of War, Houston stressed the advantages to the government and its "interprising citizens" of his plan. No doubt Houston hoped to be one of those "interprising citizens."[5]

Houston's reputation and his close association with the President insured him special status at Cantonment Gibson. He is reported to have established close relations with the officers of the garrison, frequently joining in their poker and drinking bouts. Although Colonel Arbuckle seems to have resented Houston's interference, he not only allowed the former governor to participate in negotiations with the various tribes, but he also entrusted him with the task of preventing a coalition of tribes from attacking the Plains Indians. On July 7, 1829, after conferring with Arbuckle, Houston attended a Creek-Cherokee war council. A number of the younger Cherokee warriors, against the advice of the former governor and most of their chiefs, decided to attack the Pawnees and Comanches. Houston learned that some 250 Osages, Choctaws, Shawnees, Delawares, and Cherokees intended to invade the Plains within fifteen days. He advised Arbuckle that he would continue his efforts to dissuade the young Cherokees "until all hope is lost."[6] The general's efforts may have delayed the Cherokees, but early the next year Cherokee warriors joined in a devastating raid on a Pawnee village in Texas.

Although the Indians did not always accept Houston's advice, they seemed more willing to discuss their problems with him than with other white men. The former governor would in turn relay the Indian viewpoint to government officials. From the Cherokees Houston learned that the "most turbulent" warriors wanted Cantonment Gibson abandoned and the soldiers stationed outside Indian Territory. Houston considered the post essential to the security of Indian Territory and predicted that its removal would precipitate a "sanguinary & savage" war. After conferring with the Osages, Houston advised Arbuckle that Clermont's Osages were reluctant to comply with the terms of the 1825 treaty which required them to vacate their lands east of the Verdigris. The general warned that if the Osages were "driven to the open Prairie," it would frustrate government and missionary efforts to encourage them to take up farming. Noting the overlapping claims of the Creeks and Cherokees to the land between the Arkansas and Canadian Rivers, Houston predicted difficulties unless the government exercised great care in working out a boundary adjustment.[7] Houston's influence on the development of Indian policy is difficult to gauge, but it is significant that not long after he called these and other problems to the attention of President Jackson, a three-member Indian commission, headed by Governor Montfort Stokes of North Carolina, was established and empowered to seek solutions.

Cantonment Gibson and the Three Forks area had its own initiation rite for newcomers, and even the illustrious Sam Houston would not be excused. In August, 1829, Houston contracted a malarial fever which as he said, "well nigh closed the scene of all my mortal cares." For over a month the Cherokees nursed their stricken friend, whose condition began to improve in mid-September. Houston's convalescence afforded him time to reflect on the recent changes in his life. He had hoped that life among the Indians would divert his attention from the political arena from which he had fled. His first months on the Indian frontier convinced the former governor that the past could not be forgotten. Newspapers that arrived at Cantonment Gibson were a constant reminder of the world he had abandoned. Houston wrote President Jackson, "It is hard for an old Trooper, to forget the *note* of the *Bugle!* Having been so actively engaged for years past in politics, it is impossible to lose all interest." Rather cryptically he suggested that "I might render my aid in some future political struggle between usurpation, and rights of the people."[8] Whether Houston was offering the President his services in overthrowing Mexican rule in Texas is not clear. It does seem apparent that the former governor was not satisfied with the limited horizons afforded within the Indian country.

Not long after his recovery, tribal leaders extended Cherokee citizenship to Houston and selected him as a member of a delegation to travel to Washington to protest the corruption of Indian Bureau officials. John Jolly placed his mark at the bottom of a letter to President Jackson introducing Houston as a man whose "path is not crooked" and who is "beloved by all my people." Some of the Cherokees did not share Jolly's evaluation. John Rogers, a future principal chief of the Western Cherokees, wrote Secretary of War John Eaton that fears of what Houston and the delegation might do in Washington "are creating much anxiety and uneasiness amongst our people." Rogers implored Eaton not to listen to the designs of Houston and the delegation.[9]

Rogers' apprehensions were well founded. Attired in a manner befitting an ambassador from the Cherokees, Houston renewed his friendship with President Jackson and then used that friendship in an attempt to secure a government contract to provide rations for emigrating Indians. While Houston emphasized that his intent was "to do ample justice to the Indians in giving to them full ration," his motive did not go unchallenged. During a Congressional inquiry into the matter, several members of the House of Representatives accused the general of attempting "wrongfully, to obtain the contract . . . for the supply of rations to the emigrating Indians," and of scheming "to obtain such a contract upon terms disadvantageous to the Government." Since the House of Representatives generally supported Jackson, it is not surprising that the majority report of the investigating committee cleared Houston of the charge of fraud. The testimony of several witnesses and Houston's own correspondence, however, raised doubts concerning the objectivity of the inquiry. Duff Green, a prominent Washington editor who opposed Jackson, testified that Houston proposed a bid of eighteen cents a ration—twelve cents higher than it ought to have cost.[10]

Ultimately, lower bids forced Houston to advise his associates to reduce their price by one-third while he urged his competitors to raise their bids so "that a great fortune could be made." The controversy surrounding the contract soon prompted the War Department to reject all offers. Back in Indian Territory several months later, Houston penned a stinging indictment of the government for leaving the immigrant Indians destitute in the west "while hundreds are ready to furnish the accustomed rations at six or seven cents each."[11] This protest would have been more believable had not Houston himself proposed a bid of eighteen cents a ration.

Houston had more than Indian rations on his mind during his visit to Washington in 1830. His six-months residence in Indian Territory had convinced him that most of the agents in the Cantonment Gibson area were unworthy, and he did not hesitate to express this opinion. Within a period of six months, Cherokee agent Edward W. DuVal, Creek agent David Brearley, Osage agent John F. Hamtramck, and the chief of the War Department's Indian Office, Thomas McKenney, were removed. The general's campaign against these officials may have been motivated by his indignation concerning their treatment of the Indians, but it seems more than coincidental that most of them were obstacles to the realization of his financial schemes.[12]

Before returning to Indian Territory, Houston agreed to convey an appeal from President Jackson to Chief Jolly urging an end to the conflict between the Osages and the Cherokees. Sometime during his years with the Cherokees, perhaps while he was in Washington, Houston proposed that he, Colonel Arbuckle, and Colonel Chouteau be authorized to negotiate with the Pawnee in an effort to end their feud with the Osages. Terminating this rivalry, Houston suggested, would resolve the Indian problems on the American frontier and facilitate Jackson's removal plans. Perhaps the President was not yet convinced of Houston's emotional stability, for it would be another two years before he would entrust the general with a mission to the Plains tribes. When he returned to Cantonment Gibson, Houston suggested to Arbuckle that he and A. P. Chouteau might be useful in preserving the peace among the Indians. The colonel, obviously irritated by his meddling, informed Houston that he "was not instructed to call for his assistance or that of Mr. Chouteau." Arbuckle continued, "I am decidedly of the opinion that but few of those who visit Indian country as Traders can be relied on to negotiate with Indians, when the object of the government may interfere with their interest."[13]

Returning to the Cherokee Nation, Houston sought the assistance of his friends in a business venture. He had heard reports that

General John Nicks, sutler at Cantonment Gibson, was to be removed from his post because of a disagreement with Major Asher Phillips, the army paymaster. Acting on the belief that the position of post sutler at Cantonment Gibson would soon be vacant, Houston suggested himself to Secretary of War Eaton as a substitute. The position of sutler at a remote frontier post gave its occupant a near monopoly on the soldiers' trade and could be very profitable. Apparently certain that his appointment would be forthcoming, Houston purchased a keelboat-load of supplies from New York and Nashville and had them shipped up the Arkansas River to Cantonment Gibson. But upon reaching Arkansas, the former governor learned that his information concerning Nicks's removal was unfounded and asked that his request for appointment be withdrawn.[14]

When he returned, Houston opened a store not far from Cantonment Gibson where he pledged to provide the Indians with trade goods "at honest prices." The store and the general's home, which he called Wigwam Neosho, were located in a large log structure in an apple orchard between the Verdigris and Grand Rivers. Although he would not divorce his first wife until 1833, Houston shared his "wigwam" with a Cherokee mixed-blood named Tiana. She was the widow of a white blacksmith and related to several of the leading Cherokee families. While the arrangement seems to have been informal, Tiana was referred to as Mrs. Houston.[15]

The new proprietor informed Colonel Arbuckle that his Cherokee citizenship excused him from obtaining a license to trade with the Indians. He did feel called upon to explain that the barrels of liquor included in his shipments would not be sold to Indians or soldiers and would not be disposed of without Arbuckle's knowledge and consent. The commander of Cantonment Gibson did not concur in Houston's belief that his naturalization as a Cherokee freed him from the restrictions imposed on American citizens by the Indian Intercourse Law and requested a ruling from the War Department. The Acting Secretary of War rejected Houston's contention that his adoption by the Cherokees gave him special status. He reasoned that "an Indian tribe did not have the right to confer on such citizens any privileges incompatible with the laws of the United States."[16]

Before the end of the summer of 1830, Houston had cast another financial iron in the fire. Turning to land speculation, the former governor purchased from the Osages salt springs within the Cherokee Nation near Cantonment Gibson. Concerning the venture the general wrote an associate, "I am just about to make a grand purchase of Salt Springs, and trust in God that I will be in a way to 'do well.' My fortune must not *wane*, it must *full*." George Vashon, the Cherokee agent, claimed Houston and his partners had made the purchase "with a view and expectation of prevailing on the Government to purchase them out at an exorbitant price, by availing themselves of an undue influence over the Cherokees to induce them to demand of the Government the removal of persons unacceptable to them." Subsequent developments support Vashon's assertion. Houston drafted instructions for the Cherokee delegation that traveled to Washington in 1831. One of its demands was that all land within the nation's boundaries be transferred to the tribe. Such a transfer could have resulted in substantial government compensation, but Houston seems to have been impatient. In 1832 he sold a portion of the tract for $30 an acre. How he disposed of the rest of his land is not clear, but one authority on Indian Territory wrote, "he seems to have made a tidy profit from his investment."[17]

About the same time Houston acquired the saline springs, he launched a vitriolic attack in the *Arkansas Gazette* on those who preyed upon the Indians. Writing under the pseudonyms Tah-Lohn-Tus-Ky and Standing Bear, Houston accused Indian agents, War Department officials, and private contractors of defrauding the tribes and betraying their interest. From June to December, 1830, five letters appeared in the *Arkansas Gazette* the last so torrid that the editor printed it in a separate supplement. In particular, Houston decried the tendency of "the Agent and his friends to speculate upon the Indians," and condemned "*those who hover about these Indians more in the character of birds of prey than angels of mercy.*" His criticism was directed in part at those who speculated in the script or specie certificates often used by the government in lieu of specie in payment of annuities. The general was correct when he asserted that "An Indian does not know the value of paper in his hands," but his indictment of those who preyed on the Indians may have been less than sincere.[18]

Houston's political enemies accused him of trading in specie certificates, and the authors of a recent study of Houston's years among the Cherokees suggest that he was a silent partner of men engaged in such speculation. While not suggesting that he was a speculator, Marquis James reported that the Cherokees entrusted Houston with at least $66,000 of their certificates. Whether Houston actually speculated in Indian specie certificates remains uncertain. There is no doubt that the general was intent on improving his financial condition.[19]

Perhaps the Cherokees sensed that Houston was trying to use them. When he presented himself as a candidate for the Cherokee National Council in the spring of 1831, he was defeated decisively. Dogged by the failure of his grandiose schemes and rejected by his adopted people, Houston ultimately "buried his sorrows in the flowing bowl." His effort to dispose personally of the ten barrels of liquor he had purchased prompted the Indians to rename him "Big Drunk," which now seemed a more accurate reflection of his character than his earlier name, "The Raven." One of Houston's early biographers mentions his "occasional indulgences" during his visits to Cantonment Gibson and other white settlements. Marquis James is less charitable in his Pulitzer Prize–winning biography, *The Raven*, picturing Houston at the ebb of his fortune at Cantonment Gibson, passed out drunk among the tree stumps, an impediment to those who strolled along the paths about the post.[20]

Houston's conduct during this period was censured by the missionaries who resided in the Cantonment Gibson area. They found his unorthodox religious views, his overindulgence, and his extramarital arrangement injurious to their effort to civilize and Christianize the Indians. Perhaps even more disappointing to the missionaries was Houston's failure to seek additional funds for their work on his first trip East. The former governor respected the dedication and bravery of the missionaries, but he dismissed their endeavors as a "very poor way to go about civilizing the Indians." Houston's objection to missionary activity may have led him to support an attempt to remove Union Mission from the Cherokee lands. Cherokee agent George Vashon warned the Secretary of War that Houston had written the instructions for the Cherokee delegation going to Washington in late 1831. These instructions called "for a literal fulfilment of the Treaty of 1828 which stipulates for the removal of all persons unacceptable to the Cherokees." Vashon was certain that the delegation would demand the removal of the mission, sacrificing "the true interests of the Cherokees to gratify the private views of a few individuals."[21]

Houston's disfavor among the missionaries, his drinking, and the suspicions of the Cherokee agent certainly reduced his influence among the Indians. Yet even at the nadir of this fortune, the general continued to play an active role in the affairs of Cantonment Gibson and Indian Territory. In May, 1831, he participated in the negotiations between the Osages and the Cherokees and Creeks which resulted in two treaties that terminated the long-standing feud between the Osages and emigrating tribes.[22]

Houston's escape into an alcoholic fog was terminated abruptly in the late summer of 1831, when he learned that his mother was seriously ill in Tennessee. Rushing to her bedside, Houston arrived in time to be present when she died. The trauma of her death had a sobering impact on the hapless expatriate. Shortly after his return to Indian Territory, the general accompanied another Cherokee delegation to Washington as an official advisor. Houston's dress might still be Indian, but by this time his thoughts were increasingly focused on Texas. In 1829, pressure from President Jackson had compelled Houston to pledge to refrain from any adventures in Texas.[23] The failure of Jackson's attempts to purchase Texas from Mexico had since persuaded the President to pursue a more vigorous policy.

By 1832, Andrew Jackson seemed receptive to Houston's schemes involving Texas. Of course, the President could not openly support his friend's venture, but he could and did provide a cloak of legitimacy and, perhaps, even some financial assistance. On his return to Indian Territory, Houston stopped off at the Hermitage to confer with Jackson, who may have loaned him as much as $500. The War Department accorded Houston semi-official status by requesting that he gather information on various Plains tribes and transmit his findings to the newly appointed Stokes Commission. The department also issued him a passport requesting that all Indian tribes permit him passage through their lands and give him aid and protection. Houston returned briefly to Indian Territory, where he disposed of Wigwam Neosho, concluded his personal affairs, and conferred with Henry Ellsworth, the first member of the Stokes Commission to arrive at Cantonment Gibson. Houston then pointed his horse south and in December, 1832, crossed the Red River into Texas.[24]

Houston did not sever his ties with Indian Territory immediately. During the next six months he sent two reports to the Stokes Commission at Cantonment Gibson and in May, 1833, returned to deliver a report in person. The tribes of the Three Forks also continued to play a role in his plans. Before going to Texas,

Houston advised a friend that he could make use of "the Indians on the Arkansas as auxiliaries in the event of a change" in the situation in Texas.

But Houston provided little useful information about the Plains Indians to the Stokes Commission at Cantonment Gibson. Once in Texas he was quickly drawn into the events that were building toward the Alamo. In his first report from Fort Towson in December, 1832, Houston suggested that the Comanches roamed the plains west of Fort Towson in May and June and followed the buffalo south in the winter. He proposed to journey to San Antonio in order to make contact with them. Houston's second letter to Cantonment Gibson reported his discussions with the Comanches and informed the commissioners that he had persuaded the Comanches to meet with them at Cantonment Gibson. Houston said the tribe was "well disposed to make a treaty with the United States."[25]

In May, 1833, the month designated for the council, Houston arrived at Cantonment Gibson, but the Indians did not. Nevertheless, Houston submitted to the Government a bill for $3,520 for his expenses as a "special agent" of the War Department. The department paid Houston only $1,200 pointing out that most of the intelligence he had supplied was secondhand. Even the lesser amount seems exorbitant for the information and services he provided. Of course, if Houston's true mission really involved Texas and not the Indians, the $1,200 was well spent, for Houston gave Jackson an excellent analysis of the conditions in Texas. In early 1833, the general informed the President, "If Texas is desirable to the United States it is now in the most favorable attitude perhaps that it can be to obtain it."[26] Few intelligence assessments have been as accurate.

Houston left Fort Gibson for the last time in May, 1833. His three years among the Indians added no luster to his reputation. They were years of disappointment and failure in which the worst side of Houston's character was exposed. But Houston was no different from many of the other whites who came into contact with the Indians and attempted to exploit them economically. It was difficult for hard-driving pioneers to resist the temptation to take advantage of the unsophisticated native. The soldiers at Cantonment Gibson were no exception. But because of the nature of military service, their economic interests usually did not conflict with that of the Indian. Consequently, the army often seemed to be the only frontier agency which attempted to secure justice for the tribes in the Southwest.

Chapter 8
Command Post in Indian Territory

DURING THE YEARS Sam Houston lived near Cantonment Gibson, President Andrew Jackson discarded the Jeffersonian policy of urging the Indians to move beyond the Mississippi and adopted a new approach based on coercion. Congress enacted the Indian Removal Act in May, 1830. While the Act contained no mention of forced removal, there was little doubt concerning the methods Jackson would employ. By withholding federal protection while the states were allowed to apply pressure to the Indians, removal was assured.[1] Strategically located in the area where Jackson intended to relocate the Southern tribes, Cantonment Gibson assumed a new importance.

Manned by half a regiment of understrength companies, Cantonment Gibson was ill-prepared for the flood of immigrant Indians that would soon descend upon it. In August, 1831, army General-in-Chief Alexander Macomb decided to concentrate the entire Seventh Infantry on the Grand River. The last five companies of the regiment formerly stationed in Louisiana arrived at Cantonment Gibson in late January, 1832, increasing the force at the post to 382 officers and men. This concentration of personnel occurred just a few weeks before the War Department redesignated the Grand River post Fort Gibson. General Macomb also assigned four companies of the Third Infantry, under Major Stephen W. Kearny, the task of reactivating Cantonment Towson, which had been abandoned two years earlier. General Macomb's reinforcement of the Southwestern frontier was designed to facilitate the immigration of Eastern Indians and to provide protection for them against the attacks of unfriendly tribes.[2]

The assignment of ten companies to a facility designed for half that number necessitated a renewed building program. Colonel Matthew Arbuckle proposed replacing the wooden barracks on the west side of the post with stone buildings and erecting a stone wall to take the place of the rotting pickets of the stockade. He suggested that stone construction would cost little more than wood, since the stone could be quarried within a mile and a half of the garrison. In January, 1833, Quartermaster General Thomas J. Jesup informed the commander of Fort Gibson that he anticipated an appropriation from Congress that would enable Arbuckle to begin the proposed renovation. By April, an obviously irritated Arbuckle informed Jesup that the newspapers had yet to report a significant appropriation from Congress for construction at his post. "If a permanent work is not shortly commenced here," Arbuckle warned, "continual repairs will be required . . . which in the end may cost more, than the construction of good Buildings."[3] The warning was probably accurate, but Congress appropriated no more than the minimum required to maintain the post. The plans for reconstructing Fort Gibson encountered determined opposition, and until its deactivation in 1857 improvements and enlargement of the post were financed out of its meager annual allocation.

Meanwhile, the residents of western Arkansas, who opposed reconstruction of Fort Gibson, had begun agitating for the reactivation of Fort Smith after the territory's western boundary was relocated forty miles to the east in 1828. While they stressed the exposed nature of their frontier settlements to Indian depredations, economics seems to have been even more important than military considerations. In a frontier community where money was scarce, a military post was a major source of specie and a stimulus to the economy.[4] The residents of Arkansas Territory waged a long and eventually successful campaign to persuade Congress to reopen Fort Smith. The first phase of this campaign was to prevent any major construction at Fort Gibson. However, despite political opposition, the strategic location of the rough-hewn and decaying fort on the Grand made it the logical choice as the command post from which the army would supervise the immigration of the Southern tribes.

The refusal of Congress to appropriate funds for construction at Fort Gibson did not slow the Jackson administration's removal plans. While negotiators applied pressure on the Eastern tribes, the garrison stood by to assist the new arrivals. In September, 1830, Arbuckle ordered Captain Benjamin L. E. Bonneville to conduct an armed reconnaissance into the territory southwest of the post. The force was to "apprehend lawless characters; and to make a Survey

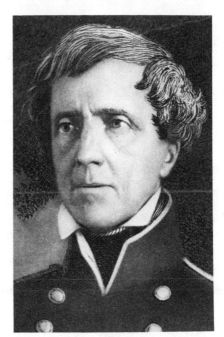

Stephen W. Kearny, a professional officer with years of frontier military experience who served as second-in-command of the Dragoons. From a mezzotint engraving in the Library of Congress, taken from an original daguerrotype engraved by J. B. Welch for *Graham's Magazine*.

of the Canadian river" as far west as the Cross Timbers. The primary objective of the expedition was to gather information on the "country intended for the Indian Tribes East of the Mississippi." For twenty days the company marched without encountering friends or enemies, through a country the captain described as "nothing but a barren waste, having no cultivable land, no game no timber."[5]

Government agents had already persuaded Choctaws and Chickasaws in Mississippi and Alabama to examine the area Bonneville explored. The Chickasaws had negotiated a removal treaty the previous August which would be annulled if their exploring party could find no land in the Indian country suitable to the needs of their people. In September the Choctaws also negotiated a removal treaty at Dancing Rabbit Creek in Mississippi. The exploring parties of both tribes reached the Indian Territory in late fall. Colonel Arbuckle assigned officers to accompany both parties while they explored the valleys of the Canadian, Blue, Washita, and Red rivers. The Chickasaws, who were dissatified with the government's plan to unite their people with the Choctaws on land between the Canadian and Red rivers, expressed dissatisfaction with the land above Red River and rejected it as unsuitable for their people. The rejection nullified the treaty and delayed their removal. The delegation did suggest that land south of the Red River in Mexican Territory would be acceptable to them.[6]

In persuading the Southern tribes to remove, the government had pledged to provide protection and security in the Indian country. Colonel Arbuckle knew that Fort Gibson alone could not secure the entire region. Anticipating the need for additional forts, he directed Lieutenant James L. Dawson to submit recommendations based on observations he had made while escorting the Chickasaw exploring party. Dawson concluded that a garrison located where the Blue River joined the Red River would provide adequate protection for the emigrating tribes and could be maintained without major logistical difficulties. Before Dawson's departure, Arbuckle had tentatively concluded that a post on the Canadian near the Cross Timbers would be preferable to one located on the Red. Dawson acknowledged that the latter location had some advantages, but he suggested that it would leave "a wide space unprotected in the cordon of posts which are intended to protect the frontier." The unsettled state of affairs in Texas and the Indian and white adventurers living along the Red River, the lieutenant believed, required the presence of the military below the Canadian.[7]

Removal would require not only the construction of new posts in Indian Territory but also the reactivation of several that had been abandoned. Large numbers of Choctaws would soon be traveling to their new home, where they would be dependent on government subsistence until they cleared their land and harvested a crop. The vacated facilities at Fort Smith were selected to be a supply depot for the tribe. To assist in obtaining and safeguarding the rations and supplies, Colonel Arbuckle ordered Lieutenant Gabrial Rains and a five-man detachment to Fort Smith. Their arrival on April 26, 1831, gave new life to the post at Belle Point, which the Seventh Infantry had abandoned in 1824 when it established Cantonment Gibson. A month earlier Lieutenant James R. Stephenson had been ordered to Cantonment Towson on similar duty. His assignment anticipated War Department plans to regarrison the post on the Red River to protect the southern flank of the Indian country.[8]

After the reoccupation of these two posts, the War Department authorized the Western Choctaw agent to call on Colonel Arbuckle

Benjamin L. E. Bonneville, career officer with long service on the Southwestern frontier. Courtesy Denver Public Library Western Collection.

for assistance in improving the route between Fort Towson and Fort Smith. In March, 1832, Lieutenant Colonel James B. Many, commanding the post while Arbuckle was on furlough, ordered Captain John Stuart to construct a road from Fort Smith to the Red River to facilitate the transportation of the immigrating Choctaws. The army had begun work on a similar route in 1828, but had abandoned the project because of lack of manpower. By 1832, there were more troops at Fort Gibson, but the post's funds were limited. Many provided Stuart with $200, rations for ninety days, and two wagons. The captain considered two wagons "totally unsufficient to transport the baggage and provisions of the detachment," but his requisition for five additional wagons was rejected. Colonel Many suggested that the Indian Department might provide additional transportation.[9]

Stuart sent his two wagons overland, and the rest of his forty-man command left Fort Gibson on March 22, 1832, by keelboat. They reached Fort Smith four days later, where Stuart learned that the Indian Department had "made no arrangements of any kind . . . towards opening the Road." After conferring with Colonel Robert Bean, who had been commissioned to survey the road, Captain Stuart began construction on March 28. Progress was slow at first because of heavy rains which turned the newly cut road into a quagmire. Stuart had to assign one-fourth of his force to escort the two wagons shuttling supplies to the work crew. After a month the road had been opened to Cavanal Mountain, some thirty miles southwest of Fort Smith. The captain had decided that he would not "employ the men any longer in playing the part of oxen" when he learned that four wagons and teams had been sent from Little Rock for his use.[10]

Beyond Cavanal Mountain, Stuart instituted stringent defensive measures to prevent surprise attack by western Indians who were reported to be active in the area. A mobile gun rack advanced with the work crew, and a stockade was constructed to protect equipment not needed immediately. As the road progressed toward the southwest, even greater precautions were required. The construction crew was ordered to stay together; an armed sentinel stood ready to cover the workers in case of attack, and at night Stuart posted a heavy guard around the camp and a mounted sentinel near the livestock. The Kiamichi Mountains slowed the rate of progress and compelled Stuart to narrow the roadbed. By the end of May, it became apparent that the rations would not last until the road was completed. A party was sent to Fort Towson to obtain additional provisions. They returned with food for six days; Fort Towson had not received its annual supplies and was able to provide no more. Stuart had no alternative but to put his men on half rations. Fast running out of food, the force worked frantically to complete the route, cutting only "such trees as were most likely to be in the way" and making only those improvements that could be accomplished "without detaining the wagons." The construction force reached Horse Prairie on the Red River June 16, with less than a week's rations left. A few head of cattle were purchased in the area, and several days later the detachment marched for Fort Smith on the

147-mile road they had just completed. Despite three months of backbreaking labor, the route was primitive even by nineteenth-century standards.[11]

The inadequacy of the roads was not the only problem complicating removal. The careless manner in which Western land had been awarded to immigrating tribes also hampered the government's plans. Overlapping boundaries had created conflicts that gave Eastern tribes justification for their reluctance to emigrate. The Secretary of War wanted this problem resolved at once. After the passage of the Indian Removal Act, the Reverend Isaac McCoy and President Jackson's nephew, John Donelson, were sent to the Indian country to survey boundaries between the tribes. When the surveying party assembled, McCoy complained that he was not able to obtain "Men and means to carry on our business from Fort Gibson." Further frustration arose from the unwillingness of the Cherokees and Creeks to resolve their boundary dispute.

Despite these problems, McCoy and Donelson began surveying in July, 1831, along the Arkansas border where the threat of Indian attack was minimal. When McCoy reached the Osage agency, he was met by Captain Edgar S. Hawkins and an escort of twenty-five soldiers. McCoy then proceeded through the Osage reservation, which he believed would be suitable to the Chickasaws, who had rejected a tract below the Canadian. He suggested that the Osages be shifted north to a reservation on the Kansas River.[12]

The military escort of the McCoy party was not merely ceremonial; there was a real danger of hostility in much of Indian Territory. In the autumn of 1829, warriors from the Red River killed six or seven Osages, all members of the family of Chief Tally. The Osages planned "swift and decisive vengeance," but were dissuaded by agents of the government, who hoped to arrange a settlement to the long-standing antagonism between the Osages and tribes living near the Red River. In the spring of 1830, a council was held at Cantonment Gibson, at which the government indemnified the Osages for the losses they had suffered.[13] While these arrangements restrained the Osages, they had little effect on the Red River tribes. On May 23, 1830, an Osage was wounded by a party of Indians whom Arbuckle learned were Kickapoos from the Red or the Sabine River. A month later a party of ten to fifteen Indians killed a Creek warrior about eight miles south of Cantonment Gibson. Arbuckle ordered Captain Nathaniel G. Wilkinson and a detachment of mounted soldiers, accompanied by 180 Creeks under the command of General Roley McIntosh, to pursue the band. Their trail led 150 miles to the southwest before it was obscured by tracks of wild horses and buffalo. Arbuckle could only guess about the identity of the attackers, but he speculated that they were Caddoes or some other tribesmen who resided along the Red River.[14]

The hostility of the Indians living along the Red River prompted Colonel Arbuckle to recommend to the Secretary of War the acquisition of an area sixty to eighty miles wide south of the Red River, extending from Louisiana to the 100th meridian. Arbuckle explained, "The different Bands now there are without restraint, and produce most of the disorders on this frontier." Its annexation to the United States would satisfy the needs of the emigrant Indians and "*insure peace between them and the United States,*" the colonel asserted.[15]

The resources of the Seventh Infantry were already strained in July, 1831, when Colonel Arbuckle received orders to hold his companies in readiness for service in Louisiana, where they might be required to suppress "disturbances on the part of the colored population." The colonel reminded his superiors that he had almost a company escorting McCoy's survey team and a detachment at Fort Smith guarding Choctaw subsistence stores. Under these circumstances he reported "it out of my power to promptly prepare my command for the service anticipated to the south."[16] Fortunately for Arbuckle, the difficulties in Louisiana subsided before it became necessary to call on the troops at Cantonment Gibson.

In the fall of 1831, McCoy again called on the army for assistance. In October, Lieutenant Dawson and a detachment of eight men accompanied a small survey team through the Creek country to the mouth of the Cimarron River. McCoy, who had learned of a Pawnee attack on a Delaware hunting party, decided not to explore the Canadian valley. He explained to Dawson that "it was a point of importance that he should pass through the country unmolested in any way by the Pawnees." He feared that the opponents of removal would use any incident to support their claim that the immigrating "Indians would find no security in their new homes." Following a safe return route, the party reached Cantonment Gibson without incident. Based on his observations, Dawson reported that the Creek country could not sustain a dense population. North of the Arkansas River, the good land was restricted to the river and creek bottoms, and on the other side the prairie was "of an inferior quality." Even the bottom lands along the Arkansas were not as rich as earlier reports indicated.[17]

McCoy, whose enthusiasm for removal may have obscured his judgment, did not share Dawson's opinion. He reported that the Creek lands were "sufficiently large and good for all the tribe, including the Seminoles." Moreover, he was convinced that "there is more land already assigned to the Cherokees than will be sufficient for all the tribe on both sides of the Mississippi."[18] Differences of opinion concerning the quality of land assigned to the immigrating tribes were academic. President Jackson had already decided that whether the land was good or bad, the Eastern Indians were going to live on it.

Despite Arbuckle's best efforts, conflict continued west of Cantonment Gibson. In the late fall of 1830, an Osage party was attacked "high up the Arkansas" by a band of Pawnees. Forced into retreat at first, the Osages rallied and routed the attacking Pawnees in a "short but bloody contest." The Osages, who used rifles, lost only two men, while the Pawnees, armed with spears and battle axes, left eighteen of their men dead on the field. Although no other major skirmishes were reported between immigrant and Plains Indians that autumn, hunting parties from the Eastern tribes were encroaching on the buffalo range with increasing frequency.[19]

Incursions onto the Plains by the Osages and immigrating Indians were bound to prompt retaliation. In the spring of 1831, three hundred Pawnees appeared in southeastern Indian Territory. Before they withdrew they killed a Choctaw and "skinned his head all over." About the same time, rumors of imminent Pawnee attack prompted several thousand Osages to evacuate their villages and set up a temporary camp within three miles of Cantonment Gibson, where their women and children would be safe. Most of the Osage warriors and two hundred Creeks then marched to confront the Pawnees. Apparently the invaders encountered no substantial resistance, for neither the missionaries nor the editor of the *Arkansas Gazette* reported a clash. But the growing conflict prompted one of the ministers at Union Mission to observe that the Osages' "wars with their western enemies continue with unabated fury."[20]

The Plains Indians were often indiscriminate in their retaliations. In early 1831, a Pawnee attack inflicted heavy casualties on a Delaware village on the Canadian River. The War Department ordered Arbuckle to provide "efficient protection" for the immigrants settling in the Creek Nation. With his resources already strained, the colonel could do no more than provide a small amount of ammunition for the Creeks. Such countermeasures were ineffective against the Comanches and Pawnees, who appeared "in great numbers on the borders of the Cross Timbers." Disturbances near Cantonment Gibson in the fall of 1831 spurred the commander of the Western Department to suggest that Arbuckle inform the hostile parties that the army would "punish as enemies all who shall in future dare to commit outrages of warlike nature near us."[21]

The threats and promises of the army provided little comfort for the immigrant Indians who bore the brunt of the depredations of the Plains tribes. On October 29, 1831, the Creeks appealed to the President for help. In a memorial they reminded Andrew Jackson that the government had pledged "vigorous support and protection" for those who elected to move to the Western wilderness. That promise had not been kept. "Wild Indians" from the Southern and Western frontiers constantly harrassed Creek settlements and endangered their people. The Creeks, who said they were also speaking for the Cherokees and Osages, urged the government to send commissioners to the Plains tribes to establish peace. Secretary of War Lewis Cass concurred and recommended that the President ask Congress to establish a three-member commission. Its mission would be to bring peace to the Indian country and resolve difficulties encountered by the immigrating tribes. Cass also proposed that Congress authorize a mounted force which could "strike terror" in the Plains Indians and provide the immigrating tribes the "protection they have a right to expect from the Government."[22] The President submitted both recommendations to Congress, which acted with unusual dispatch.

On July 14, 1832, legislation authorizing an Indian commission was approved; the same day Lewis Cass sent letters of instruction to several prospective members. These letters directed the commissioners to proceed to Fort Gibson to adjust existing difficulties between the tribes, recommend locations for tribes yet to immigrate, and persuade the Osages to accept a reservation on the Kansas River. Finally, the commissioners were to establish a permanent peace with the Plains tribes.[23]

Montfort Stokes, governor of North Carolina, accepted the chairmanship of the commission. Stokes was seventy years old at the time of his appointment, but he was still vigorous and alert. Although his major qualification for the position was his political

Nathan Boone, frontier army officer and son of Daniel Boone.

support of President Jackson, he undertook his assignment with determination. Despite rumors about his failing health, he accompanied several expeditions into the Indian country and soon became personally acquainted with the tribes and their problems.[24] Other commissioners were Henry L. Ellsworth, a Hartford, Connecticut, businessman, and the Reverend John F. Schermerhorn of Utica, New York, a persistent applicant for government appointment.

Colonel S. C. Stambaugh, editor of a Harrisburg, Pennsylvania, newspaper was appointed commission secretary.

To assist the commission in bringing peace to the Indian country, the Secretary of War directed several companies of mounted rangers to proceed to Fort Gibson. The ranger companies were part of a battalion of mounted troops created by Congress in June, 1832, in response to Cass's recommendation. The companies were to be manned by volunteers who were recruited for one year and were to provide their own arms, horses, and uniforms. Each company was composed of four officers, fourteen noncommissioned officers, and one hundred privates. Most of the rangers were backwoodsmen, many of whom regarded their enlistment as an opportunity to spend a year of adventure away from the farm. Besides the regiment's commander, Major Henry Dodge, the only experienced officers in the battalion were Captain Nathan Boone from Missouri and Captain Jesse Bean from Tennessee. All three had served under General Jackson in 1815 at New Orleans. The training, discipline, and efficiency of the rangers were inferior to that of regular troops, but they suffered no lack of *esprit*.[25]

In notifying Colonel Arbuckle of the assignment of part of the ranger battalion to Fort Gibson, the Adjutant General urged decisive and prompt action at the "first appearance of hostility." He reminded the commander of Fort Gibson that "The army must do its duty—The President expects it, and so do the people." Arbuckle, who had been endeavoring to prevent conflict between the Plains and immigrating Indians, seems to have decided that the depredations of the Plains tribes should be answered. He made no effort to stop a hundred-man Cherokee-Delaware war party which marched against the Pawnees and Comanches in the summer of 1832. Although they were seeking revenge against Pawnees who had earlier robbed a Cherokee merchant, the party killed three Wacos and captured two others.[26] The immigrants' retaliation was as indiscriminate as the raids of the Plains tribes. The expedition may have provided some satisfaction for the Cherokees, but it did little to restrain the Comanches and Pawnees. Arbuckle hoped the rangers would be more successful in bringing these tribes to terms.

The ranger company raised in Arkansas by Captain Jesse Bean was the first to reach Fort Gibson, arriving on September 14, 1832. The Stokes Commission was to assemble there on October 1, but none of the members arrived on schedule. Arbuckle, who intended to use Bean's company "in protecting the Indian Tribes in this quarter . . . from depredations by the Comanchee and Pawnee Indians," waited until October 6, and then ordered the rangers to march west. The route designated would take the force past the mouth of the Cimarron, through the Cross Timbers to the Red River, and then back to Fort Gibson. Bean was to try to make contact with the Western Indians and invite them to a meeting at Fort Gibson or Towson the following spring.[27]

When the ranger company marched from Fort Gibson, Henry Ellsworth and his party were nearing the post. En route the commissioner had met Washington Irving, Joseph Latrobe, and Count Albert-Alexandre de Portales—all were on a sightseeing tour of the West. Latrobe, an Englishman, and Portales, a Swiss, had become acquainted with Irving during their voyage from Europe. Both were financially independent and seeking adventure. When Ellsworth invited them to accompany him to Fort Gibson, they were unable to resist the opportunity "of seeing the remnants of those Great Indian Tribes . . . the pristine wilderness, and herds of buffaloes scouring their native prairies, before they are driven beyond reach of a civilized tourist." Upon reaching Fort Gibson, Ellsworth found that his fellow commissioners had not yet arrived and that the ranger company had marched two days earlier. The commissioner decided that he could best familiarize himself with the Indians' problems by accompanying Bean's force onto the Plains. Arbuckle dispatched an express with orders for Captain Bean to wait for Ellsworth.[28]

The commissioner invited his traveling companions to accompany him on the expedition. On October 10, 1832, the party left Fort Gibson escorted by a ranger officer and fourteen men; after four days they reached Captain Bean's company, which then resumed its march up the Arkansas River. Ellsworth, Irving, and Latrobe kept journals during the expedition and agreed that the rangers acted more like they were on an unorganized hunting trip than on a military expedition to overawe the Indians. Latrobe commented that "neither the officers, nor the men, were considered to belong to any class of regular troops; and that neither one nor the other had any great idea of military discipline." Irving observed that the rangers were "a raw, undisciplined band . . . without a tradition of military service, without training, without uniforms or commissary, without consciousness of rank." Insofar as ability to accomplish their mission was concerned, Ellsworth said the rangers "strike no awe." Nor did they have an opportunity to do so, for

Bean, who was able to penetrate only as far as the eastern limits of present Oklahoma City, encountered no Plains tribes and thus failed in his mission to invite them to a council with the Stokes Commission. The jaded condition of his horses forced the captain to return by the most direct route to Fort Gibson in early November. In view of the performance of the rangers in the field, perhaps it was well that they did not encounter a hostile force.[29]

Prior to the departure of the Bean expedition, Major Dodge had ordered two more ranger companies, commanded by Captain Boone and Captain Lemuel Ford, to proceed to Fort Gibson. That post, already crowded by the arrival of the five companies from Louisiana earlier in the year, was not large enough to accommodate the rangers. Arbuckle had ordered Bean's company to construct a camp on the Grand about seven miles above the fort near the northern boundary of the military reservation. Since there was not enough space to accommodate two more companies at Bean's location, Arbuckle ordered Boone and Ford to encamp a mile and a half below Fort Gibson on the west side of the Grand.

Although the colonel was pleased that his request for mounted troops had been granted, he had reservations concerning the rangers, whom he reported "have come down upon us without funds tools or anything etc to build their own quarters." The colonel noted that the men could not be adequately trained before their one-year enlistment had expired. The companies were undisciplined because of the fraternization between officers and privates. Since the men had to provide fodder for their horses, they were frequently unavailable for duty. In Arbuckle's opinion the army would be better served if the rangers were converted into a "regular Cavalry" manned by soldiers enlisted for five years.[30] Congress apparently agreed with Arbuckle, for it was already considering the organization of a permanent regiment designed to avoid many of the problems encountered by the ranger battalion which had been organized hastily during the Black Hawk War.

In April of 1832, the Sac chief Black Hawk had led two thousand of his followers across the Mississippi to land in Illinois that other chiefs had ceded to the United States. Alarmed by the return of the Indians, state and federal officials mobilized the military to repel the invasion. The four-month conflict was hardly a war. It was, in reality, a lopsided encounter which ended in the slaughter of most of Black Hawk's followers.

Although Fort Gibson was almost eight hundred miles from the

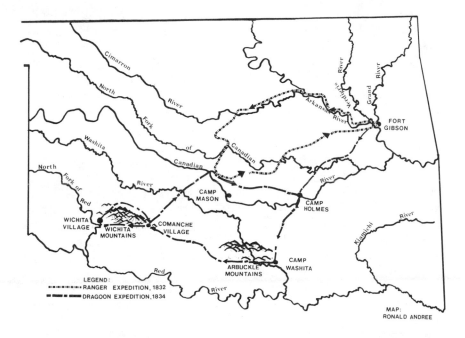

Routes of the 1832 Mounted Ranger Expedition and the 1834 Dragoon Expedition of the Plains.

scene of the Black Hawk uprising, rumors circulated that the Indians were attempting to build an alliance on "the western frontier from Michigan to Texas with a view to a simultaneous attack on the whole of that frontier." Colonel A. P. Chouteau confirmed that Sac emissaries had tried unsuccessfully to win the support of the Osages residing near Fort Gibson. General Gaines, commander of the Western Division, warned Colonel James B. Many, interim commander of Fort Gibson, to instruct his men "in rifle and light infantry service and hold themselves ready for action." Gaines, who implied that the British had a hand in stirring up the Indians, did not mention the white pressure on the tribe to move beyond the Mississippi as a possible cause of resistance. When it became clear that the uprising was not a frontier-wide war but rather a localized uprising, Colonel Arbuckle was informed that his regiment probably would not be required for service in Illinois.[31]

The Indians near Fort Gibson did not support Black Hawk, although Arbuckle learned that many "feel much displeasure towards the United States, and that some of them do not hesitate to declare, that when the whole of the Tribes east of the Mississippi have arrived, they will take satisfaction of the white people for the injuries they have received." Arbuckle attributed these feelings to the full-bloods, who generally held to traditional ways and owned little individual property. He urged the government to adopt a generous policy towards the Indians, but stressed the need for an adequate military force in Indian country to discourage uprisings.[32]

To safeguard the citizens of Western Arkansas Territory, Arbuckle suggested constructing a strong work at Fort Smith where arms and munitions could be stockpiled to equip the population in the event of an Indian uprising. In January, 1833, the War Department responded to Arbuckle's suggestion by ordering him to send one company to man Fort Smith. From there the troops were to expel intruders from Indian Territory and enforce the laws against the introduction of whisky. In March a company of the Seventh commanded by Captain John Stuart joined Lieutenant Rains's detachment, which had been at Fort Smith about a year assisting with the Choctaw immigration.[33]

While many of the immigrant Indians did harbor deep resentment against whites, their chiefs understood that resistance would be suicidal. The tribes that kept Indian Territory unsettled were from the Plains and the Red River region. Their incursions became more frequent as the immigrating tribes settled near their hunting grounds. A large Choctaw settlement had already been established in the Kiamichi valley, and new arrivals were pressing up the Red River to the mouth of the Boggy. White settlements extended up the river about the same distance on the Texas side. The commanding officer at Fort Towson described the inhabitants across the Red as "of the very worst kind—men who have fled from justice and who are now engaged in kidnapping negroes—horse racing, gambling and selling whiskey to soldiers and Indians." The Choctaw and white pioneers were settling on land already occupied by dissident bands of Cherokees, Delawares, and several other tribes. The area was a breeding ground for trouble. During the winter of 1832–33, the Cherokees reported that two of their hunters had been killed by Plains Indians near the Red River. The tribe's agent doubted that skirmishes between the immigrants and Plains tribes could be prevented, but he suggested that additional garrisons higher up the

Arkansas and Red Rivers might "prevent such occurrences leading to disastrous consequences."[34]

Another episode that attracted wide public attention also underlined the need for more vigorous action to police the Plains tribes. In December, 1832, a party of twelve traders returning from Santa Fe by way of the Canadian River valley encountered a band of Kiowas in Mexican Territory. The Americans, who had about $10,000 in specie, attempted to avoid conflict, but when one member of the party ventured out to retrieve some mules, the Indians attacked. Two traders were killed and another wounded, but for thirty-six hours the survivors held the Kiowas at bay. Finally they decided to attempt an escape under the cover of darkness. After filling their pockets with all the silver dollars they could carry, the traders buried the remainder and crept past the Indians on foot. Hundreds of miles separated them from the nearest friendly outpost, and it was mid-winter. After forty-two days, five of the traders were found by Creek Indians near the Arkansas River, and eventually two others arrived in the settlements.[35]

After the escape of the traders, the Kiowas found a few coins. Unaware of the function of money, the Indians pounded the silver dollars into ornaments. On the way back to their village the warriors encountered a band of Comanches, who explained the value of these coins. The Kiowas returned to the scene of the attack and unearthed the thousands of dollars the Americans had been forced to abandon.[36]

Arbuckle's orders directed him to take decisive action at "the first appearance of hostilities." Accordingly, in the spring of 1833, the colonel planned a campaign to demonstrate the military might of the United States to the Plains Indians. Lieutenant Colonel James B. Many was selected to lead two companies of the Seventh Infantry and three ranger companies up the Red River through the Cross Timbers to the western boundary with Mexico. The force's principal mission was to "give security to the Indian Tribes ... now settling on this Frontier, as well as to prevent difficulties between these Tribes, and between them and our citizens." Many was given the delicate assignment of persuading the Pawnees and Comanches to send representatives to Fort Gibson to negotiate with the Stokes commissioners and also of forcing warriors of those tribes to remain west of the immigrant Indian settlements.[37]

Many's force, the strongest yet to enter the country southwest of Fort Gibson, crossed the Arkansas River May 7, and proceeded without incident toward the Red River between the Washita and Blue. Before reaching the Red on June 2, an Indian band, possibly Wichitas, seized a member of Captain Boone's company, Private George B. Abbay. The entire force pursued the Indians to the eastern slopes of the Wichita Mountains, where lack of food, fatigue, and illness forced Colonel Many to abandon the chase and return to Fort Gibson. The expedition of 1833 was an even greater failure than that of the year before. Captain Bean's rangers did not make contact with Plains Indians in 1832, but at least they returned intact. Colonel Many not only failed in his mission, but he also lost one of his men. Many's futile pursuit convinced him that it would be useless to negotiate treaties with the Plains tribes unless a post was established between them and the settlements of the immigrant Indians.[38]

Arbuckle had drawn the same conclusion; while Many was still trying to contact the Plains Indians, the commander of Fort Gibson submitted his recommendations concerning frontier defense to General-in-Chief Alexander Macomb. Observing that Fort Towson was too far west to protect the Arkansas frontier and too far east to provide security to the immigrant Indians, Arbuckle recommended a fort on the Red River at the mouth of the Washita as best calculated "to preserve peace and good order between the Indian Tribes." Since the Creek country lay entirely west of Fort Gibson, Arbuckle suggested that it would be better protected "if a military post, was established on the Arkansas River, at the mouth of the Red Fork [Cimarron]; and another on the North Fork, of the Canadian, about the same distance west." If the expense of maintaining these posts was too great, the colonel proposed the less costly alternative of regular reconnaissance of the prairies by military patrols. Still concerned about the loyalty of the immigrating Indians, Arbuckle also urged that "a *strong work*" be constructed at or near Fort Smith to protect the frontier of Arkansas Territory and to restrain the Indians "from going to war; against the United States."[39]

Again, the colonel was trying to ease the desperate strain on his resources; a strain which made the conduct of his many charges virtually impossible. In addition to the colonel's other responsibilities, the War Department had ordered him to assist the Indian commission established in 1832. Before Montfort Stokes arrived, the commissioners had concluded a treaty with the Senecas and Shawnees by which the tribes received 60,000 acres between the Grand River and the Missouri border. During the negotiations conducted in the first week of December, 1832, the Senecas and Shawnees accused their agent of delinquency in issuing provisions promised by the government. The commissioners asked Colonel Arbuckle to investigate the charges. He sent an officer who reported that the Indians were "in a truly destitute situation." The agent was removed, and the army was placed in charge of the agency until other arrangements were made. In 1834, the Office of Indian Affairs approved a recommendation of the Indian Commission and assigned the Senecas and Shawnees to the Cherokee agency.[40]

After the arrival of Stokes in February, 1833, the commission addressed itself to the boundary conflict between the Cherokees and Creeks. Both tribes had resisted the appeals of Isaac McCoy in 1831 to compromise their overlapping claims to the rich bottom lands of the Verdigris and Arkansas rivers. Perhaps McCoy's warnings concerning the government's growing impatience made both tribes more receptive, for each negotiated a treaty with the Stokes Commission at Fort Gibson in mid-February which fixed a mutually acceptable boundary.[41]

About the same time, a Seminole delegation from Florida arrived at Fort Gibson after exploring lands assigned to the Creeks. The Seminoles, who were looking for a Western home, indicated their approval of the land between the Canadian and its North Fork, but expressed concern about the proximity of the marauding Plains tribes. Pressed by the commissioners, the Seminole delegates, who were to report their findings to their Tribal Council, signed a treaty at Fort Gibson on March 28, 1833. This document obligated the entire tribe to accept a reservation within the lands assigned to the Creeks. Although tribal leaders later repudiated the treaty of Fort Gibson, the government ignored their objections and insisted on removal. By 1835, military pressure applied against the Seminoles in Florida led to conflict. For almost a decade the tribe resisted removal in a war called by one military historian, the "bitterest episode in the annals of the frontier army."[42]

While the Seminole negotiations were under way, the commission began talks at Fort Gibson with the Osages. Negotiations were complicated by differences among the commissioners. Ellsworth and Schermerhorn favored relocating the Osages on the Kansas River. Stokes, after consulting with Colonel A. P. Chouteau, concluded that the Osages would be well advised to retain their present lands. This disagreement produced discord which disrupted the commission in subsequent negotiations. Stokes complained that "My two colleagues . . . have taken an unfounded prejudice against Colonel Chouteau, which has already embarrassed our proceedings, and may (if persisted in) finally prevent the success of some of the important objects of our appointment." The prediction was accurate; after about a month of fruitless discussion, in late March the Osages discontinued negotiations and traveled west for the spring buffalo hunts.[43]

One hunting party followed the Washita River westward into Kiowa country. The Kiowas, who were grazing their horses near the Wichita Mountains, learned that the Osages were nearby when they found the shaft of an Osage arrow in a buffalo. Since most of the Kiowa warriors were on a raid against the Utes, the band was almost defenseless. After several days without further signs of the Osages, the Kiowas drifted south along the edge of the Wichita Mountains. On Glen Creek the band established camp, pastured their ponies, and waited for the return of their warriors. Apparently confident that the Osage danger had passed, they posted no sentries and took no precautions against a surprise attack. Early one morning while most of the camp slept, a young boy tending his horses observed the Osages within a few hundred feet. His screams alerted the camp. Old men, women, and children fled to the rocky slopes on either side of their lodges, but for many the warning came too late. The Osages were already upon them. Not bothering to take scalps, the attackers decapitated their victims and placed their heads in brass buckets. Colonel A. P. Chouteau later estimated Kiowa losses at 150. A few survivors managed to reach another band of Kiowas, who alerted all other tribes in the area. The Kiowas, Comanches, and Wichitas eventually organized their defenses, but the Osages were long since safely beyond their reach, with about four hundred captured horses and a portion of the silver dollars the Kiowas had taken from the Santa Fe traders. The Osages took several prisoners, including a brother and sister of about ten and fifteen years of age. The Kiowas lost more than lives; their *taime*, a sacred medicine doll, was also carried off by the Osages. Without it the tribe could not conduct the sun dance, considered essential to the regeneration of tribal life and held each year in the spring or early summer.[44]

Unaware of the events that were transpiring to the west, the Stokes Commission continued its work after the departure of the Osages. Commissioner Schermerhorn traveled to the Quapaw

Henry Ellsworth, member of the Stokes Commission, sent by President Andrew Jackson to negotiate a treaty with the Plains tribes. Courtesy Aetna Insurance Company.

agency in Arkansas Territory and entered into discussions with representatives of that tribe. In 1824, the Quapaws had been assigned land in Louisiana on the Red River. The region flooded regularly and was unhealthy. The hapless Quapaws returned to their native land in Arkansas Territory, where the white settlers made them unwelcome. The tribe's agent, acting with the consent of the chiefs, traveled to Fort Gibson to arrange for a new reservation in Indian Territory. Schermerhorn, who returned with the agent, negotiated a treaty in May, 1833, by which the tribe relinquished its lands in Louisiana for a tract in Indian Territory adjacent to the Senecas and Shawnees.[45]

As summer approached, the commissioners, who apparently were aware of the post's unhealthy reputation, found that they were required elsewhere. Colonel Arbuckle was probably pleased to see them go, if only temporarily. But his relief was short-lived. The commissioners had not been gone long when a jurisdictional issue demanded Arbuckle's immediate attention. One of the pledges made to the immigrant tribes was that they would be allowed to administer justice within their new nations. In February, 1833, Edward Edwards, a white man residing with the Cherokees and considered a member of the tribe, killed a Cherokee. Edwards was convicted of first degree murder under the Cherokee laws and sentenced to death. Several days before the date of execution, Cherokee Chief Walter Webber notified Arbuckle of the findings of the court.[46]

Arbuckle acknowledged the right of the Cherokees to try their own people but requested that the execution be stayed until the Attorney General could rule on the status of Edwards. The Cherokees complied with Arbuckle's request and turned Edwards over to the army for confinement, but they expressed the opinion that the tribe should have jurisdiction over whites who claimed the rights and privileges of tribal citizenship. The case became more complex when several witnesses came forward saying that the killing had been in self-defense. Arbuckle suggested to Webber that Edwards be turned over to civil authorities in Arkansas Territory for trial. Apparently the Attorney General directed that Edwards be re-tried in Arkansas Territory's Superior Court. The United States District Attorney attempted to bring Edwards to Little Rock for trial but was informed that he had been released from custody and that his whereabouts were unknown. The Cherokees must have noted the unwillingness of the government to entrust their courts with the life of a white man. The United States Attorney had hoped to re-try the case "in order to give satisfaction to the Cherokees," but confusion and delay deprived him of the opportunity.[47] The Edwards case revealed the government's ambivalent attitude towards the Indian nations settling around Fort Gibson. The Indian was encouraged to establish laws and courts and was promised territorial status or even statehood, but the actions of officials in Washington and in Indian Territory appeared to reflect doubt concerning the Indian's ability in self-government.

The federal government's ambivalent policy was rendered even more confusing by the rift among the members of the Indian commission. During his absence in July from Fort Gibson, Commissioner Ellsworth traveled to Fort Leavenworth to make arrangements for negotiations with the tribes of the Missouri River. Stokes, who did not accompany Ellsworth because of illness, believed that he "might as well attempt to collect last year's clouds as to collect the Pawnees and Comanches at this time." When Ellsworth succeeded in negotiating a treaty with the Pawnees of the Platte River, Stokes claimed it was of "little importance" noting that "even now, while Mr. Ellsworth is conducting the Pawnees of the Platte to this place [Fort Gibson] the Clermont band of Osages has been driven from the great Western Prairie by the Pawnees and Comanches."[48]

Ellsworth argued that the treaty he negotiated between the Osages and Pawnees of the Platte "seems to afford *great joy* and promises much good" and asserted that Wichita and Comanche warriors he encountered had promised to open communication between the commissioners and the Indians of the Southern Plains. Stokes doubted that Ellsworth's efforts would enable the commission to establish contact with the "Arabs of the prairie" and predicted that the government's plan of sending "an imposing military force on their hunting ground . . . will have no effect."[49]

Both Stokes and Ellsworth were hasty in their judgments. While Many's expedition of 1833 had failed to locate the Plains tribes, it did not necessarily follow that an expedition in 1834 would suffer the same fate. On the other hand, the promises of the Wichitas and Comanches to carry messages to their fellow tribe members on the Red River was no guarantee that channels of communication had been opened to the Indians of the Southern Plains.

The feuding among the commissioners became vitriolic in the fall of 1833, when they disagreed over the best location for the military along the Arkansas River. Ellsworth and Schermerhorn recommended that the garrison at Fort Gibson be reduced to one company and the remainder of the Seventh Infantry be stationed at Belle Point. Stokes disagreed; he believed the location at Fort Gibson was "the most commanding position in the country, not only for the protection of whites, but also for subjugating the refractory tribes." He predicted that the abandonment of Fort Gibson "would be productive of the most disastrous consequences, as regards the peace and tranquillity of the surrounding nations. They would be at war in six months."[50]

Stokes' opinion was shared by the commanders of both Fort Smith and Fort Gibson. Captain John Stuart asserted that the proposal to relocate troops from Fort Gibson to Fort Smith was "pregnant with fraud and deception." Echoing Stokes' argument, Arbuckle predicted that the abandonment of Fort Gibson would invite intertribal hostility. The colonel suggested that Ellsworth and Schermerhorn were influenced in their decision by the prospect of personal gain resulting from their acquisition of property near Fort Smith. Arbuckle mentioned that he had heard "many reports very unfavourable to the character of Judge Ellsworth and the Revd Mr. Schimmerhorne." He also charged that the two commissioners were not only speculating in land but also misapplying government funds.[51]

Schermerhorn angrily responded that Arbuckle had been misled by "some cunning artfull & damaging men who have been very diligent in endeavoring to promote jealousy and discord among the Commissioners." He threatened legal recourse unless Arbuckle disavowed the charges. The colonel, in compliance with instructions from Washington, began gathering statements from persons having knowledge of the performance of the accused commissioners. Apparently, the testimony did not support Arbuckle's allegations, for on May 19, 1834, Arbuckle sent a letter to Schermerhorn in which he disavowed his charge that the commissioner had been "influenced by improper motives in your concurrence with Mr. Ellsworth in the settlement of his public accounts or in the recommendation of measures for the adoption of the government." When the commissioner refused to accept Arbuckle's letter repudiating the charges, the colonel accused Schermerhorn of vindictiveness. Apparently Arbuckle's repudiation was motivated by fear of legal action threatened by Schermerhorn, for the colonel continued to harbor suspicions concerning the actions and motives of the two commissioners. These suspicions were apparent in a letter to Schermerhorn in which Arbuckle wrote that "at present" he was able to "furnish no evidence on your part of an intention to do injustice to the Government."[52]

The rift which allied Arbuckle and Stokes against Ellsworth and Schermerhorn reached no formal conclusion. Arbuckle left the post in June to recuperate from a lingering illness, and the next month the two-year term of the Indian commission expired. When Arbuckle returned to Fort Gibson in the fall, Stokes was there, but Ellsworth and Schermerhorn were gone; the garrison on the Grand River remained in place.

The decision of the War Department to leave troops at Fort Gibson may have been influenced by the recommendations of General Henry Leavenworth, who was appointed commander of the Southwestern Department in 1834. He saw no reason for stationing troops on the Arkansas line, since the military had no jurisdiction over the residents of the territory and the Indians were not hostile. The general, who had no economic interest in either Indian Territory or Arkansas, was not swayed by the financial considerations that colored the recommendations of the civilian population. He was able to evaluate proposals for the relocation of the post on the basis of military desirability. In the four years since the passage of the Indian Removal Act, the intensified tempo of activity at Fort Gibson had emphasized the necessity of maintaining sufficient troops within Indian Territory to insure the peace. Like Arbuckle, Leavenworth urged that facilities at Fort Gibson be improved and expanded and cited the post's "central and important position in relation to the Agency and government of the Indians."[53] Thus Fort Gibson remained, for the time being, the major guardian of the pathway of the immigrant Indians.

Henry Dodge as he appeared some years after the expedition. Photograph courtesy of The Iowa State Historical Society.

Chapter 9

The Dragoon Expeditions of 1834

IN THE SPRING of 1834, Fort Gibson became the staging area for a major army expedition whose mission was to bring the Indians of the Southern Plains to terms. To improve the prospects for success, the War Department assigned the elite First Dragoon Regiment to spearhead the expedition. This regiment, authorized by Congress in March, 1833, had been organized at Jefferson Barracks near St. Louis in response to the persistent demand of frontier officers for mounted troops.[1] The Dragoons were better equipped and trained to challenge the roving Plains bands than the slow-moving infantry or the undisciplined rangers.

The men of the First Dragoon Regiment were virtually hand-picked by their officers. Many regular units of the army were manned by soldiers described as the "scum of the population of the older States." But the Dragoons were described by Indian artist George Catlin, as "young men of respectable families, who would act . . . with feelings of pride and honour." Officers were selected with equal care. Henry Dodge was commissioned a full colonel and given command of the regiment. Dodge, who was not a professional soldier, had entered the military during the War of 1812. Because of his frontier experience, President Andrew Jackson appointed him a major and gave him command of the ranger battalion formed during the Black Hawk War of 1832.[2]

Dodge recommended that Dragoon officers be selected "by taking a part . . . from the Regular Army who understand the first principles of their profession and uniting them with Ranger officers who understand the woods service."[3] By blending the professionalism of West Pointers with the frontier experience of the backwoods militia officers, a well-balanced cadre for training the recruits was established. Only in one area were the officers ill-prepared; none had cavalry experience.

The caliber of the regiment's officers can be judged best by their later accomplishments. Dodge's second-in-command was Lieutenant Colonel Stephen Watts Kearny, a professional soldier who would lead the Army of the West during the Mexican War. Lieutenant Jefferson Davis, a recent West Point graduate, is the best remembered of the regiment's officers. He would eventually serve as United States Senator and secretary of war and later as president of the Confederacy. Captain David Hunter, another young West Pointer, commanded one of the Dragoon companies. He would later rise to the rank of major general in the Union army and chair the commission that tried the conspirators in the assassination of President Lincoln.

The qualifications of the officers and the caliber of the enlisted personnel did not alter the old-age character of military administration. When the Dragoons assembled at Jefferson Barracks, ten miles south of St. Louis, they discovered that their uniforms had not arrived; their drill weapons were obsolete muskets retired after the War of 1812, and their duties were not conquering new lands and defeating Indian foes, but chopping down trees and building stables. In their first drill the recruits were described as looking like "Jack Falstaff's ragged regiment." Morale, which was high in late spring, sagged badly by mid-summer.[4]

The drudgery of army life weighed heavily on the recruits. Many chose to escape either physically or mentally when their dreams of conquest faded into the reality of drill and fatigue duty. Some deserted, while others found relief in alcohol. Punishment was severe for either offense. Army pay in the 1830's provided little compensation for these hardships. Privates received five dollars a month, out of which they had to buy furnishings for their barracks, including kitchen utensils. The military budget in the early 1830's allowed for no frills and even neglected a few essentials.[5]

Yet despite grumbling in the ranks, the regiment had much potential. Training proceeded, and even without horses and uniforms the men gradually hardened to the regimen of army life and acquired fundamental military skills. When the Dragoons' horses arrived in October, mounted training started and morale improved as rumors spread that the regiment was about to march for the frontier. Finally, on November 20, 1833, Dodge led half of the regiment from Jefferson Barracks through the sparsely settled areas of Missouri and Arkansas into the land recently designated as Indian Territory.[6]

"Artillery, Infantry, Dragoon (Full Dress), 1835-1850," a lithograph by H. A. Ogden in the *Army of the United States*, 1888, courtesy Yale University Library.

Little preparation had been made for the arrival of the Dragoons at Fort Gibson. Neither rations for the men, nor corn for their mounts, nor housing for either was available there. Dodge ordered construction of a camp about a mile and a quarter west of the fort near a canebrake where the horses could graze. Each company constructed a barn-like barracks of logs covered with oak shingles which afforded some protection from the elements. The winter was particularly bitter; temperatures dropped to twelve below zero, preventing the delivery of supplies to the ice-choked Arkansas River. Although the sixty-man barracks were warmer than the tents they replaced, they were poorly caulked. Only those soldiers fortunate enough to have procured buffalo robes succeeded in staying dry. Particularly leaky were the chimneys, through which quantities of water poured into the Dragoons' beans, making them "somewhat less strong than common."[7] Dodge did not let inclement weather interfere with training. Mounted and dismounted drill continued throughout the winter.

The Dragoons' uniforms and weapons eventually reached Fort Gibson. Each trooper was armed with a sabre, a Hull breech-loading carbine, and a pistol.[8] The uniforms were specifically designed to do justice to the army's elite unit. Described as "better suited to comic opera than to summer field service," the uniforms' double-breasted coats were trimmed in yellow with two rows of gilt buttons. The trousers were blue-gray with a yellow stripe running down the outside seam of each leg. The eagle perched atop their infantry-type hat was blinded by a drooping white horsehair pom-pom. If the uniforms appeared a little mildewed, it was because they were not properly dried by the salvage crew which recovered them from the bottom of the Arkansas River after the steamboat on which they were being transported sank.

Although the regiment was now adequately equipped, it was not yet prepared for a summer campaign. Half the regiment was still training at Jefferson Barracks when the commanding general of the army ordered Brigadier General Henry Leavenworth to assume command of the Southwestern military region. In selecting the general, the War Department passed over Colonel Matthew Arbuckle, who had commanded Fort Gibson since its establishment.

Although these two officers had never met, Arbuckle had suspected for several years that Leavenworth was attempting to displace him at Fort Gibson. In 1831, the colonel had heard unofficially that the general was attempting to persuade the War Department to transfer the Seventh Infantry to the Red River and to relocate his regiment, the Third Infantry, at Fort Gibson. A rather agitated Arbuckle informed his superiors that he would regard the assignment of Leavenworth to Fort Gibson as an indication that the War Department was not satisfied with his conduct as commander of the Seventh Infantry. Officials in Washington reassured Arbuckle that they had no intention of assigning any portion of the Third Infantry to Fort Gibson or displacing him as commander.[9]

Leavenworth was apparently persistent, for again in 1834, rumors reached Fort Gibson that he had renewed his efforts to secure command of the post. Arbuckle responded by informing the commanding general of the army, Alexander Macomb, that if he were replaced by Leavenworth, his junior in terms of service, he would request an investigation by general court martial. Arbuckle's protest was too late. More than a week earlier Macomb had ordered Leavenworth to assume command of the Southwestern frontier, which included Arbuckle's Seventh Infantry. When the news reached Fort Gibson, the colonel announced that he was "suffering under a dangerous disease from which I fear I cannot be recovered here," and asked for a leave of absence until his health had been restored. When Leavenworth reached the post, Arbuckle relinquished command of the Seventh Infantry because of his health, thus sparing himself the indignity of serving under the general. Arbuckle did not give up his command without a struggle. He fired volleys of letters to his superiors attempting to block execution of Leavenworth's orders, urging his own brevet promotion to brigadier general, and proposing that Leavenworth's brevet rank be vacated.[10]

Arbuckle's requests went unheeded; General Leavenworth reached Fort Gibson on April 18, 1834. Immediately after his arrival, the general had a "private conversation" with Arbuckle in which Leavenworth explained the manner in which the command was conferred upon him. The explanation apparently soothed the colonel's injured pride or at least "materially changed" his impression concerning the reasons for the change or command. However, on the matter of brevet rank, Arbuckle told Leavenworth, "my opinions . . . have undergone no change whatever."[11]

Relations between the two officers remained proper, but cool. On June 12, when the officers of the post gave their former commander a public dinner, General Leavenworth tendered his regrets, explaining that he was "compelled by the nature of my public

Brigadier General Henry Leavenworth, commanding officer of the Southwestern Military Depart ment and the 1834 Dragoon expedition. Photograph courtesy of the Office of Public Information, Fort Leavenworth, Kansas.

duties, and indisposition, to ask you to excuse me from attending." The dinner was described as "the largest party ever convened at Fort Gibson upon any occasion," and the officers and civilians residing at the post were lavish in their praise of Colonel Arbuckle's service to the country. To the strains of martial and patriotic tunes, the guests proposed toasts to everyone from George Washington to the absent post surgeon. Conspicuously missing among the names of those toasted was that of General Leavenworth.[12] Afterward, Colonel Arbuckle may have left Fort Gibson expecting never to return, but he would be recalled to duty there within the year.

General Leavenworth was described by one of his men as "a plain-looking old gentleman, tall yet graceful, though stooping under the weight of perhaps three-score winters." His friendliness quickly endeared him to the troops. His mild manner was somewhat deceptive, for Leavenworth was a strict disciplinarian and a thorough planner with extensive military experience.[13]

While the general's excuse for not attending the farewell dinner may have been contrived, he was indeed fully occupied with public duties. The War Department had directed him to dispatch the Dragoons into the Comanche country in the spring of 1834. Officials in Washington hoped that an impressive military expedition would persuade the Plains tribes to respect the immigrating Eastern Indians, the Arkansas settlers, and the Santa Fe traders.[14] The expedition was also to try to obtain the release of the ranger private captured the year before.

At Fort Gibson, General Leavenworth conferred with the members of the Indian commission. Although torn by dissension, the commission continued to lay plans for a meeting with the Plains tribes. In February they offered their assistance in attempting to obtain the release of Ranger George Abbay. They hoped to win his freedom and arrange a meeting with the Comanches in June or July through the intervention of the Pawnee Picts (Wichitas) or Pawnees of the Platte. Henry Ellsworth had conducted successful talks with members of these two tribes the previous winter, and they promised to aid the commissioners in their mission. The commissioners also suggested that the Dragoons might establish friendly relations with the Plains tribes by returning tribal members abducted by the Osages. Leavenworth agreed and obtained a Kiowa girl and two Wichita women who would be restored to their tribes as a gesture of good will.[15]

While Leavenworth planned the expedition, several civilians at Fort Gibson offered their advice and cooperation. Sam Houston warned Secretary of War Lewis Cass in March that an armed expedition would result in the certain execution of Abbay and would fail to accomplish its mission. In fact, Houston predicted, "The display of a force on the Prairies, would unite all the Indians that inhabit them, and over whelm it at once!" He recommended that a small party of skilled woodsmen be sent to negotiate with the Plains tribes.[16]

Samuel C. Stambaugh, secretary of the Indian commission, also proposed a method of establishing communications with the Plains tribes. He had learned that the immigrant Indians were holding a council on the Trinity River in Texas at which the Comanches would be present. "This meeting," Stambaugh suggested, "appears to me to be the most favorable that has yet been offered to approach the Wild Tribes of Pawnees & Comanchees." The secretary informed Leavenworth of the meeting and offered his services in negotiating with the Indians. He also suggested that Governor Montfort Stokes would be willing to accompany the expedition to the Trinity if his presence would be helpful. Leavenworth accepted Stambaugh's advice but not his offer to go to Texas. Lieutenant William Eustis was ordered to go to Nacogdoches to deliver letters from the Indian commissioners and the general, requesting Mexican assistance in arranging a meeting between the Comanches and Colonel Dodge on the Washita River. Despite Leavenworth's efforts to enlist Mexican support, he was unsuccessful in establishing communications with the Plains tribes.[17]

Leavenworth's main concern, however, remained the expedition. Logistical support was assigned to the infantry units at Forts Gibson and Towson. Soon after his arrival at Fort Gibson, Leavenworth instructed the commander of the Seventh Infantry to lay out a series of military roads, one along the north bank of the Arkansas to the Cimarron, another directly to the mouth of Little River on the Canadian, and a north-south road that would connect these two routes with the one being built from Fort Towson to the Washita. On June 2, he ordered the creation of three posts to serve as forward bases for the expedition. The most northerly, Camp Arbuckle, was to be located at the junction of the Cimarron and Arkansas rivers. To the south, Camp Holmes (also known as Camp Canadian) was established at the confluence of Little River and the Canadian, and on the southern flank, at the mouth of the Washita River, Camp Washita was to be garrisoned by troops from Fort Towson.[18]

Preparations for the campaign continued into the spring. Warmer weather not only brought relief from the hardships of winter but also posed a serious new peril. Fort Gibson had earned a reputation as one of the most unhealthy posts in the American army, and the rainy spring was the worst season of the year. Even before the expedition began, men were reporting to sick call with a malarial-type fever.[19]

Despite frantic preparations the Dragoons were not ready by the first of May, the date originally set for beginning the march. In fact, on that date the second battalion was still being formed at Jefferson Barracks. The last three companies of this battalion did not reach Fort Gibson until June 14, just one day before the departure of the expedition.[20]

About the same time, news reached Fort Gibson that the Pawnees had moved through the Cross Timbers and attacked Gabriel

Martin, an Arkansas judge, and his party. Leavenworth dispatched a detachment which found the bodies of the judge and one of his Negro slaves near the Washita River. It was assumed that the judge's young son, Matthew, had been kidnapped by the attackers. The recovery of the boy was added to the list of objectives to be accomplished by the Dragoons.[21]

On June 15, 1834, over five hundred officers and men of the First Dragoon Regiment embarked upon their campaign to contact the tribes of the Southern Plains. They were an impressive force as they marched from Fort Gibson. Forming a column a mile in length, the regiment was the most powerful military force the United States had ever sent onto the Southern Plains. The expedition was not exclusively military. The secretary of war had authorized several civilians to accompany the Dragoons. George Catlin went to sketch and paint the Plains Indians. Joseph Chadwick, a St. Louis merchant and trader, hoped to secure the permission of the Plains tribes to establish trading posts in their country. And Count Carl Beyrick, a German botany professor, and his assistant planned to collect specimens of Southwestern flora. Over thirty Indians accompanied the Dragoons, including the women being returned to their people by General Leavenworth as a gesture of good will. The Cherokees, Delawares, Osages, and Senecas sent warriors who served as guides and hunters for the Dragoons and carried messages of friendship to the Plains tribes.[22]

The expedition moved slowly at first in a southwesterly direction. The route, through country occupied by the immigrant Eastern Indians, was well marked, and the regiment advanced with little difficulty. The landscape was a mixture of woodlands and prairies which Catlin described as "one of the richest and most desirable countries in the world for agricultural pursuits." But appearances were deceptive. Before they reached the Canadian River, the men began to complain about the scarcity of good water. A sergeant in G Company reported, "We would travel whole days at a time without coming to any water at all[;] what we came to occationally [sic] was of the worst kind, the top all covered with green slime . . . perfectly muddy and unfit for use by man or horse." Even the Canadian was reported to be unusually dry for so early in the summer. Already disease, which would plague the expedition, was exacting a heavy toll. At a camp established on the Canadian River, twenty-seven ill men were left under the care of the Dragoons' assistant surgeon.[23]

Twelve days from Fort Gibson, General Leavenworth, Colonel Dodge, and a party of forty left the regiment under the command of Lieutenant Colonel Kearny and proceeded to Camp Washita at the mouth of the Washita River. The remainder of the regiment followed at a slower pace. Unencumbered by the slow-moving wagons, the advance party made rapid progress until the first sightings of buffalo. Leavenworth, Dodge, Catlin, and several other officers spurred their horses and galloped toward the lumbering animals. After a headlong chase the hunters killed one buffalo, but the fat cow sought by Catlin escaped. The next day, noting the aches and pains caused by his exertions, Leavenworth told Dodge, "This running for buffaloes is a bad business for us—we are getting too old, and should leave such amusement to the younger men."[24]

As the party topped the next small hill, Leavenworth forgot his resolution. Just across the knoll a small herd grazed peacefully. Shouting orders to his companions, Leavenworth galloped full speed after a calf. The animal dodged, and the general's horse fell. When Catlin reached the downed rider, he was struggling to get to his feet. With Catlin's assistance, Leavenworth stood up and then fainted; he recovered in time to prevent the artist from opening a vein, a standard first aid procedure. After a few hours, Leavenworth rejoined the party with no apparent injuries, but Catlin later observed that "from that hour to the present, I think I have seen a decided change in the General's face; he has looked pale and feeble, and been continually troubled with a violent cough." Several days later Leavenworth told Catlin that "he was fearful he was badly hurt."[25]

When the advance party reached Camp Washita, Leavenworth was informed that Wichita warriors had been observed in the area. A reconnaissance patrol was dispatched while the general waited for the main body of the expedition to arrive. When Colonel Kearny reached Camp Washita on July 1, Catlin reported, "nearly one-half of the command . . . have been thrown upon their backs, with the prevailing epidemic, a slow and distressing bilious fever."[26] General Leavenworth was among the sick. Although he refused to admit his illness and insisted that he would personally lead the expedition, he had a burning fever and a marked shallowness of breath. Leavenworth was finally forced to acknowledge the extent of his sickness. After crossing the Washita River, he abandoned his plans to lead the Dragoons and ordered a reorganization of the regiment into six companies of forty-two enlisted men each.

These six, under Dodge, were to proceed by forced marches into the Plains Indians country unencumbered by baggage wagons or livestock. Leavenworth planned to follow in a few days with the wagons and reinforcements. Before the advance party marched, Leavenworth urged Dodge to "take great pains to avoid the use of your arms" against the Indians. If attacked, however, Dodge was directed to "chastise them as severely as possible."[27]

As Colonel Dodge's force proceeded almost due west, the landscape began to change. The regiment traveled across expanses of flat, grassy prairies where trees and thickets grew only along the creek banks. Signs of Indian activity, such as fresh pony tracks and embers of recent campfires, increased, and an Indian scout was observed reconnoitering the Dragoons' camp. The soldiers attempted to capture him but were unsuccessful.[28]

Sentinels were particularly edgy on the night of July 7. One of them believed he saw an Indian creeping out of the bushes and fired. His Indian was a strayed Dragoon horse returning to camp, but the wounded animal's cries, the shouts of the sentry, and his gunfire caused momentary panic in the camp. Hasty fortifications were thrown up, and the regiment tensely awaited attack. Finally order was reestablished, but during the commotion the regiment's horses stampeded and scattered across the countryside. It took a day for the Dragoons to recover most of their mounts.[29]

Before continuing, Dodge sent Kearny back to take charge of the sick camp in compliance with orders from Leavenworth. Ten soldiers whose horses had not been recovered after the stampede returned with him. The command resumed the march west on July 9, and soon encountered a small party of mounted Indians, believed to be Wichitas. A forty-man patrol led by Captain Hunter was dispatched under a white flag to intercept them. After pursuing the Indians for a few miles the patrol returned, reporting that the Indians had eluded them. The next day the regiment entered the Cross Timbers. This natural border separating the Plains Indians from their immigrant neighbors was described as a great thicket "composed of nettles and briers so thickly matted together—as almost to forbid passage."[30] The Dragoons divided into three columns and picked their way through the thicket for three days before reaching the western limits of the Cross Timbers and the open Plains.

On July 14, the Dragoons broke camp at 8:30 A.M. and had marched half a mile when they sighted a band of about thirty Indians. After identifying them as Comanches, Dodge ordered a

Hisoosanches, the first Comanche warrior to greet the Dragoons. From the George Catlin painting "His-oo-san-ches (The Little Spaniard)" in the Bureau of American Ethnology Collections, The Smithsonian Institution.

A sketch portraying the first official meeting between representatives of the United States and members of the Comanche tribe in 1834. From George Catlin, *Letters and Notes on the Manners, Customs, and Conditions of the North American Indians*, 1857.

white flag advanced. Despite this gesture of friendly intentions, the Indians maintained their distance from the Dragoons. Finally, Dodge halted the regiment while he and several members of his staff advanced. When they were within half a mile of the Comanches, Dodge sent the white flag forward again. One of the Indians, with a white buffalo skin on his lance, left the band and cautiously approached the waiting Dragoons. After assuring himself that the soldiers intended to honor the white flag, he approached the column and offered his hand in friendship. Upon seeing this, the other warriors galloped full speed toward the Dragoons and greeted them enthusiastically.[31]

After a prolonged greeting ceremony, a pipe "was lit, and passed around." Communication was difficult, but by a double translation from English to Spanish to Shoshonean, Dodge was able to convey the idea that he was on a mission of peace on behalf of the President. The Comanches told Dodge that they were on a hunting excursion and offered to take him to their village located a few days' march to the west. Dodge accepted, and the march was resumed with the Comanches leading the way. In further discussions Dodge learned that the Comanches were allied with the Kiowas and the Wichitas. The latter were reported to have a village several days' journey west of the Comanche camp. The Comanches promised to send for the Wichita chief so that he, too, might take part in discussions with Dodge.[32]

For the first time, the members of the expedition were able to observe Plains Indians at close hand. What they observed was a little disquieting; the Comanches were formidable looking warriors. Their dress and weapons seemed perfectly adapted to mounted hunting and warfare. Each carried a quiver on his back and a bow in his left hand, ready for instant use. They were also armed with fourteen-foot lances and rifles carried in buckskin covers.[33]

The warrior who had ridden up to the Dragoons was a Spanish mixed-blood named His-oo-san-ches. Normally he would have been held in contempt by full-blooded Comanches, but he had earned the respect of his tribe by repeated acts of bravery in warfare and on hunting expeditions. The mixed-blood gave Dodge his first real clue concerning the fate of Judge Martin's son. He reported that the Wichitas were holding a black man and a white boy. With this information and positive intelligence concerning the location of the Wichita village, prospects for a successful conclusion of the mission improved. But despite the apparent friendliness of the Comanches, Dodge remained apprehensive. He cautioned his officers and men to remain on the alert.[34] The colonel's fears were not realized; the Indians displayed no hostility, and the Dragoons arrived at the Comanche camp in two days without incident.

The village of six to eight hundred skin lodges was located in a valley at the foot of a range of mountains which the Dragoons believed to be a spur of the Rockies. The regiment stopped several miles from the village while Comanche messengers went forward to inform the camp of their arrival. Dodge formed the regiment into three columns and positioned himself and his staff in front to await the Indians.

Several hundred mounted braves galloped out to meet the visitors and formed a line within thirty feet of the first echelon of

After their initial encounter, the Comanches and the Dragoons marched for the Comanche camp. En route the warriors gave chase to a herd of buffalo, pursuing them through the ranks of the Dragoons. George Catlin sketched the scene and later painted it. Photograph courtesy of Gilcrease Institute.

Dragoons. For half an hour the two forces stood their ground gazing at each other. Finally, one of the Comanche chiefs rode up to Dodge and shook his hand. Followed by the other warriors, he then proceeded down the ranks of Dragoons, shaking hands with each man. During these formalities, which took about an hour, the Comanches invited the Dragoons to camp in their village. Dodge declined the offer, preferring to establish camp across the creek from the Comanches in an area bordered on all sides by steep gullies. One of the tents pitched in the Dragoons' camp housed the hospital for the twenty-nine latest victims of the fever. One of these was George Catlin, who diagnosed his malady as fever and ague.[35]

As the fear of surprise attack lessened, Dodge allowed a few of the men to enter the Comanche village. Since they were the first official representatives of the United States to meet the Comanches, the visitors were surprised to find an American flag flying over one of the lodges. They speculated that the Indians might have captured it from a Santa Fe caravan.[36]

Despite the Comanche's willingness to discuss peace and to send messages to the Wichitas, Dodge was unable to arrange negotiations. He was ready to open talks with Ta-wah-que-nah (The Mountain of Rocks), a three-hundred-pound warrior who represented himself as the Comanche chief, until it was learned that the tribe's actual leader was on a buffalo hunt and would return within a day or two.[37] After waiting two days, Dodge began to suspect the sincerity of the Comanches and decided to proceed to the Wichita village.

The march was resumed at 11 A.M. on July 18, with an Indian guide from the Comanche camp leading the way. The number of sick had increased to thirty-three, many of whom were litter cases. Since the route the guide selected wound through rugged mountain country, Dodge decided to establish another sick camp to enable the regiment to move more rapidly. The command, now reduced to 183 men, passed beneath granite peaks five hundred to a thousand feet in height. These were the same mountains seen from the Comanche village. Later explorations would prove that they were not a spur of the Rocky Mountains but an isolated range of much greater geologic age. They would eventually be named the Wichitas, after the tribe the Dragoons were trying to locate. The boulder-strewn route made progress difficult. The Dragoons were forced to dismount and lead their horses, whose shoes had been completely worn down.[38] Although the mountains abounded in wildlife, Dodge pushed his men forward too rapidly to allow time for foraging. Rations were almost exhausted by the time the regiment reached the level Plains once again.

As the Dragoons were setting up camp on the evening of July 20, a single mounted Indian was observed about two miles away. A lieutenant and several of the Osage scouts were sent to capture him. The Indian attempted to escape, but when his pursuers overtook him, he offered no resistance. One of the Wichita women accompanying the expedition identified him as a relative. Her ability to translate facilitated communications; the prisoner said he was returning to his village about five miles from the Dragoon camp. Dodge assured the Wichita that he was on a peaceful mission and

A Catlin sketch illustrating the Wichita camp on Red River where the first formal negotiations between the United States and the Plains tribes were held. From George Catlin, *Letters and Notes on the Manners, Customs, and Condition of the North American Indians*, 1857.

that he would like to meet with the tribal leaders. The Indian agreed to relay this message and was released.[39]

Morning broke without sign of Indians. Just before the march was resumed, the father of the Wichita hostage rode into the Dragoon camp. His joyful reunion with his daughter was the first indication that the Wichitas intended to receive the expedition. The Dragoons had gone a mile or two toward the Wichita village when they were met by about sixty warriors who were soon reinforced by hundreds of men.[40] This meeting was friendly, and the Dragoons were invited into the camp.

As the expedition approached the Wichita camp, it marched through cornfields enclosed by fences of brush. The sight of cultivated fields and meat drying on racks in the village greatly improved the morale of the troops. The Wichita camp contained four hundred thatched lodges which looked like beehives thirty feet high and forty feet in diameter. The village was located between a six-hundred-foot granite bluff and the north fork of the Red River. In the village, populated by about two thousand Indians, Dodge realized that the regiment's safety depended upon maintaining amicable relations. Accordingly, he ordered that no food be taken without the consent of its owner. The soldiers, who had earlier swapped two-dollar knives for Comanche horses, were now trading good cotton shirts for two ears of corn. The Dragoons literally tore the buttons from their uniforms and took the clothes off their backs to purchase corn, melons, green pumpkins, squash, plums, and horse and buffalo meat. The men ate their first substantial meal since leaving the Comanche camp three days earlier.[41]

Although the principal chief of the Wichitas was not in camp, a council was arranged for the next day. Thus the first formal negotiations between the Plains Indians and the United States began on the morning of July 22, 1834, in a thatched Wichita lodge near the Red River. Merely by meeting with these tribes, Colonel Henry Dodge had succeeded where two earlier expeditions had failed. However, Dodge's orders called for him to pacify the Plains tribes and recover several Americans captured by them. Surrounded by hundreds of armed Indians, it was clear that Dodge would have to rely on diplomacy.

During the first day's negotiations, the American colonel told the Wichita council he had been sent by the Great American Captain who wished to establish peace among all people under his jurisdiction. Dodge explained that the President would like for them to visit Washington and make a treaty which would insure lasting peace. After such a treaty had been concluded, Dodge promised they would receive many presents and white traders would be sent among them to provide blankets, rifles, and other trade goods. Before concluding, he told his hosts he had learned they had captured a white soldier last summer and kidnapped a white boy in the spring. Dodge demanded return of the boy and positive information concerning the man. He reminded the Wichitas that he had obtained one of their women from the Osages at great expense and trouble. She would be returned only after these demands were met.[42]

In the absence of their chief, the Wichita council was headed by We-ter-ra-shah-ro, a Waco chief. He denied any knowledge of the white boy and accused the Comanches of seizing the soldier. Dodge remained adamant and restated his demand for the boy and definite information concerning Private Abbay. The chief conferred with his council and informed the colonel that a tribe called Oways, not the Comanches, had captured the ranger and killed him when they returned to camp. Dodge accepted this explanation but continued to press the chief concerning the return of the kidnapped boy. During the discussion, the Dragoons found a black man living among the Indians who said that a white boy had recently been brought into their village. When this information was announced, a long period of strained silence followed, during which the Indians consulted among themselves and finally ordered that the boy be brought in from the cornfield where he had been hidden. When he arrived, he told Dodge his name was Matthew Martin, the son of the murdered judge. After the excitement over the return of the boy subsided, Dodge questioned the Indians concerning attacks on the Santa Fe traders. The chief accused a "roving tribe of very bad Indians called Wakinas" of being the culprits.[43] Dodge did not press this point, and eventually the meeting was adjourned.

The next morning negotiations resumed in Dodge's tent with We-ter-ra-shah-ro and two of his principal warriors representing the Wichitas. The leaders of the Indians who accompanied the Dragoons were also present. Dodge opened the discussion by asking if the Wichitas had reached a decision about visiting the President. After prolonged discussion, one of the Indians agreed to return to Fort Gibson with the expedition. Reiterating his promise of many presents for those who would visit the Great American Captain, the colonel asked his guests to accept some rifles and pistols. For the first time, the Wichitas acted without long deliberations; they accepted immediately. But no others appeared anxious to return with the expedition.[44]

Later the same day the Comanche chief, who had been leading a hunting expedition when the Dragoons visited his village, arrived at the Dragoons' camp. Dodge explained the purpose of his mission and invited the Comanches to go to Washington to see the President. The Comanche chief seemed no more anxious to make the journey than had the Wichitas, but he reluctantly agreed to send his brother. While these discussions continued, an armed party of twenty or thirty Kiowa warriors galloped into the Dragoons' camp. Their menacing appearance sent the women and children scurrying for safety. The sight of Dodge's Osage guides infuriated the

Kiowas, who had been brutally attacked by an Osage war party the year before. The Kiowas demanded the return of a girl whom the Osages had kidnapped. The Dragoons, with rifles in hand, waited nervously. Dodge completely disarmed the Kiowas by agreeing to their terms. The girl, who had accompanied the expedition, was returned to her tribe, and the Kiowas readily accepted an invitation to a final conference the next day.[45]

With the major Southwestern Plains tribes assembled, the last day of negotiations began in a wooded area about two hundred yards from the Dragoon camp. Two thousand armed Indians in a state of great excitement gathered at the meeting place. The Kiowas seemed particularly aroused. They "embraced Colonel Dodge, and shed tears of gratitude for the restoration of their relative." The meeting was opened with the ceremonial smoking of pipes, after which the colonel once again asked the Indians to consider his invitation to return with the Dragoons who were to depart the next day. The Kiowa chief agreed immediately; he further promised that all white men who came to his country would be treated kindly. Since the other tribes had already agreed to send representatives with the Dragoons, Dodge's mission was accomplished. The council adjourned. The Indians returned to their encampments to decide upon representatives, and the Dragoons prepared for the return march.[46]

Early on the morning of July 25, the chiefs of the three tribes visited the Dragoon camp and were presented with rifles and pistols. Fifteen Kiowas, led by their chief, waited to accompany the Dragoons. The Comanches were represented by the Spanish mixed-blood, a woman, and two other warriors. The Wichitas designated We-ter-ra-shah-ro and two warriors to represent them. The expedition then marched eastward. One of the Wichitas led them through a broad valley and across the open plains north of the mountains.[47]

On July 27, the command returned to the sick camp near the Comanche village. There the situation had not improved; one man had died, and Catlin and several others were seriously ill. Supplies at the sick camp were almost gone, and the men returning from the Wichita village had eaten most of the provisions purchased there. The supply wagons and reinforcements had not arrived. With game scarce in the vicinity of the sick camp, Dodge decided to march by the most direct route to the Canadian River, where the Indians said great buffalo herds were grazing. He dispatched an express to

Leavenworth with a report of his conference at the Wichita village and news of his plans to move to the Canadian.[48]

Despite his fever, General Leavenworth had pushed forward with the baggage wagons and reinforcements, leaving Lieutenant Colonel Kearny and a small detachment of the able-bodied men at the Washita River camp to care for the sick. By the time Leavenworth's column reached the Cross Timbers, the general was critically ill from a combination of the fever, the fall from his horse, and the hardships of the march. He died on July 21, the same day Dodge reached the Wichita village. The supply column was attempting to penetrate the Cross Timbers when the messenger dispatched by Dodge informed them of the movement of the advance party. The next morning the ranking officer ordered the command back to Camp Washita.[49]

Dodge and his command, unaware of the happenings in the supply column, broke camp on July 28, and marched to the northeast across the Plains. Progress was slowed by forty-three sick men, seven of whom were on litters. Catlin reported that most of the creeks were dry and that the primary source of water was stagnant pools "so poisonous and heavy" that horses "sucking up the dirty and poisonous draught . . . in some instances . . . fell dead in their tracks." Catlin and Chadwick found one pool inhabited by frogs who could walk on the surface of the water. Chadwick's elation over this biological curiosity was shattered when it was discovered the unique ability was caused by the thickness of the scum on the pool, not by mutation of the frogs' webbed feet.[50]

On July 30, the regiment crossed the Washita River and continued through a rolling prairie broken by deep gullies. By August 1, the Dragoons reached the Canadian and established a temporary camp about twenty miles south of where Oklahoma City stands today. For the next few days, most of the able-bodied Dragoons dispersed in small groups to replenish the supply of buffalo meat. The hunt was successful, but the men were tiring of their monotonous diet. Years later Jefferson Davis's wife recalled that since the expedition her husband regarded buffalo meat as the "most distasteful of all foods."[51]

The men quickly killed enough animals to fulfill their needs, but the hunters continued shooting just for sport until several hundred carcasses surrounded the camp. Apparently the August heat soon gave the area around the camp the smell, as well as the appearance, of a slaughtering ground, for the expedition's adjutant reported that the camp was moved a mile for reason of "police." In the camp every tent had been turned into a hospital. Catlin was sure the water caused both horses and men "to be suffering and dying with the same disease, a slow and distressing bilious fever, which seems to terminate in a most frightful and fatal affection of the liver."[52]

The regiment broke camp on August 6, and marched eastward along the Canadian River through the Cross Timbers. The closeness of this belt of trees and undergrowth seemed to alarm the Plains Indians. In many places the thicket was so dense that men with axes had to clear a path before the horses could pass. The regiment was further slowed by the litters of the sick. The difficult terrain and the heavy burdens began telling on the horses. Many collapsed and had to be abandoned, but Dodge pushed the regiment forward rapidly and in the evening of August 9, reached an outpost where supplies had been stockpiled. The next day the men drew their first rations since leaving the baggage wagons. With the end of the expedition in sight, the morale of the Dragoons improved.[53]

On August 16, the regiment established camp near Fort Gibson. A week later Kearny and his command returned. Small parties of the sick continued to straggle into Fort Gibson for several weeks. Unfortunately, the return to the post did not provide immediate relief for the sick. The maladies which afflicted the Dragoons were shared by the residents of the Three Forks. Missionaries at Union wrote in late August, "the sickness around abates but little as yet. Sixteen have died in the Hopefield settlement, mostly of cholera." Deaths among the soldiers continued at the rate of about four to five a day. From his room in the Fort Gibson hospital, Catlin heard the "mournful sound of 'Roslin Castle' with muffled drums, passing six or eight times a day under my window, to the burying-ground." He estimated that as many as 150 had died since June and speculated that the death rate must have been equally high in the infantry regiments. Among those who died at Fort Gibson were Count Beyrick, the German botanist, and his young assistant. Calculated in human lives, the cost of the expedition was staggering. Dodge wrote, "Perhaps their never has been in America a campaign that operated More Severely on Man & Horse."[54]

Colonel Dodge was not the only Dragoon officer who led an expedition from Fort Gibson in 1834. Shortly after assuming command of the Southwestern frontier, General Leavenworth had sent a Dragoon lieutenant to determine whether the Santa Fe traders desired a military escort. Anticipating an affirmative answer, the general ordered Company A of the Dragoon regiment under the command of Captain Clifton Wharton to march north to join the caravan en route. Encumbered by a wagon, the fifty-man force marched from Fort Gibson on May 13. Three weeks later the company reached the Cottonwood Creek crossing on the Santa Fe Trail where it remained until June 8, when the traders from Missouri arrived. Wharton's offer to escort the eighty-wagon caravan to the international boundary was accepted by Josiah Gregg, captain of the traders.[55]

The caravan proceeded west for a week without disturbance until the night of June 17, when a sentinel's shot alerted the camp. No intruders were discovered, but the next morning Wharton found moccasin tracks near the sentry's post. Later the same day, reports of the approach of Indians caused another flurry of excitement among the traders. The small party proved to be friendly Kansa warriors, but Wharton was hard-pressed to restrain a few "irresponsible" traders. Even though the tribe had negotiated a peace treaty with the United States almost a decade earlier, their relations with the Santa Fe traders remained strained. Captain Wharton was compelled to conduct talks with them well away from the Missourians. From his discussions with the Indians, Wharton concluded that the disturbance the previous night was caused by a party of Kansa warriors attempting to steal horses without the approval of their chiefs.

No further difficulties were encountered with the Kansa Indians, and the caravan resumed its march west. On the morning of June 26, as the column approached the Arkansas River, Wharton was informed that Comanches were approaching the wagons. Leading forty soldiers, Wharton moved ahead of the caravan, where he intercepted a party of forty Indians who in Spanish, broken English, and gesture indicated their peaceful intentions. When the Indians retired, the traders, still apprehensive about the Comanches, proceeded to the Arkansas and established camp on the north side.

Wharton discovered the Indians' village about a mile beyond and estimated that it contained about a hundred warriors. The peaceful disposition of the Comanches prompted Wharton to arrange a meeting for later in the afternoon. In the meantime, the Missourians had wheeled an artillery piece onto the riverbank and were planning to fire on the Comanches assembled on the other side. When one of

Wharton's officers attempted to intervene, the traders abused and threatened him. The intervention of the captain of the caravan was required to restrain the belligerent traders from firing.

Wharton, who had been at Fort Gibson during the planning for the Dodge-Leavenworth expedition, was fully aware of the objectives of the government concerning the Plains tribes. Although he had no authority to negotiate with the Comanches, the captain regarded his meeting with them as "a most fortunate and opportune one, to promote . . . the views of the Government." Specifically, he hoped to convince the Indians of the government's desire for peace and of the friendliness of the Dragoon expedition that would be marching from Fort Gibson onto the Plains in June. Wharton also hoped to obtain information about Ranger Abbay.[56]

Wharton's prospects of conducting a friendly dialogue with the Comanches were dashed when Gregg and several other traders crossed the Arkansas River and met with the Indians. While they assured the Comanches that they had come as friends, the traders warned that the soldiers would fire if Indians approached the caravan. The threatening tone of the Missourians frustrated Wharton's plans for an amicable meeting with the Comanches. Wharton, obviously upset by the action of the traders, announced that they had reached the international boundary and that the escort would continue only as long as there was a real danger of attack. At the same time, the captain's subordinates reported that rations were dwindling and that the company's draft and pack animals were in poor condition. Gregg cited the Indian menace as justification for further military protection, but Wharton dismissed the danger of Indian attack as minimal and announced that he would accompany the caravan no farther than the Cimarron River. A new captain of the caravan, selected after Gregg's resignation, told Wharton that unless the military escort could go as far as the Canadian River, the traders did not want further military protection. Accordingly on June 28, the day after crossing the Arkansas, the Dragoons left the caravan and began their return march to Fort Gibson without their slow-moving wagon.

En route the force encountered parties of Pawnee, Kansa, and Osage warriors, all of whom proved friendly. On July 19, with horses worn and food supplies nearly exhausted, Company A reached Fort Gibson. In his report Wharton indicated that there was little danger of attack on a caravan as long as the Indians remained at peace. In fact, he suggested, the presence of an escort could cause "negligence and a lack of vigilance" among the traders which might render them even more vulnerable when their military protectors were forced to turn back."[57] Reaction to Wharton's report in the War Department is unknown, but it would be nine years before another military escort was assigned to protect the Santa Fe traders.

There is no such lack of information concerning the reaction of officials in Washington to the Dodge-Leavenworth expedition. President Andrew Jackson in his annual message informed Congress that the frontier had been pacified by "Colonel Dodge and the Troops under his command." He also reported an arrangement with the "Indians which it is hoped will assure their permanent pacific relations with the United States and the other tribes of the Indians on that border."[58] At last an expedition into the Plains had met with some success.

Chapter 10
Treaties with the Plains Tribes

THE EXPEDITIONS OF 1834 were only the first step in establishing the permanent pacification of Indian Territory. Colonel Henry Dodge had hoped to demonstrate American might to the representatives of the Plains tribes who accompanied him to Fort Gibson by sending them to Washington. Neither War Department officials nor the Indians, however, appeared anxious to conduct a meeting in the nation's capital. Lack of funds prompted the Secretary of War to direct that the representatives of the Plains tribes not be sent, and the Indians themselves indicated their reluctance to continue to Washington. Instead, Colonel Dodge arranged a meeting at Fort Gibson between Kiowa, Wichita, Comanche, and Waco warriors and Indians residing near the fort.[1]

When the conference opened on September 2, 1834, the Plains Indians were joined by representatives of the Cherokees, Creeks, Choctaws, Osages, and Senecas. The United States was represented by Major Francis W. Armstrong, Superintendent of Indian Affairs for the Western Territory, who presided at the meeting, Colonel Dodge, and Governor Montfort Stokes, who had no official capacity since his commission had expired in July. The American representatives were hampered in the negotiations by their lack of authority to conclude a treaty. They attempted to convince the Indians of the value of maintaining the peace and accepting the protection of the United States. The council continued three days, during which numerous speeches were delivered and presents awarded. Armstrong promised that the results of the meeting would be reported to President Andrew Jackson and that another council would be held in 1835 on the prairies, where more tribes would be able to participate.[2]

Two days after the conference ended, the Plains Indians departed for their homes beyond the Cross Timbers. Enroute several died, probably from cholera contracted at Fort Gibson. The Indians had their own theories concerning the deaths; some suspected that their food had been poisoned, while others believed Governor Stokes, who had peered at them through strange glass lenses perched on his nose, had cast an evil eye at them and was responsible for the deaths. Despite these suspicions, the frontier remained tranquil, and Dodge predicted that the government would be able to negotiate "a lasting peace between all parties on this frontier." Reports of the Dodge-Leavenworth expedition and the Fort Gibson council convinced the Commissioner of Indian Affairs that the army's efforts had made "a deep and durable impression" on the Plains tribes.[3] In Washington and at Fort Gibson, officials began laying plans for a major council of all the tribes in the southern half of Indian Territory.

At Fort Gibson the responsibility for such planning was assigned to Matthew Arbuckle. On September 9, 1834, the War Department ordered Arbuckle, who was recuperating from a chronic intestinal malady in Virginia, to return to Fort Gibson to take command of the entire Southwestern frontier with the rank of Brevet Brigadier General. Although his health was not completely restored, Arbuckle accepted the assignment and resumed command of the post on November 5, 1834. The letter accompanying Arbuckle's orders informed him that General Henry Leavenworth had exceeded his instructions in establishing new posts in Indian Territory. The secretary of war felt that the positions had been "unnecessarily pushed into Indian Country." Because their maintenance entailed "considerable expense" he was "anxious that they should be abandoned." Arbuckle was directed to withdraw the troops stationed there if the removal could be accomplished "without injury to the public service." By the time Arbuckle reached Fort Gibson, Colonel James B. Many had already ordered the recall of the troops from those posts. The infantry companies serving at Camp Holmes and Camp Washita were withdrawn completely, and at Camp Arbuckle on the Cimarron only a small detachment remained to guard public property that could not be removed immediately. While the scattered companies of the Seventh Infantry were returning to Fort Gibson, most of the Dragoon regiment was departing for service elsewhere; only three Dragoon companies under the command of Major Richard B. Mason remained at Fort Gibson.[4]

Encouraged by the improving relations with the Plains tribes, a party of eight men left Fort Gibson with a large stock of trade goods just after the council held in September. It was their intention to "amass, at once, an immense fortune, being the first traders and trappers that have ever been in that part of the country." Of course, this party was by no means the first in the area. Several weeks earlier another party of traders led by Holland Coffee had preceded them west and established a trading post beyond the Cross Timbers on the north side of the Red River.[5] The presence of Coffee's trading house provided General Arbuckle an important source of information about the Plains Indians.

Relations with the Plains tribes were closely connected to the impoverished conditions of the Osages. Driven by hunger, Osage warriors raided the herds of the immigrant Indians and encroached on the hunting grounds of the Plains tribes. To reduce this obstacle to the pacification of Indian Territory, a treaty with the Osages was negotiated at Fort Gibson on January 5, 1835, by Major Armstrong. By the terms of the document, the Osages ceded to the Cherokees a strip of land twenty-five to thirty miles wide in return for an annuity of $20,000 for twenty or twenty-five years and other monetary considerations. Armstrong asked General Arbuckle to inform the War Department of the importance of the document. The general noted that during the past two years, the scarcity of game had prompted the Osages to raid the herds of the Creeks and Cherokees. If such depredations continued much longer, Arbuckle warned, "it will be found impossible to prevent their neighbors from resorting to acts of hostility against them." The general foresaw two possibilities. The Osages could follow the buffalo to the west, where their bitterness against white men and immigrant Indians might cause them to join the Plains tribes in terrorizing the frontier. Or the government could ratify the treaty and provide annuities to encourage the Osages in "the cultivation of the earth, and raising of domestic animals." With the encouragement of the government, Arbuckle predicted, the Osages' "habits will be greatly changed for the better and that the United States may confidently rely on their permanent friendship."[6]

Officials in Washington apparently did not share Arbuckle's belief concerning the necessity of the treaty. When he learned that it had been rejected, the general reemphasized his fear that impoverished Osages would disrupt the peace of the frontier. Arbuckle's opinion was corroborated by Osage warriors who periodically raided the herds of the immigrant tribes and whites residing nearby. In the fall of 1835, the frequency of these raids increased, and relations with the tribe were further aggravated by the murder of a white blacksmith employed by the Osage Nation. Arbuckle vowed to use "every exertion in my power to prevent the Osages from committing further depredations." In the spring he sent a patrol to recover horses stolen by the Osages from the Creeks and the army. About the same time, Captain David Hunter led his Dragoon company from Fort Leavenworth through the Osage country to Fort Gibson in a show of force.[7]

Although intertribal strife would continue to disturb the tranquility of the eastern portion of Indian Territory, records at Fort Gibson suggest that by this time the army was being called upon increasingly to protect the tribes from non-Indian interlopers. Arbuckle sent out frequent patrols to apprehend or expel white troublemakers and return runaway slaves. One of the officers at the post complained that armed commands were sent out almost daily to police the illicit whisky trade or to escort "villianous white people out of Indian country."[8]

During the meeting with the Plains Indians in September, 1834, Dodge and Armstrong had promised that a council would be convened the next year. Accordingly, on February 1, 1835, General Arbuckle urged the War Department to appropriate funds for the purchase of presents for the Indians. He suggested that the council should be held in June at Fort Gibson. In April the general learned that the Plains tribes favored a meeting at Coffee's trading house on the Red River. This location Arbuckle considered too remote for the tribes residing near Fort Gibson.[9]

Direct communications with the Plains tribes began on April 15, when two Wichitas and a Waco arrived at Fort Gibson apparently seeking information about the time and place of the council that Colonel Dodge had proposed. Since the Indians did not speak English, discussions were delayed until an interpreter was obtained from the Osage village. When talks began, the general was unable to give the Plains Indians definite information concerning the council because the War Department had not yet responded to his recommendations. A few days later a letter arrived from Washington appointing Arbuckle, Stokes, and Armstrong as commissioners, authorizing them to conduct a council with the Plains Indians and neighboring tribes at Fort Gibson, and allotting funds for presents for the Indians. Arbuckle recalled the Plains Indians who were visiting Clermont's village and informed them that the government was anxious to conclude treaties with the Comanches and other wandering tribes of the Plains. On May 14, 1835, the three commissioners decided to send Major Mason's Dragoon squadron onto the Plains to establish communications with the Comanches, Kiowas, and other Plains tribes. The seventy-four-man Dragoon column marched from Fort Gibson on May 18, closely followed by Colonel Auguste P. Chouteau, who was to serve as interpreter and advisor. [10]

Before the departure of the Dragoons, Isaac Pennington, an Indian trader, informed Arbuckle that Mexican authorities had demanded the evacuation of Coffee's trading post. He also reported that they were encouraging Indians residing in Texas to attack the Plains tribes living north of the Red River. The general found the report difficult to believe, but he ordered Mason to protect Coffee's trading post and directed Colonel Many, now commander at Fort Jesup, to investigate the charges. [11]

By June 3, Mason had selected a location near the Canadian River in what is now central Oklahoma. The position, designated Camp Holmes, was about 150 miles from Fort Gibson. As soon as Arbuckle was informed of its location, he ordered Lieutenant Augustine F. Seaton and thirty men from the Seventh Infantry to open a wagon route to the camp to facilitate transportation of supplies and personnel. Among the members of Seaton's column was Assistant Surgeon Leonard McPhail, a physician recently assigned to the Dragoons. He maintained a diary during the expedition to and from Camp Holmes which adds color to the rather impersonal account recorded in the official journal. His description of the hardships of frontier travel are similar to those reported by the Dragoons the previous summer. Just a few days after leaving Fort Gibson he wrote, "A soldier is taken sick and a plague of flies descends upon us, tormenting horses and men. The heat is terrific and not a breath of air stirs." Unseasonable rains soon broke the heat but delayed Seaton's column, which arrived at Camp Holmes a month after leaving Fort Gibson. [12]

McPhail's diary discusses the diseases suffered by the soldiers on the expedition. Their maladies were similar to those that had plagued the Dragoons the year before. The most common were dysentery and malarial fever. The surgeon blamed a change in the weather for an increased number of "intermittent fever" cases in early August and reported "the winds prevailing blow over a large bottom and marsh a little ways from camp wafting the 'mal-aria' over us." The remedies he discussed were little superior to the herbs employed by the Indians, but compared to the 1834 expedition, the troops at Camp Holmes in 1835 enjoyed good health. McPhail felt the previous year's high death rate had been the result of the drastic medication used in treating dysentery and the "frightful doses" of calomel, a mercurial purgative, which he believed caused gangrene of the jaws and face.[13] Despite McPhail's claim that better medical practices kept the death rate low at Camp Holmes, most of the credit probably belongs to chance. The epidemic that swept the prairies in 1834 had run its course by the time Mason and his men left Fort Gibson in the summer of 1835.

Major Mason had ascertained that the Comanches wanted the council to convene by July 22. Arbuckle and Stokes believed that this date did not allow adequate time for the nearby tribes to assemble and reach Camp Holmes. They suggested that August 10 was the earliest day that the council could be conducted. This delay apparently upset the Comanches, for Mason's Osage hunters reported that they intended to attack Camp Holmes. Although Arbuckle questioned the accuracy of the report, he dispatched Captain Francis Lee and a one-hundred-man force from the Seventh Infantry to reinforce Mason's command. The general warned Major Mason not to "place full reliance" in the Osages, who displayed little interest in concluding a treaty with the Plains Indians. It is difficult to judge whether or not Arbuckle was correct, because Lieutenant Seaton's arrival at Camp Holmes on July 11 had a calming effect on a Comanche chief who McPhail reported had "made great exertions to induce the other bands to join him and wipe out Major Mason's men." A few days later Captain Lee's command arrived and fired a demonstration with a four-pounder, a sight which further reduced the danger of an Indian uprising.[14]

The Indian unrest apparently resulted from disappointment at the delay in opening the talks. Many bands had traveled to the Camp Holmes area at the request of Major Mason only to find that there were no definite arrangements for a conference. A rumor that the meeting would not be held until September caused some of them to drift away in late July as the buffalo grew scarce near the army camp. Mason persuaded most of the bands to remain by promising that the meeting would be held soon. He informed Arbuckle that the Western tribes were well disposed to negotiate but warned that they were growing restless. Arbuckle had hoped to delay this meeting until September, when the weather would be cooler and more of the civilized Indians would be present. However, in view of Mason's warning that many of the Plains Indians were threatening to leave, Arbuckle scheduled the meeting for August 20 at Camp Holmes.[15]

Invitations were extended to the agents of the Cherokees and Creeks to assemble delegations to take part in the council, and arrangements were made to secure the participation of the Osages, Senecas, and Quapaws. Preparations did not proceed smoothly. The Plains Indians remained restless and renewed their threats to leave Camp Holmes unless the meeting began at once. The wagons to be used in transporting the commissioners to Camp Holmes were not immediately available, and Governor Stokes considered the money appropriated by the Congress for presents to have been "far short of what might have been reasonably ... expended in furthering this great object." Finally, both Armstrong and Stokes were so ill that it appeared doubtful that either would be able to participate in the council. Armstrong's health did not improve, but Stokes was sufficiently recovered to accompany General Arbuckle to Camp Holmes.[16]

By August 6, Stokes and Arbuckle had concluded arrangements for the meeting: presents had been purchased and shipped, the local Indians had been notified, and Camp Holmes had been adequately provisioned and reinforced. The two commissioners crossed the Arkansas River and began their journey to the council grounds accompanied by two companies of the Seventh Infantry under the command of Major George Birch. As he left, Arbuckle dispatched an express to Mason with last minute instructions to construct a brush arbor and log benches near the camp for the conferees. Creeks, Osages, Senecas, Quapaws, Cherokees, Delawares, and Choctaws left the Fort Gibson area for Camp Holmes about the same time the commissioners departed.[17]

At least one person acquainted with the Indian situation along the Fort Gibson frontier questioned the ability of the two commissioners. The Reverend Isaac McCoy, a social reformer who deplored the traditional treatment of the Indians, considered Arbuckle to be a good military leader but "just about equal to *nobody* in a business of important negotiations." The minister had an even less flattering opinion of Governor Stokes, whom he considered "an ignorant, profane old man in his dotage, a mere sot in drunkeness, and a card-player. He is therefore ten degrees worse than a *nobody*."[18]

When Stokes and Arbuckle arrived at Camp Holmes on August 19, they learned that the Kiowas had already departed because of the lack of food and did not plan to return. The *Arkansas Gazette* had another explanation for the Kiowas' departure. It reported, "The Ki-a-ways left the council ground" because of Osage misinterpretations that the whites intended to kill them. Whatever the reason, their absence diminished the significance of the treaty to be negotiated, even though the other Plains Indians assured the commissioners that the "Kioway's will also agree to any Treaty we may make."[19]

On August 22, the first formal meeting was held between the commissioners, the tribes residing east of the Cross Timbers, and the Comanches, Wichitas, and their associated bands. Stokes opened the meeting by reassuring the Indians that the President of the United States had "promised to cherish and protect them in all their just rights." Next, Arbuckle told the conferees, "We have prepared a Treaty which we believe will best secure peace between your nations and the United States, and between your people and the red nations now present." The proposed treaty was then translated and explained to the Plains Indians. Arbuckle asked them to consider the document carefully and make changes if they objected to its provisions.[20]

The treaty contained ten articles, including pledges of perpetual peace and friendship between the United States, the tribes represented at the meeting, and members of tribes not party to the treaty. Americans engaged in trade with Mexico were to be allowed to pass through the Plains unmolested; the Osages and immigrant tribes were promised free access to the hunting grounds beyond the Cross Timbers, and the Plains Indians were to continue their friendly relations with the Mexican government.[21]

Negotiations with both the Plains tribes and those residing near Fort Gibson were a delicate business. Both seemed primarily interested in the largess of the government. Arbuckle had spent over $6,000 on presents to be distributed to the Indians at the meeting, but their demands for gifts far exceeded the funds allocated for that purpose.[22] All of the Indians asked for presents almost every time they met Indian commissioners. Arbuckle, whose long service on the frontier had given him an insight into the Indian character, conceded to the Indians' demands for immediate gifts just enough to whet their appetites while holding out promises of future reward.

When the council reconvened on August 23, the Wichitas expressed concern over the article which required them not to let the signing of the treaty "interrupt their friendly relations with the Republic of Mexico." They explained that Mexicans had attacked several of their villages and murdered a number of Wichitas. The commissioners suggested that to wage war on the Mexicans under these circumstances would not be a violation of the treaty. The Wichitas also requested that no tribes settle in the area immediately west of the Cross Timbers, to insure that game in this area would remain plentiful. Otherwise, the Wichita representatives approved the treaty, particularly article eight, which promised gifts for the Plains tribes. The Comanche chief raised no objections and told the council his people "wished nothing but peace, and friendship."[23]

On August 24, the commissioners obtained the signatures of the chiefs and representatives of the Comanches, Wichitas, Cherokees, Creeks, Choctaws, Osages, Senecas, and Quapaws. The following day, representatives of the immigrant tribes were invited to address the council. Most of them praised the wisdom of the Great Father and expressed their happiness that peace had been established. On the afternoon of August 27, they began their return trip to Fort Gibson, accompanied by the infantry. Two days later Major Mason and the Dragoons broke camp and followed. By September 12, the last unit reached Fort Gibson.[24]

The treaty of 1835 was enthusiastically received in Washington. After examining its provisions, Lewis Cass privately informed Governor Stokes and General Arbuckle of his satisfaction and hope that it would "lead to permanent tranquility." Publicly, he expressed his belief that "it will have a salutary tendency . . . in preserving peace among all the Indian tribes west of the Mississippi." The major weakness of the treaty was that the Kiowas, one of the most important of the tribes of the Southern Plains, had not signed it. In late September, General Arbuckle informed the Secretary of War that the tribe might visit Fort Gibson later in the fall or next spring to negotiate a treaty with the government. During the winter, several parties of Plains tribes visited Fort Gibson and informed Arbuckle that more Plains warriors would be coming to the post soon. Arbuckle and Stokes sent Major Paul Ligueste Chouteau to establish contact with the Kiowas. After locating them in what is now the southwest part of Oklahoma and overcoming their initial suspicion, Chouteau obtained the Kiowas' promise to visit Fort Gibson in May. On his return Chouteau reported the results of his talks to the Indian commissioners.[25]

When the Kiowas failed to arrive on schedule, Arbuckle sent Osage scouts to determine what was delaying them. The scouts reported that some of the Kiowas had reached Camp Holmes and were awaiting the arrival of others before selecting a delegation to proceed to Fort Gibson. On June 7, the principal chief of the Kiowas and two of his warriors reached the post and explained that the delegation had remained at Camp Holmes after the Delawares had warned them that Fort Gibson was very sickly and that most of the troops had left. Arbuckle sent Major Chouteau to persuade the reluctant delegation to come to the post.[26]

Despite his close relationship with the Kiowas, Chouteau's efforts to persuade the tribe to send a delegation to Fort Gibson that summer failed. In fact, he reported that there was widespread unrest among the Plains Indians. During the winter of 1836–37, Major Chouteau sent his son, Edward, and a small party of men from Camp Holmes to visit the Plains tribes in their winter camps. The younger Chouteau confirmed the reports that the Western tribes were upset. They were angered by the provisions of the 1835 treaty that allowed the immigrant tribes access to the Plains hunting grounds. Major Chouteau predicted that friction between the Eastern and Western tribes might soon produce open warfare. Although the Comanches remained unreceptive to Chouteau's attempts to reassure them, the principal chiefs of the Kiowas, Kiowa-Apaches, and Wichitas accepted his invitations to go to Fort Gibson to negotiate a treaty. Since Arbuckle had just left the post for the East, the government was represented by Governor Stokes and Colonel A. P. Chouteau when negotiations began at Fort Gibson in May.[27]

After several weeks of talks, on May 26, 1837, the participants signed a document similar to the 1835 treaty which pledged perpetual peace and friendship. Stokes and Chouteau, who signed for the United States, believed that the treaty would allow Santa Fe traders and other whites to enter the Southern Plains without fear of molestation if its provisions were faithfully observed by the government.[28] Although none of the parties to the treaty would faithfully observe its provisions, the negotiation of the document did bring to a successful conclusion the five-year-long effort of the government to establish formal relations with all the major tribes of the Southern Plains.

Chapter 11

Reverberations from Texas

THE GOVERNMENT'S EFFORTS to bring peace to the Southern Plains received a major setback because of developments in Mexico, where an influx of American settlers had swelled the population of Texas and aroused suspicion in Mexico City. By 1835, strained relations between the central government and the American residents in Texas flared into open rebellion. The Texans sought and secured substantial assistance from the residents of the United States, and the Mexicans actively wooed the Indians on both sides of the Red River. As headquarters of the Southwestern military frontier, Fort Gibson became a command post and staging area for the force mobilized to guard the international boundary and preserve American neutrality.

On November 24, 1835, General Matthew Arbuckle warned the commanding officers of Forts Jesup and Towson that the newspapers were reporting that "organized companies of armed citizens of the United States are passing up the Red River on their way to the province of Texas; with the object of joining the people of that province; who are opposing with force, the Government of Mexico." Although the general directed that these parties be turned back, the few regulars assigned to the border could not possibly stem the flow of adventurers pouring into Texas. Nor was Arbuckle any better able to control Mexican agents attempting to persuade the tribes residing in East Texas "to commence war" on the rebellious Americans. The Indians in Texas rejected the Mexican proposal, but Arbuckle learned that the Creeks had been promised an extensive tract of land if they would cross the Red River and support the Mexicans in their efforts to crush the Texas rebels.[1]

Rumors that reached Fort Gibson in March, 1836, suggested that similar Mexican overtures to the Plains Indians had met with success. A Choctaw hunting party reported that Holland Coffee's trading post on the upper Red River had been destroyed and Coffee and

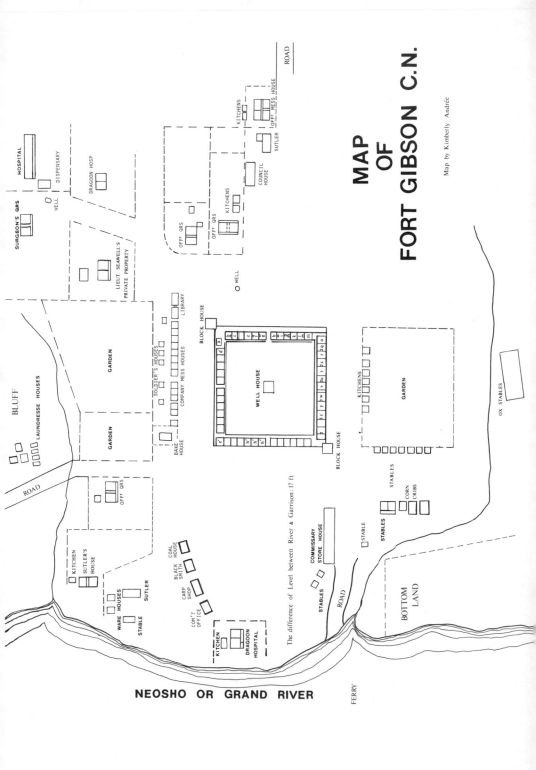

MAP
OF
FORT GIBSON C.N.

Map by Kimberly Andrée

NEOSHO OR GRAND RIVER

ROAD

HOSPITAL

DISPENSARY

SURGEON'S QRS

WELL

DRAGON HOSP

LIEUT. SEAWELL'S PRIVATE PROPERTY

BLUFF

LAUNDRESSE HOUSES

ROAD

GARDEN

GARDEN

SOLDIER'S HOUSES

LIBRARY

BLOCK HOUSE

COMPANY MESS HOUSES

BAKE HOUSE

WELL HOUSE

BLOCK HOUSE

OFF QRS

OFF QRS

KITCHENS

WELL

COUNCIL HOUSE

KITCHENS

SUTLER

OFF MESS HOUSE

KITCHENS

OFF QRS

KITCHEN

SUTLER'S HOUSE

WARE HOUSES

STABLE

SUTLER

COAL HOUSE

BLACK SMITH

CARP SHOP

COM'T OFFICE

KITCHEN

DRAGOON HOSPITAL

The difference of Level between River & Garrison: 17 ft

COMMISSARY STORE HOUSE

STABLES

ROAD

STABLE

KITCHENS

GARDEN

STABLES

CORN CRIBS

STABLES

OX STABLES

BOTTOM LAND

FERRY

Fort Gibson, about 1835, adapted from a drawing by Lieutenant Arnold Harris, Seventh Infantry.

Key to Map 4, Fort Gibson about 1835:

-a — Magazine
-b — Acting Assistant Adjutant General's Office
-c — Officers' Quarters
e, f, g — Officers' Quarters, upper and lower room
h — Officers' Quarters, lower room, Quartermasters's Office
i, k, l, m — Officers' Quarters, lower room, Soldiers' Quarters
-o, q — Company Store Rooms
-p — Company Store Rooms, lower room, Soldiers' Quarters
r, s, t — Soldiers' Quarters
u, v, x, y — Officers' Quarters
-d', e' — Company Store Rooms
h' — Guard House and Cells
All the other rooms, Soldiers' Quarters

several others killed by Comanches. Subsequent reports proved the rumor to be unfounded but indicated that the Comanches were angered by Choctaw violations of the Treaty of 1835. Although the Comanches took no immediate retaliatory measures, General Arbuckle could not dismiss the possibility that they might transfer their allegiance to the Mexicans.[2]

If the Comanches were incited to attack the Texans, Arbuckle feared that they would not be restrained by the international border unless the American forces there were augmented. Officials in Washington had already reached the same conclusion and had ordered the Sixth Infantry at Jefferson Barracks to proceed to Fort Jesup. General Edmund P. Gaines, the commander of the Western Division, was directed to assume personal command of the Southwestern frontier in order to safeguard American citizens from Indian uprisings and insure that residents on both sides of the border respected American neutrality. Fearing that Gaines might be detained in Florida, where he was directing campaigns against the Seminoles, the War Department directed Arbuckle to assume personal command of the troops assembling in Louisiana until Gaines arrived. On April 20, Arbuckle relinquished command of Fort Gibson to Lieutenant Colonel William Whistler and proceeded to Fort Jesup. At Little Rock he learned that General Gaines had already reached Natchitoches, Louisiana. Arbuckle decided to return to Fort Gibson, where his experience was needed in dealing with the Plains and immigrant Indians.[3]

In Arbuckle's absence Colonel Whistler had received orders from General Gaines to dispatch all Dragoons and most of the infantry from Fort Gibson to Fort Towson. In strengthening the force along the Texas border, Gaines recognized that he had depleted the strength of Fort Gibson. He therefore authorized General Arbuckle to ask the governor of Arkansas Territory for volunteers if they were needed to maintain peace along the "heterogeneous border" guarded by Fort Gibson. Six companies of infantry were already en route to Fort Towson when Arbuckle returned; the Dragoons marched several days later. Colonel Whistler, freed from his duties as post commander by Arbuckle's return, was ordered to assume command of the infantry companies transferred to Fort Towson.[4]

Lieutenant William W. Mather, who commanded D Company, reported that the Seventh Infantry made "something of a shew" on its twelve-day march to Fort Towson. If the troops from Fort Gibson restrained the dissident Indians along the Texas border, it was not by virtue of their appearance. Soon after leaving Fort Gibson, Mather observed that the soldiers had "left off their uniforms and every other one wears such clothing as he chooses." By the time the troops arrived at Fort Towson, news of the Texans' victory over the Mexicans at San Jacinto had reached Indian Territory. Finding the area "perfectly quiet," Mather suggested that the men would "have nothing to do but return."[5]

The lieutenant was apparently unaware of news from Texas which indicated that the Indians of that region remained a threat. An Indian trader told Arbuckle that fifteen hundred warriors had assembled within seventy miles of Nacogdoches "for the purpose of going to war and destroying all the inhabitants of Texas, as far north as the Red River, including... Miller county, and perhaps other counties in Arkansas Territory." As a reward for their loyalty to the Mexican government, the Indians were promised "all the country between the River Trinity and the Red River." Arbuckle had doubts concerning the magnitude of the Indian threat in Texas, but in early May a story in the *Arkansas Gazette* which reported five hundred hostile Indians at the Cross Timbers gave additional credence to reports from Texas. Arbuckle also had to acknowledge the possibility that the extravagant Mexican promises of land might spur warriors residing in Indian Territory to join the uprising. Confronted with the possibility of Indian hostilities, General Gaines ordered a thousand troops from Fort Jesup to the Sabine and alerted commanders in Indian Territory concerning Indian unrest in Texas.[6]

Fear of an Indian uprising along the international boundary abated temporarily when the rumors were proven exaggerated or erroneous. The Indians in the Fort Towson area remained quiet, and farther up the Red River, the Plains tribes professed "much friendship for the United States." Captain John Stuart, commander of Fort Coffee, wrote a lengthy letter to the editor of the *Arkansas Gazette* in which he attempted "to allay,... all unnecessary or unjustifiable apprehensions" concerning the immigrant tribes. Stuart asserted that "reports and conjectures... touching the probability of the existence of an unfriendly feeling towards the people of the U.S., on the part of... the Cherokees, Choctaws and Creeks... are entirely destitute of truth or probability."[7]

Despite such assurances residents of the Southwestern frontier remained apprehensive that Mexico would arouse the tribes of Texas and Indian Territory in an effort to crush the republic's claim of independence. On June 28, 1836, reports that a Mexican army was advancing on Texas spurred General Gaines to ask the governor of Arkansas Territory to raise a regiment of mounted gunmen to augment the regular troops guarding the Texas frontier. Governor William S. Fulton approved the request and issued a proclamation calling for a volunteer force to serve six months.[8]

The United States–Texas border was not the only critical area on the Southwestern frontier in the summer of 1836. General Arbuckle believed the drastic reduction of troops under his command had gravely imparied Fort Gibson's effectiveness in keeping the peace. The approach of immigrant Cherokees, Creeks, and Seminoles who were reported to have "very unfriendly feelings towards the United States" worried the general. Accordingly, he ordered the commander of Fort Towson to return the companies of the Seventh Infantry stationed there just as soon as conditions in that region would permit and informed the War Department that "at least two Regiments of Infantry and five companies of Dragoons" would be required to maintain the peace in Indian Territory.[9]

Officials in the War Department, faced with military threats in several areas, did not have additional regular troops for Indian Territory, but they authorized Arbuckle to request volunteers from Arkansas. The general had already alerted the governor to the possibility of an Indian uprising and informed him that the militia "should be organized without delay and [should be] in readiness to turn out at the shortest notice." When Arbuckle learned that General Gaines had also requested Arkansas militia units, he reminded the governor of the possibility of an uprising within Indian Territory and requested that militia units in the counties of northwestern Arkansas remain available for service along the Arkansas River frontier.[10]

Despite Arbuckle's conviction that troop strength in Indian Territory should not be reduced, General Gaines ordered the six companies of the Seventh Infantry and the Dragoon squadron recently transferred to Fort Towson to proceed to Nacogdoches, Texas. The occupation of Nacogdoches was in response to rumors that a Mexican force was advancing on Texas and that Indian bands, already assembled below the Red River, would support the invasion. Finding East Texas peaceful, one of the infantry officers who occupied the town asserted that rumors of Indian unrest were false and suggested that the Americans assigned to Texas could be more profitably employed in protecting the Southwestern frontier from "the scalping-knife of the Red man."[11]

Stressing the same point, Arbuckle warned General Gaines that "the force now at this post is entirely insufficient to ensure a continuance of peace on this Frontier." Unless regular troops reinforced Fort Gibson by November or earlier, Arbuckle believed it would be necessary to request a battalion of militia from the governor of Arkansas. The situation deteriorated more rapidly than Arbuckle had anticipated. In mid-August reports reached Fort Gibson that twenty-three hundred Creeks who had recently been at war with the United States were immigrating to Indian Territory. Arbuckle feared that the new arrivals might precipitate an intratribal civil war because of their grievances against Creeks already settled in Indian Territory.[12]

Faced with the prospect of confronting the angry Creeks with only three companies, Arbuckle invoked authority just received from the Adjutant General to request that Arkansas raise ten companies of volunteers. Governor Fulton, who had just mustered a regiment to fill the request of General Gaines, initially rejected Arbuckle's levy, explaining that he lacked authority to raise more troops. The governor suggested that some of the volunteers requested by General Gaines might be assigned to duty at Fort Gibson if they were not needed farther south. But new instructions from the War Department prompted the governor to reverse his position, and on September 5 he issued a call for ten companies of volunteers to reinforce Arbuckle's command.[13]

Before the first volunteers reached Fort Gibson, Chief Bowles of the Texas Cherokees had assembled four thousand immigrant and Plains warriors below the Red River for employment as allies of the Mexicans against the Texas rebels. Sam Houston warned that Plains Indians and Mexicans were about to attack East Texas and asked for volunteers to reinforce the United States troops General Gaines had sent to Nacogdoches. Arbuckle feared that a successful invasion of Texas might encourage the Mexican government to "commence depredations on our frontier citizens."[14] Confronted with potential hostility along the Texas frontier and within Indian Territory, the reduced force at Fort Gibson could do little more than protect itself.

Despite the obvious dangers, for the moment Indian Territory remained tranquil. The two thousand Creek immigrants who arrived in early September "much humbled, . . . naked and destitute" did not produce the intratribal conflict Arbuckle had anticipated. In fact, relations between the old and new settlers appeared to be cordial. Yet rumors persisted that the early settlers, the McIntosh faction, were "very unfriendly towards some of the Creeks expected to arrive" later in the fall. The continued possibility of intratribal hostility prompted Arbuckle to report that his post must be reinforced within five or six weeks.[15]

One resident of the post echoed Arbuckle's feelings. He informed the editor of the *Arkansas Gazette* that there was not "a sufficient regular force on this frontier to keep the Indians quiet." He maintained that the "people of Arkansas are entitled to protection" from "Indians, who have imbibed the most bitter feelings, not only against our government but our citizens, on account of the wrongs they have suffered east of the Mississippi." Creek warriors had already participated in a number of provocative incidents when the first Arkansas militia unit, a sixty-three-man cavalry company, reached Fort Gibson in early October. Twelve days later another militia company of mounted volunteers arrived to assist in keeping the peace among the immigrant Indians.[16]

After the chiefs of the dissident Indian bands in Texas rejected Chief Bowles's proposal to wage war on the Texans, Arbuckle asked General Gaines to transfer the Arkansas militia serving at Fort Towson to Fort Gibson, where it would be needed to maintain peace when twelve thousand additional Creek immigrants arrived in November or early December. One of the principal chiefs of the immigrants, Opothleyaholo, was "greatly displeased with the McIntosh party in consequence of threats" they had made against him. Arbuckle predicted, "there will be much difficulty in preventing the parties from resorting to acts of violence against each other." Should hostilities occur, the general warned, "the Traders and white men in the Creek Nation would be in much danger, and . . . without protection in consequence of the force here . . . being too small to benefit them."[17]

Although General Gaines had relinquished personal command of the troops on the Texas border to Arbuckle, as division commander he continued to supervise operations in the area. By November, Gaines had neither authorized General Arbuckle to order major troop movements nor responded to Arbuckle's request that Fort Gibson be reinforced. Obviously frustrated, Arbuckle appealed directly to the War Department for reinforcements and asserted that his depleted garrison could do nothing more than talk in an effort to maintain peace in Indian Territory.[18]

The failure of the government to pay tribal annuities on schedule threatened the fragile relations with the Creeks arriving in Indian Territory. Arbuckle advised the governor of Arkansas that "a greater evil will soon be felt here if money is not received to enable the contractors to subsist the Creek Indians." In order to bolster his command, Arbuckle deliberately ignored channels. On November 15, the general notified the commander of the militia in Washington County, Arkansas, that he would muster his company of militia into federal service immediately and "notify the Government of the fact." But even the arrival of the militia company eleven days later did not increase the strength of Fort Gibson enough to satisfy Arbuckle.[19]

The general had long believed that there was a greater possibility of hostilities in Indian Territory than in Texas. Arbuckle's opinion was supported by the evaluation of some of the officers serving in Texas. One maintained, "There is something singular in our occupation of Nacogdoches. There *never has been*, nor is there likely to be, any difficulties with the Indians." Another called rumors of Indian hostility "all humbugs" originated by land speculators. General Gaines did not concur; before he left the Southwestern frontier Gaines expressed his "belief that many of these Indian tribes [along the Texas border] are in a state of excitement calculated to lead to disastrous results."[20]

In view of the opinion of his superior, Arbuckle had been reluctant to order major troop movements without specific permission. In late November he received instructions from the War Department which authorized him to remove Colonel Whistler's command from Nacogdoches unless there was imminent danger of Indian hostilities. Arbuckle, who had advocated the removal of troops from Texas for some time, immediately transmitted these orders to Colonel Whistler. A few days earlier the general had ordered an Arkansas mounted militia regiment at Fort Towson to proceed to Fort Gibson without delay. Before it arrived two more companies of mounted gunmen from northwestern Arkansas reached Fort Gibson in response to Arbuckle's call for volunteers.[21] Their arrival helped insure the continued peace of Indian Territory even though the Arkansas militia regiment at Fort Towson and the regulars in Texas would not arrive at Fort Gibson for a month or more.

Opothleyaholo and the first parties of the twelve thousand immigrating Creeks reached Indian Territory in early December. The chief had promised military officials in Alabama that the immigrants would stop in Arkansas until the animosity between his faction and the McIntosh Creeks could be resolved. The governor of Arkansas denied the immigrants permission to stop in his state. To keep the feuding factions apart, Arbuckle directed the Creek immigrants to camp on the Fort Gibson reservation while their leaders settled affairs with the old settlers. The arrival of Opothleyaholo and a four-thousand-man contingent of immigrants in early December produced no disturbances, and General Arbuckle brought Roley McIntosh and Opothleyaholo together at a meeting during which "the pipe of peace was puffed."[22]

Lieutenant Colonel Whistler reported from Nacogdoches that everything was "perfectly quiet," and on December 19, the American forces remaining in Texas began their return march to Fort Gibson. A week later the Arkansas militia regiment from Fort Towson reached the post. Thus reinforced, Arbuckle permitted the Creek immigrants to leave the Fort Gibson reservation for the Canadian River valley where they planned to settle.[23]

Opothleyaholo expressed concern over the wretched condition of Creeks still on the trail from Alabama. General Arbuckle directed the officer escorting the tribe to insure that his charges "not Suffer for want of Provisions." The order was a little late. One observer at Fort Gibson reported thousands of Creeks had already arrived "entirely destitute of shoes;... many of them are almost naked; and but few of them have any thing more on their persons than a light dress." Some left behind by the side of the road to be aided by government contractors remained "until devoured by the wolves." This inhumane treatment on the immigrating Creeks, according to the observer at Fort Gibson, resulted from the attitude of the government contractors, who regarded their obligations to the Indians as "a matter of speculation." He concluded that "no portion of American history can furnish a parallel of the misery and suffering at present endured by the emigrating Creeks."[24]

Although the incoming bands of Creeks may have been embittered, they did not constitute an immediate danger. Consequently, after the return of the regular troops to Fort Gibson in January, 1837, Arbuckle began mustering out companies of the Arkansas militia. His decision to discharge the volunteers before their term of service had expired may have been influenced by problems caused

Opothleyaholo, Creek chief who led a large contingent of his tribe to Indian Territory in 1836. From McKenney and Hall, *History of the Indian Tribes of North America*, 1838.

by the unruly militiamen. One incident that began on February 5, 1837, almost provoked open conflict between the militia and the Cherokees. Two or three members of the Arkansas volunteers attended "a frolic given at a house of ill fame" located three miles from the post on Bayou Menard. A number of Cherokees and Negroes were also present. "Becoming excited by spiritous liquors, and perhaps other causes . . . they fell to fighting." The outnumbered volunteers "were compelled to leave the evening's entertainment with a severe drubbing." The next day the victims returned with reinforcements to even the score. Unable to find their assailants, the soldiers beat a number of Cherokees and made "menacing threats towards them as a people." A group of angry Cherokees gathered at Bayou Menard, and rumors spread that the Cherokees intended to attack the militia camp. When General Arbuckle learned of the incident, he disciplined the militiamen involved and ordered the volunteers' camp moved closer to the post. He also reported that "the Indian women who were the main cause of the affray have also been punished."[25]

Harmonious relations between the army and the Cherokees were quickly restored, but Arbuckle must have had second thoughts about the value of militia as a peacekeeping force. Not long after the incident, Arbuckle urged the paymaster to "make all prudent dispatch to hasten to this post with the necessary funds to pay off the Volunteers." The general hoped that the last companies could be mustered out no later than March 27. However, the paymaster did not have sufficient funds to discharge the entire force by that date. Three companies and the regimental staff remained on active service until mid-April.[26]

As the volunteer units were being discharged, Arbuckle advised the War Department that a realignment of military personnel was necessary to give "the South Western Frontier such additional force as may be required . . . for its security." The general reminded his superiors of the impending arrival of Cherokees "with feelings little friendly to our Government" and informed them of reports of increased restlessness among the Creeks. Some of the dissident warriors from these tribes, Arbuckle believed, would gravitate to Texas, where they might incite the turbulent bands already there. To provide adequate military protection for the Texas boundary, the general urged the War Department to station a Dragoon force along the Red River.[27]

In late December hunters employed by Israel Folsom, a mixed-blood Choctaw, returned from the prairies. They reported that the Comanches had killed and scalped a white man just beyond the Cross Timbers and that the Plains tribes were uniting against the United States with the support of the Mexicans. General Arbuckle questioned the accuracy of the report of Folsom's hunters, but subsequent accounts from the Choctaw agency confirmed that the Plains tribes were aroused. The Choctaw agent reported that he would "not be surprised if we have some difficulties in the West" in view of the encroachment of Eastern Indians on hunting grounds claimed by the Plains tribes.[28]

Whites and friendly Indians who traveled beyond the Cross Timbers reported "that the Comanches, Pawnees and other wild Indians are preparing to attack the Indian frontier." One soldier with years of experience in Indian Territory predicted, "there will be some difficulty, the ensuing spring and summer, with the Camanches and other of the wild tribes." The validity of this prediction was soon demonstrated by the robbery of an Indian trader by Comanches and reports that Mexican officials were encouraging unrest among the Plains tribes. One resident of the Choctaw Nation warned that an immediate war could be prevented only by "the prompt gathering of a military force at some point on Red river." General Gaines concurred. He considered the reinforcement of the Western Department as "very desirable, if not essential to the safety of a large, exposed and feeble section of the frontier." The War Department must have agreed with General Gaines's assessment, for during the summer over three hundred replacements arrived at Fort Gibson. Their presence may have restrained the Plains tribes—at least no major clashes were reported in the *Arkansas Gazette* or dispatches from Fort Gibson.[29]

General Arbuckle had been complaining intermittently about his health since he assumed command of the Southwestern frontier in 1834. Although the War Department had repeatedly approved the general's request for leave, turbulence on the frontier had compelled him to remain at his post. In view of Fort Gibson's reputation as the charnel house of the army, it is not surprising that the general's health did not improve. In December, 1836, he informed the Adjutant General that he "had a return of the Diarrhea last fall, a disease with which I have been much afflicted." He requested permission to visit the East in order to recover his health. His request was granted, and on May 11, 1837, Arbuckle relinquished command of Fort Gibson to Lieutenant Colonel Whistler. The command of the Southwestern Department fell to Colonel James B. Many, the commander of Fort Jesup. In his instructions to Many, Arbuckle ordered prompt military retaliation against any tribe residing within the United States which committed hostilities in Texas. Still convinced that unrest in Indian Territory constituted the primary threat to peace, the general specifically prohibited Colonel Many from withdrawing any troops from Fort Gibson.[30] Although Arbuckle considered the Southwestern Department peaceful enough to entrust to a subordinate, he clearly wished the fort to remain strong. His foresight proved correct. It would be several more years before the turbulence resulting from the Texas Revolution would subside.

Chapter 12

A Turbulent Haven

TURBULENCE SPAWNED BY the Texas Revolution, Indian removal, and dissident Plains tribes supported General Matthew Arbuckle's conviction that a significant military force at Fort Gibson was essential to the peace of Indian Territory. Officials in Arkansas, however, did not share the general's opinion. As the territory moved toward statehood, the legislature renewed its efforts to secure the relocation of troops from Fort Gibson to a point closer to the Arkansas border. In March, 1836, a memorial drafted by that body was referred to the Military Affairs Committee of the House of Representatives, which was already considering a comprehensive plan proposed by Secretary of War Lewis Cass to realign the military along the entire frontier from the Red River to Canada. Cass notified the chairman of the Military Affairs Committee that numerous complaints concerning the unhealthful site of Fort Gibson had persuaded him that it should be abandoned.[1]

The commanding general of the army, Alexander Macomb, suggested Fort Coffee as a healthy and convenient location for a new post. Arbuckle disagreed, noting that "Fort Coffee will prove *very* unhealthy to any force over one or two companies, as it is surrounded on three sides by extensive River Bottoms, and on the South . . . low and sour prairie." From a tactical point of view, Fort Coffee's location was undesirable in Arbuckle's opinion because it was too far from the most troublesome tribes, which resided north of the Arkansas River. After giving the matter further thought, Arbuckle concluded that "the removal of this garrison at present would be very unfavorable to the continuance of peace on this frontier." Before Fort Gibson could be abandoned, Arbuckle believed that the Osages, still residing on Cherokee lands, would have to be moved to their reservation, and the Cherokees and Creeks would have to become more friendly to the United States. He also argued that there was no position between Fort Gibson and the

Arkansas boundary on the Arkansas River that would be any more healthful than Fort Gibson.[2]

Captain Joseph A. Phillips, a company commander in the Seventh Infantry, did not concur with Arbuckle's evaluation. In a letter to the chairman of the House Committee on Military Affairs, the captain urged that the Seventh Infantry be assigned a new post and charged that prolonged service at Fort Gibson had impaired the health of the troops and diminished the regiment's effectiveness as a military force. Phillips also questioned Arbuckle's objectivity in defending the location of the post. He suggested that Arbuckle's ownership of a plantation on the Arkansas River had "*some* effect in influencing his motives." In an earlier letter Phillips had written that Arbuckle's "principal objection" to the removal of Fort Gibson "is that he is afraid *he will die* if the regiment is ordered to the North!"[3]

Despite the opposition by Arbuckle, on July 2, 1836, Congress formally adopted Cass's plan, which called for the construction of a military road along the frontier from Fort Towson to Fort Snelling in what is now Minnesota. Troops were to be concentrated at strategic points along the route. Since Fort Gibson lay west of the proposed route, Congress earmarked funds for its removal, and the Secretary of War instructed a three-member military commission, assigned to survey the road, to find an appropriate site for a new post along the Arkansas River.[4]

News of the passage of the Frontier Defense Bill produced mixed reactions in the Southwest. A Dragoon officer claimed that "every one here is rejoiced to see that Fort Gibson is to be broken up—it was indeed a grave yard for our soldiers." An unsigned editorial in the *Arkansas Gazette* in December, 1836, stated that the post "is undoubtedly at present, the most important military station, in every point of view, occupied by the US government." The writer suggested that the fort guarded the most volatile portion of Indian Territory and was the "only point from which we have any apprehension of hostilities."[5]

The editorial may have been designed to influence the officers charged with the task of recommending a new location for the army on the Arkansas. The commissioners, Colonel Stephen W. Kearny, Captain Nathan Boone, and Brevet Major Key F. Smith, reached Fort Gibson in early December, in advance of news of their appointment. An agitated General Arbuckle declined to accompany the commissioners in their inspection of sites for a new post. Instead, the commander of Fort Gibson assigned Captain Benjamin L. E. Bonneville to escort them. He also questioned the War Department's motives in appointing the commissioners without consulting him first.[6]

Arbuckle's brusque treatment of the commissioners did not prejudice them against his recommendations. Instead of confirming the conclusions of the general-in-chief that Fort Gibson should be abandoned, Kearny and his fellow commissioners reported that "the presence of a military force, near Fort Gibson is indispensable for the preservation of peace amongst the Indians themselves." They did suggest that the post might be moved to higher ground about half a mile to the northeast. Concerning the site for a military garrison located nearer the Arkansas boundary, the commissioners rejected Fort Smith and seconded General Macomb's selection of Fort Coffee. They also recommended that a regiment of infantry and four companies of Dragoons be divided between Fort Gibson and Fort Coffee.[7]

News of the commissioners' report evoked a memorial from citizens in the western counties of Arkansas. They protested that they locations recommended were "entirely without the limits of our state." Noting that the increasing number of immigrant Indians might constitute a real danger to their safety, the memorialists urged that a fort be constructed within the boundary of their state.[8]

The citizens of western Arkansas were probably less concerned about frontier defense than about the income which a military installation within the state would produce. Indeed, one of the major boosters of Fort Smith as a site for a post was John Rogers, a major landholder in the area. Members of the Arkansas congressional delegation worked diligently to reverse the War Department's decision. Joel Poinsett, the Secretary of War under Martin Van Buren, did not share Lewis Cass's views on frontier defense. Concerned primarily about the security of white residents of the frontier, he scrapped Cass's plan for frontier defense and with it the recommendations of the three commissioners concerning military positions on the Arkansas River. In October, 1837, Poinsett informed Arkansas congressmen that he had suspended the order for the construction of enlarged facilities at Fort Coffee and had directed that sites within the borders of the state be examined. To further reassure aroused residents of western Arkansas, the secretary informed one of the Arkansas senators that "the Department is anxiously solicitous to place the intended fort where it will afford the best protection to that portion of the country."[9]

The secretary stopped short of giving the citizens of Arkansas direct assurances that a fort would be built within the state. He was awaiting the results of a new study he had commissioned shortly after assuming office. At the direction of Poinsett, Lieutenant Colonel William Whistler and Captain John Stuart examined prospective sites for a military installation along the Arkansas. In September, 1837, they informed the commanding general of the army,

> In the first place, we are decidedly of the opinion that a
> large body of troops should be kept in the immediate
> vicinity of where Fort Gibson now stands, or even farther
> west. . . . There the troops would, if necessary, be able to
> keep in check the disaffected Creeks. They would also be
> able to prevent war between the Creeks and Osages, or the
> Cherokees and Osages, which will most assuredly occur,
> just so soon as the troops are removed from Fort Gibson.

The commissioners continued, "We would next place a considerable force at Fort Coffee. At that point the troops would, if necessary, give protection to the State of Arkansas." Whistler and Stuart argued persuasively that the western boundary of Arkansas was exposed to little danger from hostile Indians and that the troops should be garrisoned within Indian Territory, where they were really needed to preserve the peace.[10]

Despite this report, pressure from the Arkansas delegation forced the Secretary of War to subordinate the recommendation of his military commissioners to political considerations. In October, Poinsett sent new instructions to Whistler and Stuart directing them to select "a site for a large military post within the state of Arkansas." The commissioners surveyed three sites, none of which they considered particularly desirable, and finally agreed on Fort Smith as the least objectionable.[11]

The pressure from the Arkansas Congressional delegation did not relent. On February 7, 1838, the Senate adopted a resolution which required the War Department to provide a status report on the selection of a site for a post on or near the Arkansas boundary. The Secretary of War replied that it was impossible to comply literally with the Act of Congress which called for removal of Fort Gibson. Citing the conclusions of Whistler and Stuart, Poinsett asserted that peace on the frontier can be maintained "only by continuing Fort Gibson at its present site, or, at least, at some point near to it, and by the erection of another post on or near the Arkansas line." The Arkansas delegation was relentless. On April 4, they succeeded in persuading Congress to adopt a joint resolution empowering the Secretary of War to purchase land for a military reservation on or near the western boundary of Arkansas. Surrendering to the political pressure, Poinsett sanctioned the purchase of approximately three hundred acres of land adjacent to the old Fort Smith reservation and directed that construction should begin at once on facilities at Fort Smith. The land belonged to John Rogers, a long-time advocate of the reactivation of the post.[12]

When Fort Smith was reestablished, Fort Coffee was abandoned, and Captain John Stuart and his company were ordered into the Cherokee Nation. On October 29, 1838, Stuart established a post on the Illinois River in order to calm the residents of western Arkansas who feared that the arrival of the Eastern Cherokees might produce strife in Indian Territory. This installation, named Camp Illinois, proved to be particularly unhealthy. Within a few months a number of soldiers died there, including the post's commanding officer, Captain Stuart. As a result the site was abandoned, and the soldiers moved farther north to Spavinaw Creek near the Arkansas line, where they began work on a new post called Fort Wayne. From this location they patrolled the Cherokee Nation during its most turbulent years.[13]

Although the Arkansas congressional delegation had persuaded the War Department to establish two posts on or near the state's western border, General Arbuckle managed to dissuade the department from abandoning Fort Gibson. The general was not as successful in competing for funds with Arkansas congressmen, who were able to get the lion's share of appropriations for defense of the Southwest allocated for the construction of Fort Smith. As the bastions of Fort Smith rose, the pickets of Fort Gibson rotted, but the garrison on the Grand River continued to guard Indian Territory during the final phase of removal of the Eastern tribes.

The tempo of activity at Fort Gibson during the late 1830's gave convincing proof that Arbuckle's assessment of the importance of the post was correct. The negotiation of the treaties of 1835 and 1837 with the Plains tribes did not produce the "perpetual peace and friendship" the signatories had agreed to observe. The Comanches, angered by violations of the treaty of 1835 and the encroachment of hunting parties from the Eastern tribes, remained a threat to the security of the Plains. Reports that they had murdered or captured American citizens prompted the War Department to commission Colonel Auguste P. Chouteau to undertake a mission to the Comanches and other tribes in April, 1837. He was to investigate Indian grievances, explain the obligations imposed by the treaty of 1835, obtain the release of any American captives, and inform the government of any threats posed by the Indians of the Southwestern frontier.[14] Chouteau's instructions arrived just before the negotiation of the Kiowa treaty of 1837 at Fort Gibson.

During the negotiations Captain William Armstrong, the western superintendent, and Colonel Chouteau worked out plans to meet with the Comanches and other Plains tribes at Camp Holmes in October. In a report to the commissioner of Indian Affairs concerning the meeting, Armstrong suggested that a visit by the leaders of the Plains tribes to "some of the populous cities of the United States" would be the most effective demonstration of national strength. Commissioner Carey A. Harris agreed with Armstrong and directed Chouteau to collect a deputation of Plains Indians who were to be brought to Washington in the winter or spring. Just before his departure Chouteau reported that the Comanches and associated bands had thirty or forty white prisoners who had been captured in Texas and Mexico. Since his orders covered only American prisoners, Chouteau asked the Secretary of War if he were authorized to ransom these captives and was given permission to liberate any white person held by the Plains Indians.[15]

Chouteau delayed his departure until he had an opportunity to talk to General Arbuckle, who had been in the East from May to October, attempting to recover his health. Soon after Arbuckle returned to Fort Gibson in October, 1837, he ordered Captain Eustice Trenor and his Dragoon company to escort Colonel Chouteau to Camp Holmes. Although he was delayed in departing, the colonel sent his brother, Major Paul L. Chouteau, to arrange a meeting with the various Plains tribes. Colonel Chouteau and his Dragoon escort did not leave Fort Gibson until November 1. When he arrived at Camp Holmes twenty-four days later, Chouteau learned that his brother had been unable to persuade the Plains tribes to participate in talks that fall. Colonel Chouteau reported that agents of the new Texas Republic and Mexico had been vying for the support of the Plains Indians, most of whom were scattered across the country at war. While some were supporting the "Texicans" or Mexicans, Colonel Chouteau reported that a great many had gone to war "for predatory purposes alone." Chouteau decided to remain at Camp Holmes during the winter of 1837–38 and to renew his attempts to meet with the tribes in the spring. Captain Trenor and his Dragoon company returned to Fort Gibson, leaving a small detachment under the command of Lieutenant Lucius B. Northrop at Camp Holmes with Colonel Chouteau.[16]

Throughout the winter Chouteau kept General Arbuckle informed of the activity of the Plains tribes. He was particularly concerned that marauding bands of Pawnees would "keep all the different tribes at war with each other" and endanger American citizens who ventured onto the Plains. The horse-stealing expeditions of the Osages also antagonized the Comanches, who informed Chouteau that they would not "suffer these injuries to go unnoticed." Despite this intertribal feuding, Chouteau reported that he might be able to organize a deputation of Plains Indians to visit Washington by late spring. When the Plains tribes had not arrived at Camp Holmes by April, Chouteau informed Arbuckle that unless the Indians came in soon, he probably would be unable to assemble them until late fall.[17]

Chouteau's difficulty in persuading an Indian deputation to journey to Washington prompted one officer familiar with the Plains Indians to inform the Indian Office that Chouteau was "too dilatory" to succeed in his mission. Despite this pessimistic prediction, the colonel was making progress at Camp Holmes; on May 27, 1838, about one hundred Indians representing eight different prairie tribes met with Chouteau and promised him that they would assemble at Camp Holmes in the fall, prepared to go to Washington. By that time Chouteau hoped to have instructions from the government concerning depredations committed by the Pawnees, Cheyennes, and other tribes. The representatives of the eight tribes pledged to refrain from attacking the Pawnees and Cheyennes until the fall. An injured leg confined Chouteau to Camp Holmes, but he sent his nephew, E. L. Chouteau, and a military escort commanded by Lieutenant Northrop onto the Plains to try to persuade the other tribes to keep the peace and honor their treaty obligations. Northrop and the younger Chouteau learned that Cheyenne, Arapaho, and Pawnee warriors were raiding the camps of other tribes west of Camp Holmes. Although anxious for revenge, the Indians who had been attacked promised not to retaliate until they learned what the War Department planned to do to pacify the area.[18]

Chouteau's efforts to maintain peace succeeded, and during the summer the friction subsided between the Plains and immigrant tribes. In his annual report for 1838, Armstrong expressed "but little fear" of trouble "from the Wild Indians," and reports from the upper Red River indicated "no probability of the Prairie Indians, disturbing the Frontier of the United States, or that of Texas, this summer." During the summer Chouteau returned to Fort Gibson. He planned to renew his efforts to convince the Indians that they should go to Washington after the fall buffalo hunt, but his health continued to deteriorate. On Christmas Day, 1838, Colonel Chouteau died at his home at the saline north of Fort Gibson.[19]

Captain Armstrong recommended that the work of gathering the Indians for a visit to Washington be continued by Lieutenant Northrop, who was familiar with Chouteau's plans. Northrop had established personal contact with many of the Plains tribes. Confronted with the Seminole War in Florida and an international boundary dispute in Maine, however, the War Department had lost interest in the plan to bring a Plains Indian delegation to Washington. No new orders were issued concerning the visit, nor were Colonel A. P. Chouteau's instructions cancelled. General Arbuckle seems to have taken no action until John Rogers, one of the principal chiefs of the Western Cherokees, informed him of the arrival of an emissary from the Comanches who brought word of their desire to meet with representatives of the government. Rogers reported that the Plains tribes seemed disposed "to make peace with all nations as well as the Genl Government" and urged Arbuckle and Armstrong to seize the opportunity to make some arrangement with them. The general, who had already ordered Lieutenant James M. Bowman to escort the Santa Fe traders to the Mexican border, directed him to inform the Comanches that a report of their desire for talks had to be transmitted to Washington and that instructions were expected by fall.[20]

The Plains tribes had already assembled and were unwilling to await instructions from Washington. In late May, a twenty-four-member delegation of Kiowas and Comanches arrived at Fort Gibson in response to the invitation issued by Chouteau before his death. Since Arbuckle lacked authorization to send the chiefs to Washington, he sent the delegation to visit Superintendent

Armstrong at the Choctaw agency. Arbuckle recommended that at least a portion of the delegation be sent to the capital to negotiate a treaty which would "tend in a great measure to give security to our citizens in travelling through the Western Prairies." Armstrong, who expressed concern about the health of the Indians traveling in the late spring and summer, left the decision to the chiefs. They decided not to continue on to Washington, and the superintendent did not press them. Arbuckle expressed regret at the decision and suggested that the consequences of not sending the delegation "will be disastrous to our Citizens that will hereafter attempt to pass west through the grand prairie."[21] Although the extent of the danger of travel on the Plains was probably overemphasized by Arbuckle, there is no doubt that the Plains tribes would continue to endanger travelers as well as settlers for at least forty more years. Nonetheless, for the moment, the government's interest in subduing the Plains tribes had waned. By 1839, removal of the Eastern tribes was nearing completion, and the hostility of those tribes no longer constituted an obstacle to federal policy.

General Arbuckle and other officials at Fort Gibson were able to resolve another persistent irritant to removal. Caught between the warring Plains tribes and the onrush of Eastern migrants, the once prosperous Osages had grown more impoverished each year. Although they had relinquished their lands near Fort Gibson in 1825, thousands still remained on land now owned by the Cherokees. Despite lengthy negotiations in 1833, the Stokes Commission had not persuaded the Osages to move to their new reservation. Whether encroaching on land ceded to the Cherokees or hunting on ground claimed by the Plains tribes, they irritated their neighbors. In late 1837, the *Arkansas Gazette* reported that the Osage tribe was "now in rather a deplorable situation. Forbidden to hunt, or even show themselves in the settlements, and unable to cope with their enemies of the prairies."[22]

In November, Arbuckle learned of trouble between white residents of western Missouri and the Osages and was prompted to warn his superiors that the tribe "may resort to acts of hostility." Noting that the Osages had inadequate food to last until spring, the general proposed making provisions available to them from the supplies of Fort Gibson. Arbuckle's compassion for the impoverished tribe was balanced by his duty to protect the immigrant Indians and their property. In December, when he learned that Osage warriors were stealing hogs and cattle in the Cherokee settlements near Spavinaw Creek, Arbuckle immediately dispatched Captain Philip St. George Cooke with a Dragoon company to drive the intruders away from the settlements and to apprehend their leaders. Cooke marched from Fort Gibson the day before Christmas and returned a week later, reporting the successful completion of his mission.[23]

In the long run, a show of military power as a deterrent proved less effective than hunger as a motivating force. By early spring General Arbuckle ordered Captain Eustice Trenor and his Dragoon company to the Creek settlements beyond the Verdigris to remove a party of Osages who were killing livestock. By the time the Dragoons arrived, the Osages were gone, but bitter Creek settlers told the captain that they had lost over 130 hogs. Arbuckle informed the War Department that the Creeks were "much insenced" by the Osages and planned "at *once* to take satisfaction by, punishing, or killing them." He urged the government to remove Chief Clermont's band from Cherokee land and to compensate the Creeks and Cherokees who had suffered losses at the hands of the Osages.[24]

The arrival of the spring hunting season brought the Creeks and Cherokees temporary relief from Osage depredations, but the return of winter was accompanied by renewed Osage raids on the herds of their neighbors. By November, Arbuckle had again dispatched Dragoons to evict Osage raiders from Cherokee settlements. Responding to the suggestions of Arbuckle and tribal agents in Indian Territory, officials in Washington commissioned General Arbuckle and Captain Armstrong to persuade the Osages to abandon their old homes near the Three Forks. Since Arbuckle did not learn of his appointment until after the Osages had left for their fall hunt, he was unable to assemble tribal leaders until January, 1839. At the council at Fort Gibson, over seventy Osages, including Clermont and Tally, accepted—with only one modification concerning the Osages' school fund—a draft treaty prepared in Washington. By the terms of the agreement signed at Fort Gibson on January 11, 1839, the Osages relinquished title to and promised to vacate all lands assigned to other tribes. The government in return promised the Osages an annuity of $20,000 for twenty years and agreed to pay claims of those injured by Osage depredations. Arbuckle estimated that the treaty would require the removal of sixteen hundred to two thousand Osages from the Cherokee country before March 1.[25]

As that date approached, smallpox broke out among the Osages of Clermont's bands who were preparing to move from Cherokee lands. To prevent further delay in the Osage removal, Arbuckle urged a civilian physician to proceed immediately to the Osage camp to inoculate the entire village. But the epidemic delayed the departure of the Osages, whose continued raiding parties aroused the Cherokees and Creeks to threats of retaliation. On March 19, Arbuckle ordered a patrol from Fort Gibson to advise the Osages that if they had not removed themselves from the Cherokee Nation within six days, a military force would be sent to evict them. Only those infected with smallpox were to be allowed to remain, and they only until recovery.[26] The threat apparently succeeded, for the records of Fort Gibson reveal few complaints from the immigrant tribes concerning Osage depredations after the spring of 1839. After three decades, the Osage-Cherokee rivalry had been concluded.

While the Osage problem was approaching solution, discontent among the immigrating Indians posed new problems for the army at Fort Gibson. The hardships of removal and the bitterness arising from unfulfilled expectations made the Seminoles' adjustment to life in Indian Territory particularly difficult. In the summer of 1836, the first contingent of Seminoles who had agreed to leave Florida voluntarily began arriving in Indian Territory impoverished and dispirited. They were settled along Little River on lands assigned the tribe by the Treaty of Fort Gibson in 1833. The officers escorting the band during the removal reported that they were "not disposed to exert themselves" and "are exceedingly dissipated, idle, and reckless."[27] Considering the trauma of their removal, it was not surprising that the immigrants did not adjust readily to their new environment.

Two more years elapsed before the next band reached Indian Territory. This party had resisted removal and arrived at Fort Gibson in early June, 1838, in a "very naked" condition. General Arbuckle arranged a meeting between the new arrivals and the Creeks who had already begun settling the region between the Canadian and North Fork allocated to the Seminoles by the Treaty of Fort Gibson. Roley McIntosh and the other chiefs of the Creeks proposed that the Seminoles settle among the Creeks and accept their government. The Seminoles rejected the offer and demanded the land promised them in 1833. The Creeks made no effort to vacate the area, and the Seminoles refused to leave Fort Gibson. By late summer, two thousand Seminoles were encamped around Fort

Gibson. General Arbuckle reported their condition to the War Department and urged that they be transported to a location they found acceptable and be provided with tools to erect cabins.[28]

By the spring of 1839, the dispirited Seminoles were still encamped around Fort Gibson, and their demand for the land promised to them by the Treaty of Fort Gibson remained unfulfilled. The arrival of another party of immigrants from Florida prompted Arbuckle to urge Superintendent Armstrong to come to the post to help find the tribe an acceptable reservation. The general also invited Opothleyaholo, whose followers had settled on the land assigned to the Seminoles, to visit the post and discuss the Seminoles' problems.[29]

By May, Arbuckle and Armstrong had negotiated an arrangement with the Creeks by which the Seminoles were to be given a tract within the Creek Nation, between the Little River and the North Fork of the Canadian River, in lieu of the tract promised by the Treaty of Fort Gibson. Although Armstrong reported that several of the Seminoles had seen and were pleased with the area, not all members of the tribe shared their pleasure. A recalcitrant chief named Alligator refused to leave the Fort Gibson area and exerted every effort to persuade others to join him. In order to bring pressure on the Seminoles, Armstrong proposed withholding their provisions until they had reached the reservation. Arbuckle observed that such action would drive them to plunder the crops and livestock of nearby farmers, resulting in "a very serious loss to the Cherokees in this vicinity."[30]

Ignoring Arbuckle's warning, Armstrong withheld supplies promised the Seminoles—but to no avail. Alligator and other leaders who arrived later chose to remain refugees near Fort Gibson rather than to accept the land and conditions offered by the Creeks. The general's warning proved correct; deprived of government help, the Seminoles residing near Fort Gibson began plundering the property of the neighboring Cherokees. Not until 1845 did Alligator and other Seminole chiefs obtain Creek approval to allow them a distinct territory on the Little River. After nearly ten years, the displaced Seminoles began leaving the Fort Gibson area for their own home.[31]

No other tribe endured as difficult a period of readjustment as the Seminoles, but many members of other tribes reached Indian Territory bitter and vengeful. It was not surprising that some of them considered schemes of retribution or listened to the promises of Mexican agents seeking to enlist their support against the Texans.

In late 1837, a force of five hundred Choctaws, recruited by the government to serve as auxiliaries against the Seminoles in Florida, disbanded with "a show of decided chagrin" because of a disagreement over pay. The editor of the *Arkansas Gazette* expressed concern that the episode would inflame the discontent on the frontier. In the same issue a letter was published from an individual in the Cherokee Nation who claimed there was "Treason a-brewing." He believed the Cherokees were attempting to unify the neighboring tribes to gain strength and were "encouraged by white men, of bad character... who do not care for the consequences of a collision between the Indians and U.S. troops." These apprehensions were aggravated by reports that Texas had again been invaded by the Mexicans. Arbuckle feared a Mexican victory "might induce the Indians on the Sabine River and to the South of it to do our frontier settlers much injury." Prompted by the anticipation of Indian hostility near the Texas border, Arbuckle ordered Captain Benjamin L. E. Bonneville and his infantry company to reinforce Fort Towson.[32]

Large numbers of American citizens had moved into the area below Fort Towson, professing allegiance to the Texas government. Their inhumane treatment of the Indians added credence to widespread fears that the tribes would support the Mexicans in case of renewed warfare. In April, 1838, Lieutenant Colonel Josiah H. Vose, commander of Fort Towson, reported "an affray between white people and Choctaws" just below the Red River, in which one white man and a Choctaw were killed and four other whites wounded. Vose concluded that "the white people were undoubtedly the aggressors, as is generally the case in all Indian difficulties." Reports reaching Fort Towson also indicated unrest among the Chickasaws, Choctaws, and Delawares living along the Red River. Vose recommended that the entire Third Infantry be stationed at Fort Towson. With the Seminole War in progress, the army could not spare an entire regiment for service on the upper Red River, but it did send 180 recruits who reached Fort Towson on March 31, 1838. A few days after their arrival, Captain Bonneville and his company returned to Fort Gibson.[33]

The Indian unrest was not restricted to the Fort Towson area. Several secret councils were held in the early spring of 1838 near

Fort Gibson and were attended by the "influential men" of the Cherokees, Creeks, Choctaws, Chickasaws, Delawares, and Quapaws. Arbuckle learned that "a portion of the chiefs or warriors advocated "acts of hostility against the United States." There apparently was no positive decision to go to war, but the general advised the War Department that should war commence, "we will not be suitably prepared to meet it in Consequence of the deficiency of Force of any kind." Arbuckle alerted the governor of Arkansas to the possibility of Indian hostilities and asked him to prepare the state militia for possible action. The *Arkansas Gazette* reported "considerable apprehensions" in Miller County regarding an invasion by "several parties of marauding Indians" who were "stealing horses, and giving other indications of a hostile disposition." The next edition of the newspaper reported "considerable dissatisfaction" among the Creek immigrants. One old Creek woman warned, "*as soon as the green corn is fit to pull*, THE WHITE PEOPLE MUST LOOK OUT!"[34]

Several weeks later the *Arkansas Gazette* noted that dissatisfaction among the Creeks was "on the increase" and that "open violence" might break out within weeks. Subsequent reports indicated that in the event of war "Fort Gibson would be the first and most essential point of attack." Accordingly, Arbuckle ordered the post's defenses enlarged and strengthened. Several weeks passed without overt hostility, but it was learned that the Plains tribes and other Indians had reached a "general understanding." Arbuckle reported, "The subject of going to War has been fully discussed and it would appear that the time for action has been postponed on account of the scarcity of provisions in this quarter at least until after the green corn dance and the arrival of the remaining Cherokees . . . from the Old Nation." It was no secret that the Eastern Cherokees harbored "much bad feeling" toward the United States. Their arrival in Indian Territory might tip the balance in favor of those advocating retaliation against the whites.[35]

Information also reached Fort Gibson that the distinguished Cherokee warrior, Dutch, had been invited by the Texas Cherokees to join them as allies of the Mexicans against the Texans. The report indicated that Dutch and other Cherokees who had received similar offers had declined, but Arbuckle acknowledged the possibility that he might have been "deceived in this particular." The general informed the commander of Fort Towson of these developments and directed him to report any Mexican overtures to

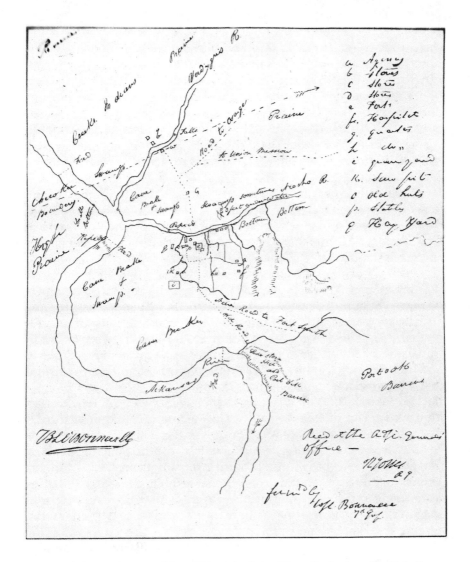

Bonneville's sketch map of Fort Gibson and the Three Forks Area in 1838. From Grant Foreman, *Pioneer Days in the Early Southwest*.

the Indians directly to Washington without delay. The tribes near Fort Towson were to be advised that the United States had recognized the independence of Texas and would not allow the Indians under its protection to resort to acts of hostility against the citizens of Texas.[36]

By early June, Arbuckle had become cautiously optimistic and was expressing the belief that "the bad feelings now existing may subside if no accident should happen to arrouse them." Roley McIntosh further assured the general that the Creeks were "perfectly friendly towards the United States." He attributed the reports that the Creeks were preparing for war to "foolish and improper remarks" of a few Creeks "at their frolicks when in a state of intoxication." McIntosh and twenty-three other tribal leaders made similar assurances to the editor of the *Arkansas Gazette*, which had carried the stories of Creek unrest.[37]

A meeting of Arbuckle and the Cherokee chiefs produced similar pledges of continued peace from that tribe. The general assured the War Department that "it is not probable that any serious difficulties will take place in this quarter until after all the Cherokees arrive in this Country and . . . not then if Treaty stipulations are regularly and fully complied with, and the tribes in this vicinity are satisfied that our government feels a proper interest in their welfare." Arbuckle, long a critic of absentee Indian agents, recommended that improved relations might result if the agents were required to visit their tribes at least semi-annually to assist them in adjusting to their new environment. Another idea advanced by the general involved the employment of volunteer units drawn from loyal Indians against hostile tribes in future conflicts. Although Indian auxiliaries were being utilized in Florida, the War Department rejected the suggestion, explaining that "there is no authority vested in the executive to engage such a force."[38]

During the summer the Cherokees invited all the surrounding tribes, except the Osages and Kansas, to meet in council in September. Arbuckle considered the invitation "to indicate something more than a renewal of Friendship" but suggested that the more militant warriors would be restrained by the principal chiefs and men of property "if the Emigrants are kindly treated by our government." Arbuckle's evaluation of the threat posed by the September council was not shared by other commanders in the area. From Fort Leavenworth, Lieutenant Colonel Richard Mason of the First Dragoon Regiment informed General Gaines, commander of the Western Division, "There is no doubt in my mind but the object of this council is to effect a union of the different tribes, preparatory to striking a simultaneous blow upon the settlements of Arkansas and Missouri, from the Red river to the upper Mississippi." Gaines, who believed the Cherokees were being incited by the Mexicans, agreed with Mason's conclusion. If the Cherokees succeeded in arousing the tribes of the frontier, Gaines estimated the Indians could field over twenty thousand mounted warriors, a force which could "lay waste the whole line of . . . settlements from the mouth of the Sabine, to the Falls of St. Anthony." The general urged the Secretary of War to empower him to call five thousand volunteers from Kentucky and Tennessee and several companies of volunteers from Arkansas "to thwart the designs of the enemy."[39]

After reading the less alarming reports from Arbuckle, Secretary of War Joel Poinsett advised General Gaines that "mere rumor and conjecture" do not authorize the executive to adopt the measures proposed. The restraint imposed by the secretary and subsequent reports of the refusal of the Delawares and Shawnees to participate in the council prompted the division commander to let General Arbuckle handle the situation.[40]

Lacking Arbuckle's years of experience in dealing with the Cherokees, Mason and Gaines had overreacted. From his vantage point within the Cherokee Nation, Arbuckle knew that "the Chiefs & Wealthy men of the Cherokees (generally) are, and will continue opposed to a rupture with the United States." Nor were the Creeks, Choctaws, or Chickasaws anxious for a confrontation. Tensions within Indian Territory diminished in mid-summer of 1838, when it was learned that removal of the Eastern Cherokees was occurring "without a resort . . . to acts of violence against them."[41] Discontent in Indian Territory was reduced even more by Congressional legislation which authorized the expenditure of $150,000 for food and supplies for destitute Indians in the West.

Congress also directed the Secretary of War to negotiate treaties with the Creeks and Osages to reduce friction and resolve grievances arising from earlier agreements with the government. The Creek chiefs were assembled at Fort Gibson in November, 1838. General Arbuckle and Captain Armstrong, representing the United States, persuaded the Creek representatives to relinquish their claims against the government which arose from their removal for a settlement of $430,103. Arbuckle, who noted that the sum was considerably less than the Creeks originally had claimed, predicted,

"If the Treaty is ratified *as made* it will no doubt be productive of much good" and will "ensure the Continuance of peace with that nation."[42]

The improving relations with the tribes in Indian Territory were jeopardized by developments below the Red River, where the encroachment of white settlers aroused the opposition of the Texas Cherokees. Reports from Fort Towson indicated that war had already commenced and that the Mexicans were actually encouraging Indian opposition. The most disquieting news from Fort Towson was contained in the translation of a journal kept by a Mexican officer who had been killed below the Red River. This document and other personal possessions of the officer were sent to Fort Towson and then relayed to Arbuckle. The journal revealed that the Mexican officer, who was visiting the tribes of Texas to persuade them to join the Mexicans in "a war of extermination of the people of Texas," had encountered little difficulty in winning the Indians to his cause. A letter found on his body authorized him to offer the Indians "the entire country" for their support.[43]

Several Americans living in Texas reported that warriors from Indian Territory were joining those of Texas. They warned of a sudden "blow to be struck, that will lay waste our country from Nacogdoches to Fort Gibson, unless an army be in readiness on our frontier immediately." Hostility in Texas, Arbuckle predicted, "will probably lead to very serious consequences to this frontier." Specifically, the general feared that the inducements offered by the Mexicans would entice tribes residing within Indian Territory to join those in Texas against the Americans. Arbuckle alerted the governor of Arkansas concerning the danger and authorized him to distribute arms and munitions from the Little Rock arsenal to increase the security of southwestern Arkansas. He also ordered two companies of Dragoons to Fort Towson to reinforce the garrison there.[44]

Subsequent reports from Forts Jesup and Towson indicating that war had not commenced prompted the general to rescind his order to the Dragoons and retain them at Fort Gibson. Although Arbuckle did not anticipate hostilities arising from the Cherokee council, he wanted as many troops in the area as possible. There had been some scattered violence in Texas, but a show of military force and Sam Houston's assurances to the Cherokees had postponed a full-fledged confrontation. Arbuckle felt there was "little certainty of the Continuance of peace in Texas" and asked the War

Department what assistance the United States was obligated by treaty to extend to Texas in restraining hostile Indians who crossed the international border. The general feared that a successful uprising of Texas Indians would inspire Cherokees and Creeks to join the fray.[45]

In Indian Territory the forthcoming intertribal council appeared less menacing. In fact, the Cherokees extended General Arbuckle and Captain Armstrong an invitation to attend. But the council, which convened on September 15, was not well attended. The Choctaws, Chickasaws, and several other tribes invited by the Cherokees did not participate. The chiefs and head men present drafted a declaration of friendship to the United States, but Arbuckle observed dissatisfaction among the "poor class of Creeks and Cherokees." He and the agents of the Cherokees and Creeks, who were also present at the council, informed the editor of the *Arkansas Gazette* that "we have no doubt of the sincerity of the Indians, in their declaration of Friendship to the United States."[46]

After Arbuckle left the Cherokee council, he learned that a party of Sac and Potawatomi Indians had threatened to exterminate the Osages unless they joined in a war against the United States. When two of the Sac warriors visited the Indian council, the general warned the Cherokees that the "Sacks at your council have come with no good intention." The Cherokees investigated the charge that their guests were planning an uprising and concluded that it was untrue. They did, however, confirm that one of the Sacs who had visited their council was the son of Black Hawk.[47]

The assurance of the Cherokees apparently satisfied Arbuckle, who advised his superiors that he did not expect serious problems from the Indians in the immediate future. The general had not anticipated the provocative action of the settlers of northern Texas who killed several Caddoes in early October. Hysteria swept the region south of Red River across from the mouth of the Washita when it was reported that the Caddoes, Cherokees, and other bands were planning retaliation. Most of the white residents of the area abandoned their homes and fled to safety. Although the retaliation anticipated by the white residents did not occur, the episode led Arbuckle to recommend the construction of a fort large enough to accommodate two or three companies at the mouth of the Washita River. The general, who had long considered Indian Territory more volatile than the Texas-Louisiana border, urged the relocation of most of the Third Infantry to the upper Red River. In

January, 1839, Arbuckle reminded the War Department "that the inhabitants on both sides of the line between the United States and Texas, including a portion of our Indians are generally of a restless and disorderly Character." Arbuckle was particularly concerned about an embittered Choctaw who had failed in a bid for reelection as chief. Blaming his loss of office on whites and mixed-bloods, the former chief invited his friends to follow him to Texas. There, Arbuckle feared, he would prove receptive to Mexican agents who remained active in the region. Emphasizing the immediacy of the danger, Arbuckle warned "that an increase of the force on Red River cannot be dispensed much longer."[48]

The general's assessment, based on reports rather than direct observation, proved to be overly alarmist. The disgruntled Choctaw chief was able to persuade no more than twenty warriors to accompany him and was forced to abandon his plans. In fact, in the spring of 1839, Montfort Stokes assured the commissioner of Indian affairs that the tribes residing in Indian Territory were at peace and constituted no threat to the Texans.[49] Three years after the Texas Revolution, the turbulence it produced among the tribes of Indian Territory had finally begun to subside.

Chapter 13

Cherokee Schism

IN THE LATTER HALF of the 1830's, Fort Gibson's manpower was stretched thin policing the growing population of immigrant Indians, restraining the war-like tendencies of the Plains tribes, and guarding the turbulent Texas border region. Considering the challenges, General Matthew Arbuckle and the meager force under his command maintained remarkable stability in Indian Territory until the last year of the decade.

Ironically, it was the arrival of the Eastern Cherokees, the most advanced of the Southern tribes, that posed the greatest threat to peace in Indian Territory. The Treaty of New Echota of 1835 had divided the Eastern Cherokees into two hostile factions. Those who signed or favored the treaty belonged to the Treaty, or Ridge Party. The Eastern chief, John Ross, and his followers, the Ross Party, considered the treaty which committed them to abandon their homelands an act of betrayal. The forced removal of the Ross faction intensified their hostility. As early as July, 1838, General Arbuckle noted the need to reconcile the Ross and Ridge parties if peace was to be maintained within the Cherokee Nation.[1] Unfortunately, some strong-willed and spiteful members of both parties did not share the general's concern for reconciliation and peace.

The thirteen thousand Cherokees who arrived in Indian Territory with John Ross in 1838 and 1839 greatly outnumbered the old settlers and members of the Treaty Party already established there. Despite the existence of a government in the west, the Eastern Cherokees had voted to transfer their own government with them. Naturally, the leaders of the Western Cherokees objected to being displaced by the newcomers. In order to resolve this impasse a general council was convened in early June, 1839, at Ta-ka-to-ka (Double Springs), four miles northwest of the newly established town of Tahlequah. About six thousand Cherokees attended, including Chiefs John Brown, John Rogers, and John Looney repre-

John Ridge, member of the Treaty Party assassinated by partisans of the Ross faction. Photograph from the Muriel H. Wright Collection.

senting the old settlers; John Ross, leader of the Eastern Cherokees; and Major Ridge, John Ridge, Elias Boudinot, and Stand Watie, members of the Treaty Party. Also in attendance were Montfort Stokes, agent of the tribe, and General Arbuckle. Although Stokes observed that the conferees did not agree, he saw little evidence of hostility. The agent's perception in this instance was not keen, for the Ridges, Boudinot, and Watie all left before the council ended because of "apprehension of danger."[2]

Ross urged those assembled to "take measures for cementing our reunion as a Nation," but the Eastern Cherokees rejected the old settlers' proposal that they participate in the existing government. The Western Cherokees, in turn, would not accept the new arrivals' plan for each side to appoint sixteen representatives to a council which would create a unified government. Unable to find a solution, the chiefs of the old settlers terminated negotiations on June 19. Ross, his supporters, and a few old settlers including

John Ross, leader of the Eastern Cherokees, whose arrival in Indian Territory precipitated a period of intratribal strife. Photogaph courtesy the Thomas Gilcrease Institute of American History and Art.

Sequoyah and Jesse Bushyhead remained at Double Springs, where they agreed to call a convention for July 1 to establish a unified government.[3]

Some of those who remained did more than plan a convention. John Ross's son, Allen, later admitted that he and other leaders of the recent immigrants plotted the murders of the leaders of the Treaty Party, whom they considered obstacles to tribal unification. On Saturday, June 22, the conspirators shot and killed Major Ridge in Washington County, Arkansas, dragged his son, John, from his house on Honey Creek and stabbed him to death, and mortally wounded Elias Boudinot at Park Hill. Stand Watie and several others marked for assassination were warned in time to escape. Throughout the investigations that followed the assassinations, John Ross steadfastly maintained that he neither participated in nor condoned the conspiracy. Years later Ross's son insisted that his father had no knowledge of the plans of the conspirators and "was angry when he learned the facts."[4]

When news of the killings reached General Arbuckle, he asked Ross and the chiefs of the old settlers to visit Fort Gibson "to put a stop to further acts of violence and outrage." The chiefs accepted the invitation, but John Ross, reluctant to leave his home at Park Hill because of threats made against his life, insisted on being accompanied by a small army of bodyguards. Arbuckle rejected this condition and sent a mounted patrol to escort him to Fort Gibson in safety. The patrol was also ordered to arrest some of the assassins, who were reported to be at Ross's home. While not denying that some of the murderers might be serving in his bodyguard, Ross claimed that "they are not known to me." He refused to accompany the Dragoons assigned to escort him to Fort Gibson for the meeting with the old settlers, suggesting instead that the convention scheduled to begin July 1 would be the appropriate place for the opposite elements of the Cherokee tribe to resolve their differences.[5]

The chiefs of the old settlers contended that the convention called by the late immigrants was "altogether irregular." Instead, they proposed an end to killings for political acts or opinions and invited the Ross faction to send sixteen men to meet with a similar number of old settlers at Fort Gibson on July 25 "to harmonize and reunite the whole Cherokee people." This counterproposal, advanced because of the "inducement" of General Arbuckle, was precisely what the Eastern Cherokees had proposed at the Double Springs council. The general urged Ross to accept the offer and warned "that two governments cannot exist in the Cherokee nation without producing a civil war." Ross ignored the proposal advanced by the Western chiefs and asserted that "*the western people*" had called the July 1 convention and that he and the leaders of the recent arrivals considered it "perfectly legitimate." Arbuckle did not concur and expressed his belief that the July 1 meeting had been called by "Mr. Ross, and some others of the late Emigrants, with a few of the unauthorized agents of the old settlers, and without the knowledge of the Cherokee Chiefs."[6]

Despite Arbuckle's objections, the convention opened on

Major Ridge, leader of the
Cherokee Treaty Party. Photo-
graph from the Muriel H.
Wright Collection.

schedule at the Illinois River campground near Park Hill. The
selection of Sequoyah, the most prominent of the old settlers, as
one of the presidents of the convention lent credibility to Ross's
assertion that the meeting was supported by them. Ross continued
to ignore the counter-offer of the chiefs of the old settlers, but, on
July 5, he invited them to "co-operate . . . in promoting the peace,
tranquility, and future prosperity and happiness of our *common
country*." Obviously frustrated, General Arbuckle accused Ross of
not giving his "efforts to restore peace to the Cherokee people . . .
the attention they merited." Even more upsetting to the general
were reports that a large number of Cherokees had been condemned to death "for political and other offences" by Ross's convention. Hoping to avoid further bloodshed, Arbuckle told the
leaders of the Eastern Cherokees that if they failed to restore peace,
all Cherokees could expect military protection at Fort Gibson.[7]

When it became apparent that Ross would not accept their offer, the Western Cherokees called a council for July 22 at the old National Council Ground near the mouth of the Illinois River. Major William Armstrong, acting superintendent of Indian affairs in Indian Territory, urged Ross to meet with the Western chiefs, but he and the other leaders of the convention ignored the appeal and unilaterally proclaimed the establishment of a unified Cherokee Nation. The convention also granted full pardons to those accused of killing the members of the Ridge Party and, on July 7, offered humiliating terms to the friends of the Ridges and Boudinot who had pledged to avenge their deaths. Members of the Treaty Party were promised pardons and amnesty if they disavowed their threats and pledged to conduct "themselves as good and peaceable members of the community." However, they were to be barred from public office within the Cherokee Nation for at least five years. Those who refused to accept the terms of the convention remained "liable to the pains and penalties of outlawry."[8]

On July 12, Ross informed Arbuckle that the Cherokee convention had adopted measures to prevent further bloodshed which were "in exact conformity with your wishes." Although Ross did not send Arbuckle copies of the decree of July 7 until later, the general had obviously learned of its provisions, for he informed Ross that the convention's action did not conform to his wishes. In fact, Arbuckle feared that attempts to punish those who refused to accept the terms of the convention's amnesty offer would result in a renewal of bloodshed. Alarmed by the opposition of Arbuckle, Ross led a delegation of his supporters to Fort Gibson to present their case in person on July 16. They failed to win the support of the general, who predicted that "civil war in the Cherokee nation is almost certain" unless the Eastern Cherokees agreed to revoke the July 7 decree and send representatives to the July 22 council of the old settlers. Ross and his followers rejected the steps outlined by Arbuckle, asserting that those unwilling to abide by Cherokee law were free to leave the nation.[9]

Several days before the council of the old settlers, reports reached Fort Gibson that Ross's adherents intended to prevent the meeting by force. Ross assured Arbuckle that the reports were unfounded, but admitted that the convention was planning to send a committee to show the old settlers "the importance of friendship and union to our future prosperity and happiness." Arbuckle was not reassured, for he authorized the distribution of government

Elias Boudinot, Stand Watie's
brother, who was assassinated
allegedly because of his opposition to the Ross government.
Photograph from the Muriel
H. Wright Collection.

arms and ammunition to Arkansas militia units in counties adjacent
to the Cherokee Nation.[10]

Despite Arbuckle's objection to the July 7 decree, on the opening
day of the old settlers' council, he urged its leaders to approve the
action of the Cherokee convention in establishing a unified tribal
government. John Looney, one of the chiefs of the old settlers, had
already approved the proceedings of the convention, and Arbuckle
suggested similar action by the other chiefs would "at once give
quiet and security to the Cherokee people." The arrival of the
committee sent by Ross did not produce the reconciliation desired
by Arbuckle. Reacting to threats against their lives, the members of
the committee fled the council grounds shortly after their arrival.
The chiefs of the old settlers suggested that they had overreacted to
"idle reports," but Ross maintained that the committee retired "to
escape the massacre of some of their number."[11]

Ross also mentioned reports that members of the Treaty Party were boasting that Arbuckle had encouraged one of the Western chiefs to resist the convention's efforts to supplant his government. The general indignantly denied the charge and told Ross, "I have urged them in substance to yield to your will and pleasure." Turning accuser himself, Arbuckle suggested that the late immigrants had created the difficulties by ignoring the repeated offers of the old settlers to meet in convention for the purpose of forming a new government. Ross denied the general's accusations, stressing the willingness of the late immigrants to seek accommodation and citing the refusal of the leaders of the old settlers to reciprocate.[12]

When Arbuckle urged the Western chiefs to accept the government established by the convention, he anticipated their rejection and urged them to renew their offer to meet with the Eastern Cherokees to establish a mutually acceptable government. On August 2, 1839, the Western chiefs informed Ross that their national council had appointed fifteen men to meet with a similar number appointed by him at Fort Gibson to "settle all the difficulties and differences" dividing the tribe. Although Arbuckle confessed that he did not fully understand the proposition, he informed Ross that he believed that a meeting at Fort Gibson would secure for the Eastern Cherokees "all they desire." Ross and the members of the convention rejected the offer and claimed that it appeared to be an effort to deprive them "of the right and privileges of freemen."[13]

Upon learning of the rejection of their proposal, John Brown and John Rogers, chiefs of the old settlers, appealed to the superintendent of Indian affairs, seeking the support of the United States for their government. Superintendent Armstrong relayed the request to General Arbuckle, who asked Ross not to take any measures to disturb the old settlers or their government until instructions were received from Washington. Ignoring this plea for restraint, Ross condemned the appeal of Brown and Rogers "as utterly inappropriate" and "a violation of the rights and liberties of the Cherokees." Almost two hundred old settlers who had transferred their support to the Ross Party approved a resolution deposing Brown and Rogers as chiefs of the Western Cherokees. Most prominent among the signatures at the bottom of the resolution was that of John Looney, who had been vacillating between the old settlers and the Ross faction for over a month.[14] The support of Looney and other old settlers added credence to Ross's claim of bipartisan participation in his convention's effort to draft a new constitution.

The members of the Treaty Party proved less amenable to the persuasion of the Eastern Cherokees. On August 20, they met at Price's Prairie, publicly announced their continuing opposition to Ross's efforts to establish a new government, and threatened civil war as a last resort to insure their own personal safety. John A. Bell and Stand Watie were chosen to carry a letter of grievance and appeal for justice and protection to the Secretary of War. In apparent response to the action of the Treaty Party, eight days later the national convention enacted a resolution setting September 4 as the last day of the general amnesty. Explaining that some of those who had ignored the amnesty offer were "endangering the peace of the country and threatening the lives of valuable citizens," the convention moved to outlaw the recalcitrant old settlers and members of the Treaty Party.[15]

As the Cherokee Nation teetered on the brink of civil war, General Arbuckle found it politically inexpedient to move decisively without explicit instructions from Washington. In a letter to the War Department, Arbuckle acknowledged that Ross had succeeded in inducing many of the old settlers to support him and predicted that deposed chiefs Brown and Rogers would not resist the new government. However, the general asserted that the methods employed in establishing the new regime "will no doubt long disturb the harmony of the Cherokee nation, and be the cause of frequent quarrels and violence." The immediate threat concerned the security of the Cherokees who were to be outlawed on September 4. Fearing further bloodshed, Arbuckle urged those who refused to take the oath of amnesty to flee to Arkansas or seek protection at Fort Gibson. Clearly outmaneuvered, Arbuckle informed Ross that the government did not consider the Cherokees who had signed the 1835 removal treaty negotiated at New Echota, Georgia, guilty of any crime for which they should seek anmesty. Arbuckle's timid response was matched by that of Superintendent Armstrong, who expressed deep sympathy for those about to be outlawed but admitted, "I have not the power of averting the danger which threatens you."[16]

Ross, now clearly dominant in the struggle for control of the Cherokee Nation, brushed aside Arbuckle's plea in behalf of the signers of the Treaty of New Echota and rejected the idea that "a few misguided individuals should be permitted to threaten and jeopardize the lives of our most worthy citizens." Because of the absence of the Secretary of War from Washington, it was not until

August 20 that the department directed Arbuckle and Armstrong to adopt the "most prompt and energetic measures . . . to discover, arrest, and bring to condign punishment the murderers of the Ridges and Boudinot."[17]

By the time these instructions reached Fort Gibson, the national convention had completed its deliberations, approved a constitution, and selected John Ross principal chief and Joseph Vann assistant principal chief. Arbuckle advised his superiors that "the murderers of the Ridges and Boudinot cannot with safety be punished without a force sufficient to keep in subjection the greater portion of the Cherokee nation, should they attempt to oppose the authority of the U States." Because of the limited number of regular troops at his disposal, Arbuckle considered it advisable to await further instructions from the War Department. He did, however, summon Superintendent Armstrong to Fort Gibson to consider means of protecting the Cherokees outlawed by the national convention.[18]

Despite Arbuckle's reluctance to attempt to apprehend the conspirators without additional troops, he and Armstrong decided that delay might "endanger the lives of others of the treaty party, who were liable to be murdered at any time." Accordingly, Arbuckle and Armstrong asked Ross to surrender those Cherokees who had participated in the murders. Failure to comply with this request, they warned, would result in the employment of a military force to apprehend the accused. Arbuckle's earlier suggestion that the Ross Party take no action against those who had signed the Treaty of New Echota was now changed to a requirement. Further, the general and the superintendent pointedly withheld recognition of the unified government established by the convention.[19]

Ross adroitly parried the demands of Arbuckle and Armstrong by questioning the right of the military to interfere in the internal affairs of the Cherokee Nation. Claiming ignorance concerning the identity of the assailants, Ross maintained that the national convention had already disposed of their case "in a manner satisfactory to the whole Cherokee people." Turning to the assertion of Arbuckle and Armstrong that "no union had taken place," Ross argued that the Cherokee people, acting for themselves, had in fact created a unified government and elected officers and a "national council composed both of the *old settlers* and *emigrants*." Arbuckle categorically rejected each of Ross's contentions.[20]

Conflicting reports reached Arbuckle concerning the reaction of

Stand Watie, a leader of the Treaty Party who narrowly escaped assassination in 1839. Courtesy Western History Collections, University of Oklahoma Library.

the Cherokees to the potential intervention of the military. Of particular concern was information that Ross was seeking the support of the Creeks and perhaps other tribes by sending their chiefs beads and tobacco. Confronted with the possibility of conflict with the Cherokees, Arbuckle requested that the governors of Missouri and

Arkansas alert units of their militia for possible action. He also asked the Creeks to ready a military force for service in case it was needed by the United States. Despite the possibility of opposition, the general ordered the Dragoons recently assigned to Fort Wayne to apprehend the accused assassins. Since the Dragoons' horses had not yet been moved to the new post, they were unable to comply immediately.[21]

In an attempt to forestall military intervention, the newly elected officials of the Ross government reassured Cherokee agent Montfort Stokes of their loyalty to the United States and expressed the "hope that General Arbuckle will not press a matter so calculated to unsettle all our efforts to restore order and good feeling among our people." Confronted with the continuing opposition of Arbuckle and Armstrong, the Ross government decided to send a delegation headed by the principal chief to Washington to adjust "all matters mutually interesting to the United States and the Cherokee people."[22]

Despite his disapproval of the methods employed in establishing the new government, Arbuckle was reluctant to take vigorous countermeasures since Ross did have the backing of the majority of the Cherokees, and the justification for intervention was not clear-cut. The Treaty of New Echota empowered the federal government "to protect the Cherokee Nation from domestic strife," but it did not indicate whether agents of the federal government had the right to punish those who caused the strife. Without such power, Arbuckle realized that "no efficient protection can be given" the Cherokees. The general therefore asked the War Department for instructions calculated to check Ross's "ambitious and selfish career." In the meantime Arbuckle seemed in no hurry to apprehend the murderers of the Ridges and Boudinot. The Dragoons assigned to arrest those accused were not given a list of their names for almost a month, and even then they were told to complete the defenses at Fort Wayne first.[23]

Arbuckle's hesitancy ended abruptly on November 10, when he learned of the approach of Colonel Stephen W. Kearny with a 250-men contingent of Dragoons. Assuming that the commander of the First Dragoon Regiment would assist in capturing the accused assassins, Arbuckle planned a coordinated military sweep of the Cherokee Nation. Kearny's abrupt departure from Indian Territory a few days after his arrival forced the general to abandon his plans. In a letter to General Gaines complaining of the "extraordinary conduct" of Kearny, Arbuckle maintained that the Dragoon force at Fort Wayne was too small to apprehend the individuals implicated in the murders. Kearny's force, Arbuckle asserted, was large enough not to invite resistance and to "insure the apprehension of at least, a portion of the criminals." To support his argument, Arbuckle reported that Captain Philip St. George Cooke, leading a fifty-man force from Fort Wayne, had just arrived at Fort Gibson after a fruitless effort to apprehend the accused men.[24]

Although the War Department did not revoke the orders to apprehend the murderers, in October new instructions were transmitted to Arbuckle and Armstrong which suggested the department was prepared to accept the Ross government. The Secretary of War urged the Cherokees to assemble and draft laws for a single nation, observing the principle that majority rule "must prevail" and the minority "must eventually yield to the great mass." Had the secretary stopped here, his instructions would have been clear-cut, but he also told Arbuckle that the department would not allow the majority to tyrannize those odious to them.[25] Based on these instructions Arbuckle continued supporting the government of the old settlers.

In October the Western Cherokees called a council at Double Springs. Despite Arbuckle's hopes that the delegates would take no action "to increase the difficulties in the Cherokee Nation," they declared the proceedings of Ross and his party unlawful, unauthorized, and null and void. The council also imposed penalties on anyone who attempted to enforce laws enacted by the Ross faction and appointed sheriffs and light horsemen to uphold their own laws. Since John Looney had joined the Ross faction and John Brown had sought refuge with the Cherokees in Texas, the council selected John Rogers, John Smith, and Dutch to lead the government of the old settlers. The new leaders promised to consult with Arbuckle and Stokes in forming a plan designed to unite the Cherokees and restore peace and justice to their nation. The general reassured the newly elected leaders of the Western Cherokees that they constituted "the only lawful government now in the Cherokee nation" and gave support to their suggestion that the late immigrants accept the existing government.[26]

Not all the representatives of the United States in Indian Territory shared the views of Arbuckle and Armstrong. Stokes had addressed John Ross as Principal Chief of the Cherokees, a tacit recognition of the legality of his government. Arbuckle, apparently annoyed by Stokes' indiscretion, told Armstrong that the agent "is no doubt much under the influence of Mr. Ross, and therefore liable to err." After the passage of the resolution of the old settlers annulling Ross's government, Stokes drafted a letter "to the people composing the Cherokee nation" in which he proclaimed himself a neutral in the struggle between the rival Cherokee government and urged "the Cherokee people to be at peace with one another."[27]

Claiming that they were carrying out their agent's recommendations to establish peace within the nation, the Western chiefs proposed a formula for unification by which "their new friends and brothers" would join the present government with assurance that the Cherokee Nation would be regarded as the common property of the entire tribe and that all Cherokees would enjoy equal rights and privileges. Arbuckle and Stokes both recommended that this latest proposal be considered by the Cherokees, but the leaders of all the factions were leaving the nation to present their cases in person at the War Department.[28]

John Ross and his delegation left for Washington on November 15; a week later the Western chiefs asked their agent's permission to send a five-man delegation to present their side of the case to the Secretary of War. Stokes forwarded their request to the secretary, who decided that it was unnecessary for the old settlers to send a delegation. The chiefs were informed that the War Department already had full information on the Cherokee situation, and the secretary assured them that "justice will be done to them in their absence."[29]

Actually, General Arbuckle had been representing the views of the old settlers most effectively. In a letter to the Adjutant General in late November, he asserted that Ross would have been placed in confinement had he not been preparing to depart for Washington. The general claimed that "the Cherokee nation cannot be restored to quiet . . . as long as he [Ross] is permitted to have the least authority." In a direct personal attack, Arbuckle claimed that Ross "has now attached to him . . . a number of the most cunning speculators of the new emigrants, and some of the old settlers, who desire to profit by his assistance in passing their accounts or claims." Arbuckle also challenged Ross's claim to widespread support among the old settlers by pointing out that only 150 of the 1,200 old settlers had joined the late immigrants.[30]

Despite his vociferous opposition to Ross, the general had discontinued his efforts to apprehend the members of Ross's party accused of the June 22 murders. In justifying his decision Arbuckle suggested that "the evidence against them . . . would not be sufficient to convict them before a court of justice."[31] The truth is that Ross had successfully blocked Arbuckle's attempt to apprehend or gather evidence against those accused.

Acting on instructions drafted in Washington almost two months earlier, on December 5, Arbuckle asked Joseph Vann, assistant principal chief of the Ross government, to consider the Secretary of War's recommendation that the Cherokee factions meet together to create a unified government reflecting the desires of the majority of the tribe. In response to Arbuckle's request, Vann ordered a council for all principal men of the late immigrants to meet in Tahlequah on December 16 and promised to do all in his power "to insure peace and security to the Cherokee people." Arbuckle hoped to induce both sides to accept a compromise while Ross was absent. In fact the general had decided that Ross was a major impediment to the settlement of the Cherokee strife and had recommended that "his authority should be dispensed with in the Cherokee nation."[32]

In mid-December, Arbuckle received new instructions from the War Department which cancelled earlier orders directing him "to adopt prompt and energetic measures to arrest those accused of murdering the Ridges and Boudinot. Henceforth, he was to confine his efforts to requesting their arrest by the Ross government. The new instructions reflected the War Department's view that the maintenance of peace constituted "a much higher obligation than the punishment of the guilty." On December 14 and 15, Arbuckle informed both factions of his new instructions and asked their support for a unified government headed by three chiefs, two from the late immigrants and one from the old settlers.[33]

The council called by Vann met at Tahlequah in mid-December to consider Secretary of War Joel Poinsett's proposal that the rival factions meet to create a unified government. Agent Stokes suggested Fort Gibson as an appropriate location for such a meeting, but Vann was unreceptive. Rather, he scheduled an election at Tahlequah on January 15 to select which government would represent the tribe. Pledging that no person, regardless of "party or politics, shall be molested or ill treated," Vann and other leaders of the Ross faction urged all Cherokees to participate in order to restore peace to the Cherokee country.[34]

Although Stokes concurred in this plan for a national referendum, Arbuckle protested that the council of the late immigrants had ignored the points raised by Poinsett's letter of October 12. Vann immediately challenged Arbuckle's assertion by pointing out that the scheduled referendum would allow the majority to indicate its will in conformity with the wishes expressed by the secretary. Arbuckle disagreed, noting that the old settlers and members of the Treaty Party were disinclined to participate in the referendum. He asserted that peace could be restored only by allowing all parties representation in the government and by annulling the July 7 decree.[35]

Despite Arbuckle's sympathy for the old settlers, his new instructions forced him to adopt a more conciliatory attitude in his dealings with the Ross faction. On January 3, he advised Vann that no further attempts would be made to arrest those accused of the June 22 murders, at least until after the meeting of the Cherokee people at Tahlequah on January 15. Although the general refused to attend the Tahlequah meeting in person, he did send an officer to observe the proceedings. He also reiterated the proposal made by Stokes in December that all factions meet at Fort Gibson to resolve their differences.[36]

Stokes addressed the Cherokees at their assembly in mid-January and reemphasized that peace would not be restored until they repealed the decree of outlawry passed at the national convention in July, 1839. Vann, who was aware of Arbuckle's new instructions, apparently decided that a gesture of conciliation would best advance the interest of the Ross Party. Under his leadership, on January 16, the Cherokees assembled at Tahlequah voted unanimously to rescind the edict of July 7 and to reaffirm their support of the Act of Union and constitution drafted by the convention during the summer of 1839.[37]

In reporting the results of the referendum to Arbuckle, Vann expressed his belief that the wishes of the government had been fulfilled. Although no more than 115 members of the Treaty Party or old settlers participated in the meeting in Tahlequah, General Arbuckle informed the Secretary of War there was no doubt that the majority of Cherokees supported the Ross government. In view of his instructions from Washington, the revocation of the July decree compelled the general to recognize the legality of the Ross Party. Personally, Arbuckle continued to favor the old settlers, whom he considered to be excluded from the Ross government. He also remained convinced that "the principal men of the late emigrants, with a few exceptions, excited their people... and caused them to murder the Ridges and Boudinot."[38]

When Arbuckle informed the old settlers of his decision to recognize the Ross government, they expressed opposition and announced their intention to claim "undisturbed possession" of Cherokee land in Indian Territory and to evict all the Cherokees who "refused to unite with them." The old settlers also asked and received permission from Arbuckle to meet at Fort Gibson early in February to consider the War Department's recognition of the Ross government. A select committee of old settlers which met at Fort Gibson drafted a resolution branding Ross's "usurpation" of the Cherokee government "unfounded in justice, law, or humanity." The resolution also asserted that the only legitimate government was the one "handed down to us by the original settlers of the Cherokee nation west." An eight-member delegation was selected by the old settlers to personally inform the Secretary of War of their opposition to the Ross government.[39]

Thus the Cherokee factions took their rivalry to the nation's capital. In early January, 1840, Ross was rebuffed by the Secretary of War, who refused to receive a man he considered "the instigator and the abbetor" in the murders of the Ridges and Boudinot. Redirecting their effort, the members of the Ross delegation submitted a lengthy memorial to Congress in which they defended the legitimacy of their government and suggested that General Arbuckle had conspired with the leaders of the old settlers to thwart the will of the majority of the Cherokees.[40]

The representatives of the Treaty Party received a more cordial reception from the War Department. In late January they submitted a recommendation to Joel Poinsett advocating a division of the Cherokee Nation in which the old settlers and the Treaty Party would be granted a tract and government separate from that of the Ross faction.[41]

Arbuckle's reports convinced the Secretary of War that the turmoil in the Cherokee Nation was a product of the tyrannical and oppressive conduct of the immigrating party towards the old settlers. Justifying his action by the provisions of the Treaty of New Echota, which required the United States to protect the Cherokee Nation from domestic strife, the Secretary of War suspended Stokes, the Cherokee agent, and placed the military in control of the region. Poinsett directed Arbuckle to take necessary and proper measures to adopt a constitution which would insure the life, liberty, and property of all Cherokee and annul the "barbarous laws" which sanctioned the execution of Boudinot and the Ridges and outlawed innocent men. Following Arbuckle's suggestion, the secretary insisted that the old settlers be represented by at least one chief in the new Cherokee government and that John Ross be excluded from participation.[42]

When Arbuckle received these new instructions, he asked the leaders of the old settlers and the Ross Party to assemble at Fort Gibson on April 20. There he informed the Cherokees of Poinsett's directive and encouraged them to prepare a constitution acceptable to the entire tribe. Recognizing the loyalty of the recent settlers to Ross, Arbuckle suggested that Ross's exclusion from the new government would be temporary. But any hopes the general may have entertained concerning a quick resolution of differences were short-lived. The Ross faction expressed their regret that the government had not chosen to accept the January referendum of the Cherokees in support of their government and reasserted their conviction that Ross was innocent of criminality and faithless conduct. However, the Ross delegation did not preclude a "friendly settlement" based on the terms outlined by Arbuckle, and Vann agreed to call a council as soon as possible to consider revision of the constitution. The old settlers and representatives of the Treaty Party appointed a select committee to explore Arbuckle's proposals, but after a day's deliberation the committee announced they were "unable to come to any satisfactory agreement."[43]

Arbuckle's hope for prompt action suffered another setback when Vann scheduled the council of the Ross faction for late May. Although the colonel charged the assistant chief with procrastination, Vann would not be rushed. When the council convened, Arbuckle requested that Vann appoint twenty-five or thirty delegates to meet at Fort Gibson on June 10 with a similar number of representatives of the old settlers to establish a new government. Refusal of the Ross Party to cooperate, Arbuckle suggested, would leave the government no alternative except division of the Cherokee Nation. Responding immediately to Arbuckle's request, the council of the Ross government instructed a twelve-man delegation to report to Fort Gibson on the appointed day. Although the delegation was not authorized to act in behalf of the late immigrants in adopting a new constitution, Arbuckle believed that the meeting of the rival delegations would "at least furnish an opportunity to judge

Aerial view of Fort Gibson, restored from construction plans found in the National Archives. Photograph courtesy Oklahoma Planning and Resources Board.

the measures necessary to be taken hereafter to give quiet and security to the Cherokee nation."[44]

By June 17, both sides were represented at Fort Gibson. The old settlers initially rejected the Act of Union and constitution of 1839, but eventually General Arbuckle persuaded them to accept the constitution "without admitting its legality, until concurred in by them."[45] The Ross faction conceded to the demand of the old settlers that a new Act of Union be drawn up. The document signed on June 26 at Fort Gibson guaranteed the old settlers equitable representation in the initial government. It recognized the Ross constitution adopted in September, 1839, and the laws enacted under its provisions. The agreement also provided that any monies received by the tribe from the United States would be shared equally by all the Cherokees. The document said nothing about the exclusion of Ross from participation in the Cherokee government and in several other particulars ignored the terms of settlement outlined by the secretary of war. Nonetheless, Arbuckle "was satisfied that nothing better could be done."[46]

Elated over the agreement and the professions of friendship from the rival faction, Arbuckle announced that the Cherokee difficulties were "brought to a final close at this post." Unfortunately, his assertion was premature; the animosities generated during the past year continued to divide the tribe and produce discord. One of the victims of the continuing bitterness may have been General Arbuckle himself. In the spring of 1841, the War Department transferred the general to Baton Rouge and gave him command of a military district including New Orleans in which there was not "a single Officer of the line of the Army or a soldier except for a few ordnance Sergts." Senator Ambrose H. Sevier of Arkansas speculated that Arbuckle had been removed "to gratify John Ross," who was in Washington prior to the general's transfer.[47]

Arbuckle protested his reassignment and demanded a Court of Inquiry to investigate his conduct as commander of Fort Gibson. But the protests of Arbuckle and his defenders in Congress were to no avail. In June, 1841, General Zachary Taylor assumed command of the Southwestern frontier. In his last report from Fort Gibson on June 21, 1841, General Arbuckle summarized the accomplishments in Indian Territory.

> In making this communication which will probably be my last official report of the state of affairs on this frontier it affords me the utmost pleasure to be able to say that although there has arrived in this Country within the last ten or twelve years about forty thousand Creek, Semenoled [sic] and Cherokee Indians and the greater part of them were removed under circumstances which rendered them anything but friendly disposed towards the United States or its inhabitants, notwithstanding which I have maintained peace on this frontier and at no period have the Whites on our border or the Red people of this frontier been in a more perfect state of quiet and Security than they now enjoy.[48]

Chapter 14
Conclusion

THE DEPARTURE OF General Matthew Arbuckle from Fort Gibson in 1841 marked the end of an era in the Southwest. Since the establishment of Fort Smith in 1817, the primary mission of the army on the Arkansas frontier had been to assist in implementing the government's Indian removal policy. For almost a quarter of a century, soldiers labored to restrain intertribal warfare, to pacify the Plains tribes, and to assist the immigrating Indians in adjusting to their new homeland. By 1841, the army's mission had been accomplished; most of the Eastern tribes had been resettled beyond the western tier of states.

Although General Arbuckle reported to this superiors that he had maintained peace in Indian Territory during the era of removal, some historians have suggested that his efforts were less than completely successful. In his brief history of the American Indians, William T. Hagan asserted that "the United States did not live up to its pledges to protect the immigrant Indians in their new locations any better than it had met other responsibilities to them." Hagan argued that "sufficient troops were never available to protect them; in 1834 there were less than three thousand along the entire Western frontier." In discussing the wrongs inflicted on the Indians in her now classic account of inhumanity, *A Century of Dishonor*, Helen Hunt Jackson began her list of culprits with the military.[1]

The widely held assumption that the normal relationship of the Indians and army was adversary in nature has been buttressed by well-publicized skirmishes and battles from the colonial period until Wounded Knee. Yet the history of Fort Gibson during the era of Indian removal does not confirm this assumption. William Hagan is correct in his assertions that the national government was not able to give the Eastern tribes complete protection from the Plains Indians and that the army was stretched so thinly along the western border that it could hardly be considered an effective de-

Rock ledge on the Grand River which forms a natural landing at Fort Gibson.

terrent. Helen Hunt Jackson is also accurate in viewing the military as the agency that implemented an Indian policy she considered to be a national disgrace. Such criticism, however, should be tempered with a realistic assessment of the capabilities of the federal government and the nature and function of the army. Absolute guarantees of security on the frontier were obviously impossible to fulfill, and while three thousand soldiers were inadequate to police the western border, those troops represented almost one-half of the men of the American army. Neither the government nor the army could redeem impossible promises, but a study of Fort Gibson suggests that many soldiers stationed on the Southwestern frontier made a sincere effort to protect the well-being of the immigrant Indians within the limits of their capabilities.

The efforts of these individuals have not been entirely overlooked. Grant Foreman, one of the most severe critics of Indian removal, observed:

> A conspicuous saving grace of this sorrowful story is the fidelity and skill with which the regular army officers and soldiers in the field discharged their unwelcome duties in connection with the removal. In nearly all instances they devoted themselves indefatigably and sympathetically to the sad task of removing the Indians with as much expedition and comfort as possible within the provisions made by their superiors in Washington. In this they contrasted sharply with the volunteer soldiers and a large class of political, civilian employees and especially those of local attachments and prejudices, and the contractors whose purpose was to realize as much profit as possible from their contracts.[2]

Francis Paul Prucha, a student of the Indians and the frontier army, credited the military with "blunting the sharp edges of conflict as two races with diverse cultures met on the frontier." At least in the case of Fort Gibson, the assessment of the frontier army suggested by Foreman and Prucha seems more accurate than the evaluations that picture the military as the unyielding foe of the Indian.[3]

The army established the first post on the Arkansas River in 1817 because of the conflict between the Osages and Cherokees. Like most frontier posts, Fort Smith attracted white pioneers and accelerated settlement of the area. When Cantonment Gibson was established in 1824, it also spurred white settlement in the region, but in 1825, the government began allotting the area west of Arkansas Territory to Eastern tribes. The establishment of a distinct Indian Territory pushed back the first wave of white settlers and made the garrison on the Grand River different from most other frontier outposts. Unlike Fort Dearborn or Fort Snelling, which encouraged white pioneers to settle and displace the Indians, Fort Gibson's mission was to guard an area in which whites were not permitted to settle permanently. The troops who served there were not the cutting edge of the "Sword of the Republic" preparing the Indians for ultimate subjugation; instead, they constituted a cultural buffer holding land-hungry settlers at bay long enough to allow the Indians an opportunity to adjust gradually to the technology and culture of white society.

From the time of its establishment the post served as a meeting place where antagonistic tribes and factions could attempt to resolve their differences without resorting to war. Over a period of years, the Indians were discouraged from attacking neighboring tribes who breached the peace and urged to seek justice through the army. Frustrations were numerous and mutual; the Indians found that justice administered by the military was slow at best and seldom gratifying to those who had been victimized. The army discovered that the Indians preferred to seek revenge in their own way and were seldom satisfied by the justice administered by white men. Nonetheless, the presence of Fort Gibson did restrain the bellicose tendencies of the tribes moving into Indian Territory and eventually compelled them to acknowledge the authority of the United States in enforcing tribal promises to live at peace with their neighbors.

Peace keeping was not the only function of the troops assigned to Fort Gibson. Much of their time was devoted to assisting immigrant tribes in the process of relocation. Military patrols were assigned to explore and map the region being considered as possible homes for the Eastern tribes. Army personnel accompanied the exploring parties sent by those tribes to reconnoiter Western land offered them by the federal government. The army cut roads to facilitate the movement of migrating Indians and occasionally assisted in distributing rations and provisions to new arrivals. When unscrupulous white men entered Indian Territory to sell whisky, gamble, or defraud the Indians, it was the army that was called on to expel them. The immigrants, embittered over their treatment by

Barracks along the south wall of restored Fort Gibson.

the government, may have resented the presence of the army as a symbol of the authority of the United States, but they made no real effort to secure its removal from the territory. On the contrary, tribal leaders frequently asked officials in Washington for additional troops and forts.

Perhaps the most difficult problem confronting the military at Fort Gibson concerned the Plains Indians. Unlike the Eastern Indians, who had lived in close proximity to Americans for years and recognized the futility of resistance, the Plains warriors were not prepared to yield their land without a struggle. Merely establishing communications with them required two years and a major military mobilization. Ultimately, treaties were negotiated with all of the major tribes of the Southern Plains, which reduced tension in Indian Territory during the final phase of Indian removal. Later, forts would be established closer to the Cross Timbers and to Plains tribes, but decades of military coercion would be required before the Plains Indians abandoned the warpath.

One of the two blockhouses commanding fields of fire along the post's outside walls, as it appears at Fort Gibson today.

As a principal enforcing agent of the government's Indian policy, the army has frequently been cast in the role of the callous adversary of the rights of the Indian. Officers and enlisted men are often pictured as bloodthirsty Indian baiters who forwarded their careers at the expense of the Indian. While there were indeed such individuals in the army, they were in a distinct minority. Unfortunately, the massacres they led and the atrocities they precipitated received widespread notoriety and overshadow the positive but unheralded accomplishments of the majority of officers and men.

During the turbulent years of Indian removal, the army at Fort Gibson exercised restraint and reason in its relations with the Indians. An understanding of the indigenous and immigrant Indians, developed over years of service on the frontier, enabled Matthew Arbuckle and his associates to gauge the Indian mood and to anticipate response. Such insight not only helped the army at Fort Gibson avoid conflict but also was available to policy makers in Washington if they chose to use it.

Most whites on the frontier, whether land-hungry settlers, merchants, or fur traders, were involved in economic competition or a seller-consumer relationship with the Indians. When their quest for profits ran counter to the welfare of the Indian, they usually pursued the former. The army, by contrast, was seldom placed in economic competition with the Indians. Consequently, the soldiers did not have to ignore their own economic interests in fostering the well-being of the Indians. Neither was the military a fervent champion of the concept of removal as the panacea for the Indian problem. The Reverend Isaac McCoy, for example, ignored the obvious danger of the Plains Indians in his reports because of his enthusiasm to persuade the Eastern tribes to relocate in the West. Army officers tended to be more objective and candid in their reports.

Few soldiers became ardent defenders of Indian rights, but living among the tribes of Indian Territory, the personnel assigned to Fort Gibson gained an insight and a compassion for the Indians and their plight not shared by most whites. They could view with detachment the almost inevitable clash as two distinct cultures converged and consequently were better able to appreciate the stress and frustration experienced by the Indians as they repeatedly gave way before the advance of white settlers. The soldiers of Fort Gibson could not halt the inexorable course of this cultural clash, but they did help establish a temporary haven where many Indians would have several more generations to adjust gradually to the new order.

Notes

Chapter 2

1. Arbuckle to Jones, June 21, 1841, Fort Gibson Letterbooks, Records of the United States Army Continental Commands, 1821–1920, National Archives, Record Group 393.
2. Francis La Flesche, "The Osage Tribe," in *Thirty-Sixth Annual Report*, Bureau of American Ethnology, 43–44. John Joseph Mathews, *The Osages: Children of the Middle Waters*, 297–99. William J. Ghent, "Rene Auguste Chouteau," in *Dictionary of American Biography* (ed. by Dumas Malone and Allen Johnson), IV, 94–95. Louis Houck (ed.), *The Spanish Regime in Missouri*, II, 101, 106–108. Richard Edward Ogelsby, *Manuel Lisa and the Opening of the Missouri Fur Trade*, 22–26, 297–98. Elliott Coues (ed.), *The Expeditions of Zebulon Montgomery Pike: To Headwaters of the Mississippi River, Through Louisiana Territory, and in New Spain, During the Years 1805–6–7*, II, 529–30, 557–58.
3. Grant Foreman, *Indians and Pioneers: The Story of the American Southwest Before 1830*, 20–21, 43, 123. Mathews, *The Osages, 517–18*. Coues, *The Expeditions of Zebulon Montgomery Pike*, II, 530.
4. Statement of the Former Spanish Commandant, June 5, 1816, *The Territory of Louisiana-Missouri, 1815–1821*, in Clarence E. Carter (ed.), *The Territorial Papers of the United States*, Vol. XV, 179. Charles C. Royce, "The Cherokee Nation of Indians," in *Fifth Annual Report*, Bureau of American Ethnology, 204, maintains that a few Cherokees dissatisfied with the Treaty of Hopewell moved to the St. Francis valley in Spanish territory shortly after the negotiation of the treaty in 1785. Emmet Starr, *History of the Cherokee Indians and Their Legends and Folk Lore*, 38. Cephas Washburn, *Reminiscences of the Indians* (ed. by Hugh Park), 61. Mary Whatley Clarke, *Chief Bowles and the Texas Cherokees*, 9–10. G. Foreman, in *Indians and Pioneers*, 26–27, relates that Chief Bowles settled south of the Arkansas River.
5. Francis Paul Prucha, *American Indian Policy in the Formative Years: The Indian Trade and Intercourse Acts, 1790–1834*, 226. Charles J. Kappler (comp. and ed.), *Indian Affairs: Laws and Treaties*, II, 96. *American State Papers, Indian Affairs*, I, 765; II, 125. G. Foreman, *Indians and Pioneers*, 33–34. Jefferson to Cherokees, January 9, 1809, *Arkansas Gazette*, June 25, 1828, p. 1. Royce, "The Chero-

kee Nation of Indians," in *Fifth Annual Report*, 203. James Mooney, "Myths of the Cherokee," in *Nineteenth Annual Report*, Bureau of American Ethnology, first part, 102. Grace Steel Woodward, *The Cherokees*, 129&31.

6. Starr, *History of the Cherokee Indians*, 38–39. G. Foreman, *Indians and Pioneers*, 34–35, footnote 38. Lovely to Secretary of War, May 27, 1815, in Carter, *Territory of Louisiana-Missouri*, XV, 49–50. Lovely to Secretary of War, October 1, 1813; Russell to Hempstead, November 1, 1813, *Ibid.*, XIV, 720–21.

7. Houck, *The Spanish Regime in Missouri*, I, 144. Clark to Secretary of War, September 23, 1808, *Ibid.*, XIV, 224–28.

8. Lovely to Clark, October 1, 1813; Lovely to Clark, August 9, 1814; Lovely to Secretary of War, May 27, 1815, *Ibid.*, XV, 51, 53, 49.

9. Lovely to Clark, October 11, 1814; Clark to Lovely, August 21, 1814; Clark to Lovely, January 25, 1815, *Ibid.*, XV, 54–56.

10. Secretary of War to the Indian Commissioners, September 17, 1816, *Ibid.*, XV, 173–75. U.S. Congress, House *Document No. 263*, Twentieth Congress, first session, 38.

11. Speech to an Osage Council, September 15, 1821, in Clarence E. Carter (ed.), *The Territory of Arkansas, 1819–1825*, Vol. XIX of *The Territorial Papers of the United States*, 320–22.

12. *Niles Weekly Register* (Baltimore), September 27, 1817, pp. 74, 80.

13. Edwin James, *Account of an Expedition from Pittsburgh to the Rocky Mountains, Performed in the Years, 1819, 1820*, Volumes XIV, XV, XVI, and XVII of *Early Western Travels, 1748–1846* (ed. by Reuben G. Thwaites), XVII, 19–20. Thomas Nuttall, *Journal of Travels into the Arkansas Territory during the Year, 1819, Ibid.*, XIII, 191–92. G. Foreman, *Indians and Pioneers*, 51–52.

14. Ed Bearss and Arrell M. Gibson, *Fort Smith: Little Gibraltar on the Arkansas*, 13–14, 17–19.

15. *Ibid.*, 23–24. Clark to Secretary of War, October, 1818, in Carter, *Territory of Louisiana-Missouri*, XV, 454–55. Kappler, *Indian Affairs*, II, 167–68.

16. Bradford to the Secretary of War, February 4, 1819; Lewis to the Secretary of War, March 16, 1819; Lewis to the Secretary of War, March 28, 1818 [1819], in Carter, *Territory of Arkansas*, XIX, 33–34, 55–56, 57–59. Nuttall, *Journal of Travels*, 253, 277–79.

17. *Arkansas Gazette*, March 18, 1820, p. 3. Lewis to the Secretary of War, January 21, 1820; Cherokee Council to Lewis and Bradford, February 10, 1820; Miller to the Secretary of War, March 24, 1820, in Carter, *Territory of Arkansas*, XIX, 136–37, 151–52, 153–55. Walter B. Douglas (ed.), "Documents—Captain Nathaniel Pryor," *The American Historical Review*, Vol. XXIV (January, 1919), 255–57.

18. *Arkansas Gazette*, April 8, 1820, p. 3. Miller to the Secretary of War, March 24, 1820, in Carter, *Territory of Arkansas*, XIX, 153–55.

19. Miller to the Secretary of War, June 20, 1820, *Ibid.*, 191–95.

20. Miller to the President, October 8, 1820; Bradford to Secretary of War, December 3, 1820; Miller to the Secretary of War, December 11, 1820, *Ibid.*, 220, 242–43, 244–46. *Arkansas Gazette*, December 30, 1820, p. 3. "Journal of Union Mission," January 22, 1821, 43.

21. Bradford to Secretary of War, February 10, 1821, in Carter, *Territory of Arkansas*, XIX, 263–64. "Journal of Union Mission," March 14, 1821. *Arkansas Gazette*, December 30, 1820, p. 3.

22. Lyon to Secretary of War, March 22 [1821]; Arkansas Cherokees to the President [March 17, 1821]; Miller to the Cherokee Indians, March 20, 1821; Lyon to Secretary of War, April 7, 1821, in Carter, *Territory of Arkansas*, XIX, 333–34, 272–75, 335–36, 336–38.

23. "Journal of Union Mission," March 28, 1821, 53. Secretary of War to Miller, June 29, 1820; Secretary of War to Bradford, May 12, 1820, in Carter, *Territory of Arkansas*, XIX, 339, 181–82.

24. Bradford to Secretary of War, August 10, 1821, *Ibid.*, XIX, 308–10.

25. "Journal of Union Mission," April 4, 1821, 56. Bradford to Secretary of War, August 10, 1821; Bradford to Cherokee Chiefs, March 16, 181 [1821]; Brearley to Secretary of War, April 26, 1821, in Carter, *Territory of Arkansas*, XIX, 308–10, 340–41, 285.

26. "Journal of Union Mission," April 7, 1821; May 17, 1821, 58–59, 62–63.

27. Adjutant General to Arbuckle, May 10, 1821, Office of the Adjutant General, Letters sent, 1800–1890. National Archives, Microcopy 565, Roll 6. *Arkansas Gazette*, September 15, 1821, p. 3. Mathews, *The Osages*, 475. "Journal of Union Mission," June 24, 1821; June 26, 1821, 67–68. Bradford to Secretary of War, August 10, 1821, in Carter, *Territory of Arkansas*, XIX, 308–10.

28. *Arkansas Gazette*, September 1, 1821, p. 3. Graham to Secretary of War, September 20, 1821; Clarimare's Speech to an Osage Council [September 15, 1821]; Arkansas Cherokee Agents to Bradford, September 28, 1821; Bradford to Secretary of War, October 22, 1821, in Carter, *Territory of Arkansas*, XIX, 315–16, 320–22, 346–47.

29. "Journal of Union Mission," December 10, 1821, 89–90. Bradford to Secretary of War, November 18, 1821, in Carter, *Territory of Arkansas*, XIX, 355–56.

30. "Journal of Union Mission," January 14, 1822; January 25, 1822, 95–96.

31. Union Mission, located about twenty-five miles above the mouth of the Grand River, was established by the United Foreign Mission

Society in 1820 to minister to the spiritual needs of the Osages.
Osage Chiefs to Miller [January 21, 1822]; Miller to Secretary of
War, March 1, 1822; Miller to Secretary of War, May, 1822, in
Carter, *Territory of Arkansas*, XIX, 408-11, 437-40. "Journal of
Union Mission," March 8, 1822; March 15, 1822; March 21,
1822; April 12, 1822, 101-102, 104-105.

32. Arbuckle to Adjutant General, March 4, 1822; Arbuckle to Secretary
of War, March 16, 1822, in Carter, *Territory of Arkansas*, XIX,
414, 417-18.

33. Miller to Secretary of War, May, 1822, *Ibid.*, XIX, 437-40. "Journal
of Union Mission, May 22, 1822, 112-13. *Arkansas Gazette*, June
4, 1822, p. 3.

34. Gaines to Cherokee and Osage Chiefs, June 24, 1822, in Carter,
Territory of Arkansas, XIX, 442-43. Washburn, *Reminiscences*,
94-95, 149. Washburn gives 1823 as the date of this episode, but
the Gaines letter was written and the peace conference was held
in 1822.

35. "Journal of Union Mission," July 22, 1822; July 30, 1822, 124-25.

36. Washburn, *Reminiscences*, 95. Bearss and Gibson, *Fort Smith*, 63-64.

37. Washburn, *Reminiscences*, 96. Bearss and Gibson, *Fort Smith*, 64.

38. *Arkansas Gazette*, September 16, 1823, p. 3. *Missionary Herald* (Boston), XX (February, 1824), p. 46. Washburn, *Reminiscences*,
96-98, 149. Washburn relates that some Cherokees, exasperated
by outrageous Osage demands, left the peace conference, raised
an eighty-man force, and invaded the Osage country. Clarke,
Chief Bowles, 13-14.

39. "Journal of Union Mission," September 19, 1822, September 21,
1822, 135-36. Arbuckle to Acting Adjutant General, September
30, 1822; Arbuckle to Acting Adjutant General, October 13,
1822; English to Arbuckle, September 23, 1822, in Carter, *Territory of Arkansas*, XIX, 462-65.

40. "Journal of Union Mission," September 25, 1822, 136. *Arkansas
Gazette*, October 29, 1822, p. 3. (Page 3 of this issue is incorrectly
dated October 22, 1822.)

41. "Journal of Union Mission," November 13, 1822; November 30, 1822,
144-46. Arbuckle to Acting Adjutant General, November 22,
1822, in Carter, *Territory of Arkansas*, XIX, 466-67.

42. Arbuckle to Acting Adjutant General, September 30, 1822; Kirby to
Arbuckle, December 12, 1822, *Ibid.*, XIX, 462-64, 472-73. *Arkansas Gazette*, November 28, 1822, p. 3.

43. Margaret L. Coit, *John C. Calhoun: American Portrait*, 131. Arbuckle
to Secretary of War, January 12, 1822 [1823]; Secretary of War to
Arbuckle, May 1, 1823, in Carter, *Territory of Arkansas*, XIX,
480-82, 510-11.

44. Arbuckle to Secretary of War, June 22, 1823; Crittenden to Secretary of War, September 28, 1823; Memorial to Congress by the Territorial Assembly [October 18, 1823]; Conway to Secretary of War, January 30, 1824; *Ibid.*, XIX, 525, 546–50, 557–58, 602–603.
45. *Arkansas Gazette*, December 17, 1822, p. 3. Miller County, established in 1820, was on Arkansas' southwestern frontier. Land in what is now southwestern Arkansas and southeastern Oklahoma was incorporated within its boundaries. *Missionary Herald* (Boston), XXI (August, 1825), p. 246. Arbuckle to Secretary of War, January 12, 1822 [1823], in Carter, *Territory of Arkansas*, XIX, 480–82. G. Foreman, *Indians and Pioneers*, 127. Foreman identified the murdered Cherokee as Red Hawk, the nephew of Thomas Graves. Correspondence in the *Territory of Arkansas* confirms the murder but not the identity of the victim. The Journal of Dwight Mission records that Graves' nephew was killed by the Osages after the establishment of Cantonment Gibson during the winter of 1824–25. Although this writer has not seen the correspondence on which Foreman based his identification, he accepts Foreman's version and believes that the missionaries at Dwight were in error concerning the date of the incident. This assumption is supported by a letter from Atkinson to Adjutant General, January 9, 1827, in Carter, *Territory of Arkansas*, XX, 361, which mentions an 1822 episode in which "an Osage Indian killed a Cherokee, son of Graves." Arbuckle suggests that the attack occurred in early January, 1823. "Journal of Union Mission," January 7, 1823; January 17, 1823, 152–53.
46. Arbuckle to Adjutant General, October 5, 1823, in Carter, *Territory of Arkansas*, XIX, 550–51.
47. Arbuckle to Adjutant General, October 5, 1823; Arbuckle to Secretary of War, November 8, 1823, *Ibid.*, XIX, 550–51, 563–64. Arbuckle to Nourse, November 4, 1823, Office of the Adjutant General, Letters Received, 1822–60. National Archives, Microcopy 567, Roll 6. Smith to Arbuckle, January 15, 1824, Western Division, 1821–1842, Letters Sent, Records of the United States Continental Army Commands, 1821–1920, National Archives, Record Group 393
48. Ginger L. Ashcraft, "Antoine Barraque and his Involvement in Indian Affairs of Southeast Arkansas, 1816–1832," *Arkansas Historical Quarterly*, Vol. XXXII (Fall, 1973), 227–28. Arbuckle to Gaines, December 3, 1823, in Carter, *Territory of Arkansas*, XIX, 570–71. *Arkansas Gazette*, June 22, 1824, p. 3; October 26, 1824, p. 3. "Journal of Union Mission," December 4, 1824, 198–99.
49. *Arkansas Gazette*, December 9, 1823, p. 2. Arbuckle to Gaines, De-

cember 3, 1823, in Carter, *Territory of Arkansas*, XIX, 570–71. "Journal of Union Mission," December 4, 1823; December 10, 1823; December 18, 1823, 198–201.

50. Arbuckle to Gaines, December 4, 1823, in Carter, *Territory of Arkansas*, XIX, 172–74. "Journal of Union Mission," December 19, 1823, 200–201. Cummings to Arbuckle, December 22, 1823; Arbuckle to Gaines, December 22, 1823, Office of the Adjutant General, Letters Received, 1822–60, Roll 12. G. Foreman, *Indians and Pioneers*, 165–66.

51. "Journal of Union Mission," March 15, 1823, 211–12. Acting Adjutant General to Scott, February 16, 1824; Arbuckle to Acting Adjutant General, February 29, 1824, in Carter, *Territory of Arkansas*, XIX, 609, 612. Arbuckle to Smith, March 14, 1824. Office of the Adjutant General, Letters Received, 1822–60, Roll 12. Cummings to Arbuckle, March 17, 1824, Grant Foreman Collection, Thomas Gilcrese Institute of American History and Art.

52. Arbuckle to McRee, March 18, 1824, *Ibid.* Crittenden to Secretary of War, September 12, 1824, in Carter, *Territory of Arkansas*, XIX, 691–94. *Arkansas Gazette*, April 20, 1824, p. 3; May 25, 1824, p. 3. "Journal of Union Mission," April 7, 1824, 214–15.

Chapter 3

1. Conway to Secretary of War, January 30, 1824, in Carter, *The Territory of Arkansas*, XIX 602. Smith to Adjutant General, January 16, 1824; Arbuckle to Gaines, September 3, 1823; Scott to Nourse, March 3, 1824, Office of the Adjutant General, Letters Received, 1822–1860, Roll 12. *Arkansas Gazette*, March 23, 1824, p. 3. Scott to Adjutant General, March 8, 1824, Western Division, 1821–1842, Letters Sent. Ed Bearss and Arrell M. Gibson, *Fort Smith*, 94–95.

2. Arbuckle to Acting Assistant Adjutant General, Western Department, April 7, 1824, typescript, Grant Foreman Collection, Thomas Gilcrease Institute of American History and Art. Galt to Arbuckle, June 18, 1824, Western Division, 1821–1842, Letters Sent. Bearss and Gibson, *Fort Smith*, 95. *Arkansas Gazette*, May 11, 1824, p. 3.

3. Although the term "cantonment" normally refers to a temporary military camp, from the establishment of Cantonment Snelling in 1817 the army used the term to designate new military installations. By 1832, the War Department apparently decided that the designation was inappropriate since Cantonments Snelling and Gibson, which were fifteen and eight years old respectively,

could hardly be considered temporary outposts. Accordingly, General Order 11, dated February 6, 1832, directed "that all the Military Posts designated *Cantonments* be hereafter called *Forts.*" Robert W. Frazer, *Forts of the West: Military Forts and Presidios and Posts Commonly Called Forts West of the Mississippi River to 1898*, xx–xxi. Cummings to Scott, May 26, 1824, Office of the Adjutant General, Letters Received, 1822–1860, Roll 17.

4. Grant Foreman, *Fort Gibson: A Brief History*, 4. Nuttall, *Journal of Travels*, 234. Nuttall recorded that there were already two trading houses on the Verdigris by 1819. *Arkansas Gazette*, April 13, 1824, p. 3. "Journal of Union Mission," December 24, 1821, 91.

5. *Arkansas Gazette*, May 25, 1824, p. 3; January 4, 1825, p. 3; May 10, 1825, p. 3. Arbuckle to Jesup, January 2, 1826, typescript, Grant Foreman Collection, Gilcrease Institute. Gaines to Arbuckle, April 11, 1826, Western Division, 1821–1842, Letters Sent. Arbuckle to Jones, April 4, 1827, Office of the Adjutant General, Letters Received, 1822–1860, Roll 25.

6. Henry Leavitt Ellsworth, *Washington Irving on the Prairies or A Narrative of a Tour of the Southwest in the Year 1832* (ed. by Stanley T. Williams and Barbara D. Simison), 4.

7. "Journal of Union Mission," April 20, 1824, 216.

8. *U.S. Statutes at Large*, IV, 135. Secretary of War to Commanding General, March 10, 1826; Arbuckle to Adjutant General, May 7, 1826; Arbuckle to Quartermaster General, May 5, 1826, in Carter, *The Territory of Arkansas*, XX, 205–206, 240–44.

9. Dawson to Quartermaster General, November 16, 1826; Resolution of Congress *Re* Road to Fort Gibson, December 12, 1826; Quartermaster General to Secretary of War, December 21, 1826; Adjutant General to Arbuckle, March 5, 1827; Dawson to Quartermaster General, August 28, 1827; Arbuckle to Adjutant General, November 20, 1827, *Ibid.*, XX, 303–305, 323, 338, 414, 519–22, 554. *Arkansas Gazette*, June 19, 1827, p. 3.

10. Quartermaster General to Secretary of War, January 20, 1826; Quartermaster General to Dawson, March 30, 1827; Quartermaster General to Arbuckle, December 19, 1827; Newell to Quartermaster General, October 24, 1828 [register entry only], in Carter, *Territory of Arkansas*, XX, 185–87, 435–36, 568–69, footnote 93, 436. *Arkansas Gazette*, June 27, 1826, p. 3. *U.S. Statutes at Large*, IV, 244. Arbuckle to Jones, August 4, 1827; Cummings to Jones, November 1, 1827, Office of the Adjutant General, Letters Received, 1822–1860, Rolls 25 and 26. Carolyn Thomas Foreman (ed.), "Report of Captain John Stuart on the Contruction of the Road from Fort Smith to Horse Prairie on Red River," *Chronicles of Oklahoma*, Vol. V (September, 1927), 333–34.

11. *Arkansas Gazette*, May 11, 1824, p. 3; May 31, 1825, p. 3.

12. Sevier to Howard, January 27, 1831; Brown to Chief Engineer, May 8, 1833; Chief Engineer to Shreve, May 9, 1833; Shreve to Chief Engineer, March 10, 1834, in Carter, *The Territory of Arkansas*, XXI, 311–12, 714–22, 723, 921–25. Louis C. Hunter, *Steamboats on the Western Rivers: An Economic and Technological History*, 200.

13. Edgar Bruce Wesley, *Guarding the Frontier: A Study of Frontier Defense from 1815–1825*, 81. Francis Paul Prucha, *Broadax and Bayonet: The Role of the United States Army in the Development of the Northwest, 1815–1860*, 121.

14. Inspector General's Report, Cantonment Gibson, August, 1827, Inspection Reports of the Office of the Inspector General, 1814–1842, Roll 2. *Arkansas Gazette*, August 24, 1824, p. 3; November 13, 1827, p. 3; October 27, 1830, p. 2.

15. Francis Paul Prucha, *The Sword of the Republic: The United States Army on the Frontier, 1783–1846*, 181–82. Arbuckle to Jones, May 24, 1833, Office of the Adjutant General, Letters Received, 1822–1860, Roll 78. Jones to Arbuckle, July 27, 1833, Office of the Adjutant General, Letters Sent, 1800–1890, Roll 8.

16. Address by the Governor of Missouri [no date, 1826]; Benton to Secretary of War, December 27, 1826, in Carter, *Territory of Arkansas*, XX, 341–43.

17. Scott to Adjutant General [November 4, 1825]; Arbuckle to Galt, December 2, 1825, *Ibid.*, XX, 149, 158–59.

18. Henry Putney Beers, *The Western Military Frontier, 1815–1846*, 95.

19. Dwight Mission was established in present Pope County, Arkansas, in 1821, by the American Board of Commissions for Foreign Missions. In 1829, after the Cherokees relinquished their lands in Arkansas Territory, the mission was relocated on Sallisaw Creek in present Sequoyah County, Oklahoma.

20. Prucha, *The Sword of the Republic*, 200. Gaines to Arbuckle, June 12, 1822, in Carter, *Territory of Arkansas*, XXI, 32–33. *Missionary Herald* (Boston), XXI (August, 1825), p. 247.

21. Arbuckle to Raone, May 13, 1829; Arbuckle to Secretary of War, December 4, 1829; Arbuckle to Roane, May 27, 1829; Roane to Arbuckle, June 6, 1829; Arbuckle to Secretary of War, July 11, 1829, in Carter, *Territory of Arkansas*, XXI, 33–39, 120–27, 53.

22. Secretary of War to Arbuckle, September 24, 1829; Arbuckle to Secretary of War, November 14, 1829, *Ibid.*, XXI, 71–72, 102–104.

23. Washburn to McKenney, February 2, 1830; Vashon to Secretary of War, April 12, 1831, *Ibid.*, XXI 182–85, 333–35.

24. Washburn to McKenney, February 2, 1830; Arbuckle to Butler, May 4, 1830; Acting Secretary of War to Arbuckle, August 6, 1830, *Ibid.*, XXI, 182–85, 221–23, 247–48.

25. U.S. Congress, Senate, *Document No. 1*, Twenty-third Congress, first session, 193. *U.S. Statutes at Large*, III, 682–83. Arbuckle to

Jones, September 2, 1832, Office of the Adjutant General, Letters Received, 1822–1860, Roll 66.

26. Vashon to Cass, November 20, 1832, Office of Indian Affairs, Letters Received, 1824–1881, National Archives Microcopy, 254, Roll 78.

27. Grant Foreman, *Advancing the Frontier, 1830–1860*, 25–29. Bearss and Gibson, *Fort Smith*, 134–36.

Chapter 4

1. *Arkansas Gazette*, May 4, 1824, p. 3. "Journal of Union Mission," April 20, 1824, 216.

2. *Arkansas Gazette*, January 4, 1825, p. 2.

3. *Ibid.*, June 22, 1824, p. 3.

4. "Journal of Union Mission," June 10, 1824, 221. *Arkansas Gazette*, June 29, 1824, p. 3.

5. Crittenden to Secretary of War, September 12, 1824, in Carter, *Territory of Arkansas*, XIX, 691–94. *Arkansas Gazette*, October 26, 1824, p. 3.

6. Arbuckle to Acting Adjutant General, November 4, 1824, in Carter, *Territory of Arkansas*, XIX, 719–20.

7. McKenney to Crittenden, November 10, 1824; Secretary of War to Crittenden, November 17, 1824, *Ibid.*, XIX, 722, 725. *Arkansas Gazette*, December 14, 1824, p. 3.

8. Crittenden to Secretary of War, December 25, 1824; McNair to the President, January 30, 1825, in Carter, *Territory of Arkansas*, XIX, 737, 762–63.

9. Secretary of War to Crittenden, March 29, 1825, in Carter, *Territory of Arkansas*, XX, 17–18.

10. "Journal of Union Mission," July 31, 1824, 226–27. Mathews, *The Osages*, 513.

11. *Missionary Herald* (Boston), XXI (February, 1825), p. 49. "Journal of Union Mission," August 5, 1824, 227.

12. *Ibid. Missionary Herald* (Boston), XXVI (September, 1830), p. 288.

13. "Journal of Union Mission," August 21, 1824, 229–30.

14. Arbuckle to DuVal, January 14, 1825, in Carter, *Territory of Arkansas*, XIX, 747. *Missionary Herald* (Boston), XXI (August, 1825), p. 246. Although the *Missionary Herald* account indicates that the murder had occurred recently, it is possible that it actually took place in early January, 1823. See note 45, Chapter 1.

15. G. Foreman, *Indians and Pioneers*, 199–200. Izard to Secretary of War, January 30, 1826; Gaines to Arbuckle, March 28, 1826, in Carter, *Territory of Arkansas*, XX, 192–93, 218–19.

16. Arbuckle to Lowndes, April 4, 1826, *Ibid.*, XX, 223–24.

17. Izard to Secretary of War, April 29, 1826; Clark to Secretary of War, January 6, 1827; DuVal to Secretary of War, May 31, 1826, *Ibid.*, XX, 323–33, 357–58, 259–62. *Arkansas Gazette*, May 23, 1826, p. 3; June 20, 1826, p. 3. *Missionary Herald* (Boston), XXIII (May, 1827), p. 149.

18. *Arkansas Gazette* May 23, 1826, p. 3. Arbuckle to DuVal, May 11, 1826; DuVal to Secretary of War, May 31, 1826, in Carter, *Territory of Arkansas*, XX, 245, 259–62.

19. Butler to Arbuckle, June 18, 1826; Gaines to Secretary of War, July 20, 1826, *Ibid.*, XX, 264–65, 272–75. Butler to Arbuckle, July 18, 1826, Western Division, 1821–1842, Letters Sent.

20. *Missionary Herald* (Boston), XXIII (May, 1827), p. 149.

21. *Arkansas Gazette*, June 27, 1826, p. 3. Arbuckle to Lowndes, July 3, 1826, Office of the Adjutant General, Letters Received, 1822–1860, Roll 18. *Missionary Herald* (Boston), XXIII (October, 1827), p. 311.

22. Arbuckle to Butler, July 29, 1826; Gaines to Secretary of War, July 20, 1826, in Carter, *Territory of Arkansas*, XX, 276–77, 272–75.

23. Du Val to Arbuckle, October 19, 1826; Clark to Secretary of War, January 6, 1827; Atkinson to Gaines, October 7, 1826, *Ibid.*, XX, 303, 357–58, 294. G. Foreman, *Indians and Pioneers*, 204–205. *Arkansas Gazette*, October 24, 1826, p. 3. *Missionary Herald* (Boston), XXIII (May, 1827), pp. 149–50. *American State Papers: Indian Affairs*, II, 673–74.

24. Atkinson to Adjutant General, January 9, 1827; Arbuckle to Butler, November 4, 1826, in Carter, *Territory of Arkansas*, XX, 361–62, 301–302.

25. DuVal to Clark, December 6, 1826, *Ibid.*, XX 319–22.

26. Osage Chiefs to the Cherokee Chiefs, February 25, 1827, *Ibid,.* XX, 462–63.

27. Clark to Secretary of War, January 6, 1827; Atkinson to Adjutant General, January 9, 1827, *Ibid*, XX, 357–58, 361–62. Clark to DuVal, January 2, 1827, Office of Indian Affairs, Letters Received, 1824–81, Roll 77. Arbuckle to Butler, January 14, 1827, Office of the Adjutant General, Letters Received, 1822–1860, Roll 25.

28. DuVal to Arbuckle, February 3, 1827, in Carter, *Territory of Arkansas*, XX, 460–61.

29. Cherokee Chiefs to the Osage Chiefs, February 9, 1827; Arbuckle to Butler, March 26, 1827, *Ibid.*, XX, 461–64. *Missionary Herald* (Boston), XXIII (May, 1827), p. 150.

30. Hamtramck to DuVal, October 5, 1827; Secretary of War to Izard, May 21, 1827, in Carter, *Territory of Arkansas*, XX, 612–13, 468–69.

31. DuVal to Hamtramck, September 4, 1827; Hamtramck to Clark,

November 1, 1827; DuVal to Hamtramck, August 18, 1827, *Ibid.*, XX, 609–12.

32. Hamtramck to DuVal, October 5, 1827; Hamtramck to Clark, December 12, 1827; Hamtramck to Clark, November 1, 1827; DuVal to Hamtramck, September 4, 1827, *Ibid.*, XX, 609–15.

33. Clark to McKenney, November 2, 1827; Hamtramck to DuVal, October 5, 1827; Clark to McKenney, February 24, 1828, *Ibid.*, XX, 550–51, 612–13, 606–607.

34. DuVal to Secretary of War, November 30, 1827, *Ibid.*, XX, 554–55. Kappler, *Indian Affairs*, II, 288–92.

35. Arbuckle to Jones, July 12, 1829; Arbuckle to McRee, December 24, 1829, Office of the Adjutant General, Letters Received, 1822–1860, Roll , 41.

36. Eaton to Macomb, March 24, 1830, The Secretary of War, Letters Sent, 1800–1889, National Archives, Microcopy 6, Roll 12.

37. Arbuckle to Prior, May 3, 1830; Prior to Arbuckle, May 4, 1830; Arbuckle to Butler, June 3, 1830, Office of the Adjutant General, Letters Received, 1822–1860, Roll 49.

38. U.S. Congress, House, *Document No. 172*, Twenty-Third Congress, first session, 9. U.S. Congress, Senate, *Document No. 512*, Twenty-third Congress, first session, II, 498–99.

39. *Ibid. Arkansas Gazette*, May 25, 1831, p. 3.

Chapter 5

1. Memorial to the President by the Territorial Assembly [n.d.]; McClellan to Secretary of War, February 16, 1827, in Carter, *The Territory of Arkansas*, XX, 162–65, 393–94. G. Foreman, *Indians and Pioneers*, 263–64.

2. Kappler, *Indian Affairs*, II, 264–68. Arbuckle to Butler, May 4, 1827, in Carter, *Territory of Arkansas*, XX, 455–56.

3. *Arkansas Gazette*, June 19, 1827, p. 3; January 15, 1828, p. 3. Baylor to Campbell, October 29, 1831; McIntosh, et al. to the President, October 25, 1831, U.S. Congress, Senate, *Document No. 512*, Twenty-third Congress, first session, II, 633–35. Brearley to Secretary of War, September 1, 1827; Adjutant General to Arbuckle, September 5, 1837, in Carter, *Territory of Arkansas*, XX, 527–28, 529.

4. *Arkansas Gazette*, February 13, 1828, p. 3.

5. *Ibid.*, March 19, 1828, p. 3. Scott to Arbuckle, March 17, 1828, Western Division, 1821–1842, Letters Sent.

6. G. Foreman, *Indians and Pioneers*, 258–61. Muriel H. Wright, *A Guide to Indian Tribes of Oklahoma* 134. John F. McDermott (ed.), "Isaac

McCoy's Second Exploring Trip in 1828," *Kansas Historical Quarterly*, Vol. XIII (February), 1945, 421–25.

7. Monroe to General Tolontusky, Chiefs, Warriors, of the Cherokee Nation of Arkansas [February, 1818]; Calhoun to Lewis, July 22, 1819; Calhoun to Chiefs of the Arkansa Cherokees, October 8, 1821, U.S. Congress, House, *Document No. 263*, Twentieth Congess, first session, 5–8. Secretary of War to Arbuckle, May 1, 1823, in Carter, *The Territory of Arkansas*, XIX, 510–11.

8. Secretary of War to Miller, March 4, 1823; Chiefs of the Arkansas Cherokees to Secretary of War, June 24, 1823; Arbuckle to Secretary of War, January 3, 1824; Secretary of War to Crittenden, April 28, 1824, *Ibid.*, XIX, 498–99, 525–27, 587–88, 653–57. *Arkansas Gazette,* January 18, 1825, p. 3.

9. Secretary of War to Izard, April 16, 1825; Izard to Secretary of War, June 18, 1825, in Carter, *Territory of Arkansas*, XX, 62–63, 78–80.

10. Jolly to Izard, August 18, 1825; Memorial to the President by the Territorial Assembly [n.d.], *Ibid.*, XX, 105–106, 127–29.

11. Arbuckle to Galt, December 2, 1825, *Ibid.*, XX, 158–59. MacRee to Arbuckle, December 10, 1825, Western Division, 1821–1842, Letters Sent.

12. Izard to Secretary of War, January 28, 1826, in Carter, *Territory of Arkansas*, XX, 191–92.

13. Conway to Secretary of War, June 3, 1824, *Ibid.*, XIX, 670–71. *U.S. Statutes at Large*, IV, 153. Graham to McRee, June 15, 1826; Arbuckle to Adjutant General, July 31, 1826; Adjutant General to Arbuckle, October 10, 1826, in Carter, *Territory of Arkansas*, XX, 263–64, 277–78, 295. It appears that the Adjutant General exceeded his authority in allowing the settlement of Lovely's Purchase, for Thomas McKenney, Commissioner of Indian Affairs, later explained, "the relaxation of the Military Order of 1818, which prohibitted (sic) sett'lers on a tract of land claimed by the Cherokees called Lovely's purchase, has been construed into a permission to the white sett'lers to occupy those lands.—But such it is believed was not the intention of the Secretary of War." McKenney to McLean, March 18, 1828, *Ibid.*, XX, 624–25. *Arkansas Gazette*, April 10, 1827, p. 3. *Arkansas Acts: Acts Passed at the Fifth Session of the General Assembly of the Territory of Arkansas*, 6–8.

14. Memorial from Arkansas Cherokees to DuVal, July 24, 1826; McKenney to Cooke, December 15, 1826, in Carter, *Territory of Arkansas*, XX, 331–32, 326–29.

15. Memorial to the President by the Territorial Assembly [Received December 24, 1827], *Ibid.*, XX, 570–73. *Arkansas Gazette*, January 15, 1828, p. 3.

16. "The Cherokee Nation of Indians," in *Fifth Annual Report*, 247. Cherokee Deputation from Arkansas to Secretary of War, Feb-

ruary 2, 1828, U.S. Congress, House, *Document No. 263*, Twentieth Congress, first session, 32–37. Secretary of War to the Arkansas Cherokee Delegation [March 27, 1828], in Carter, *Territory of Arkansas*, XX, 633–34.

17. John Quincy Adams, *Memoirs of John Quincy Adams Comprising Portions of His Diary from 1795 to 1848* (ed. by Charles Francis Adams), VII, 499, 502–503.

18. Royce, "The Cherokee Nation of Indians," in *Fifth Annual Report*, 247–48. Kappler, *Indian Affairs*, II, 288–92.

19. *Arkansas Gazette*, June 25, 1828, p. 3; July 2, 1828, p. 3. Brearley to Porter, September 27, 1828, Office of Indian Affairs, Letters Received, 1824–81, Roll 77.

Chapter 6

1. Izard to Secretary of War, January 30, 1826, Hamtramck to Clark, February 8, 1827, in Carter, *The Territory of Arkansas*, XX, 192–93, 411. *Arkansas Gazette*, August 29, 1826, p. 3. The Caddo Hills are located in what is now Bryan County, Oklahoma.

2. Cummings to Arbuckle, March 4, 1827; Arbuckle to Butler, April 7, 1827, in Carter, *Territory of Arkansas*, XX, 413–14, 444–45.

3. Cummings to Arbuckle, April 3, 1827, *Ibid.*, XX, 457.

4. Cummings to Arbuckle, April 14, 1827; Greenwood to Cummings, April 21, 1827, *Ibid.*, XX, 457–59.

5. Cummings to Arbuckle, April 24, 1827; Arbuckle to Butler, May 4, 1827, *Ibid.*, XX, 459, 455–56.

6. Gray to Secretary of War, June 13, 1827, *Ibid.*, XX, 479–81.

7. Gray to Secretary of War, July 3, 1827; Secretary of State to Izard, September 6, 1827, *Ibid.*, XX, 500–501, 529–30. *Arkansas Gazette*, July 31, 1827, p. 3; November 6, 1827, p. 4. John Hugh Reynolds (ed.), "Official Correspondence of Governor Izard," *Publications of the Arkansas Historical Association*, Vol. I. (1906), 451. Pecan Point is located just across the Red River from present McCurtain County, Oklahoma.

8. Secretary of War to Izard, September 6, 1827; Izard to Secretary of War, October 16, 1827, in Carter, *Territory of Arkansas*, XX, 529–30, 543. *Arkansas Gazette*, November 6, 1827, p. 4. Colquhoun to Cummings, June 21, 1827, Office of the Adjutant General, Letters Received, 1822–1860, Roll 25.

9. Arbuckle to Butler, August 27, 1827, Office of the Adjutant General, Letters Received, 1822–1860, Roll 26.

10. Gaines to Secretary of War, August 25, 1827; Cummings to Adjutant General, September 1, 1827, in Carter, *Territory of Arkansas*, XX, 517–18, 526–27.

11. Petition to Governor Izard by Citizens of Miller County [March 20, 1828]; Pierson to Izard, March 22, 1828; Izard to Rector, April 7, 1828, *Ibid.*, XX, 629–30, 632, 640–41.

12. Rector to Izard, May 8, 1828; Hyde to Adjutant General, November 17, 1828; Hyde to Arbuckle, May 6, 1828, *Ibid.*, XX, 677, 784–85, 786. *Arkansas Gazette*, May 7, 1828, p. 3.

13. Bradford to Secretary of War, March 28, 1818 [1819], in Carter, *The Territory of Arkansas*, XIX, 59–60.

14. Grand Jury presentment in Hempstead County [April, 1820], *Ibid.*, XIX, 196–98.

15. Cummings to Adjutant General, January 18, 1826, *Ibid.*, XX, 184–85.

16. *Arkansas Gazette*, May 23, 1826, p. 3; December 5, 1826, p. 3. Cummings to Gaines, June 22, 1826, in Carter, *Territory of Arkansas*, XX, 266–67.

17. Hamtramck to Clark, February 8, 1827, *Ibid.*, XX, 411.

18. *Arkansas Gazette*, January 16, 1827, p. 3. Cummings to Arbuckle, April 14, 1827; Cummings to Arbuckle, April 24, 1827; Arbuckle to Butler, May 4, 1827; Gray to Secretary of War, June 13, 1827, in Carter, *Territory of Arkansas*, XX, 457–58, 452–53, 455–56, 479–81.

19. Gray to Secretary of War, July 3, 1827; Izard to Secretary of State, October 16, 1827, *Ibid.*, XX, 500–501, 543. The abortive expedition mentioned in this paragraph was the one organized by Burkman and Robbins described in greater detail earlier in this chapter.

20. Hamtramck to Clark, September 1, 1827; Langham to McKenney, June 16, 1827, *Ibid.*, XX, 607–609, 487–88.

21. Francis Paul Prucha, ed., *Army Life on the Western Frontier: Selections from the Official Reports Made Between 1826 and 1845 by Colonel George Crogham*, 159–61.

22. Hamtramck to Clark, September 1, 1827, in Carter, *Territory of Arkansas*, XX, 607–609. *Arkansas Gazette*, September 4, 1827, p. 3. G. Foreman, *Indians and Pioneers*, 244. Prucha, *Army Life on the Western Frontier*, 160–61.

23. Hamtramck to Clark, December 12, 1827; Hamtramck to Clark, January 13, 1828, in Carter, *Territory of Arkansas*, XX, 614–18.

24. *Cherokee Phoenix* (New Echota, Ga.), October 29, 1828, p. 2. *Cherokee Phoenix and Indians' Advocate* (New Echota, Ga.), March 18, 1829, pp. 2–3. A slightly different version of this episode is related in Carolyn Thomas Foreman, "The Cherokee War Path," *Chronicles of Oklahoma*, Vol. IX, (September, 1931), 233–35.

25. *Arkansas Gazette*, September 23, 1828, p. 3. Birch to Arbuckle, September 3, 1828; Arbuckle to Galt, October 1, 1828, Office of the

Adjutant General, Letters Received, 1822–1860, Rolls 33, 37. Izard to Secretary of War, September 21, 1828, in Carter, *Territory of Arkansas*, XX, 748–49.

26. G. Foreman, *Indians and Pioneers*, 244.
27. *Arkansas Gazette*, January 27, 1829, p. 3. Galt to Adjutant General, February 20, 1829, in Carter, *Territory of Arkansas*, XX, 851–52. Newell to McRee, January 28, 1829, Office of the Adjutant General, Letters Received, 1822–1860, Roll 41.
28. *Arkansas Gazette*, February 3, 1829, p. 3.
29. *Cherokee Phoenix and Indians' Advocate* (New Echota, Ga.), February 25, 1829, p. 2.
30. Newell to McRee, January 18, 1829; Arbuckle to Jones, January 1, 1829, Office of the Adjutant General, Letters Received, 1822–1860, Roll 41. Sevier to Secretary of War, March 13, 1829, in Carter, *The Territory of Arkansas*, XXI, 5–6.
31. *Arkansas Gazette*, July 15, 1829, p. 3. G. Foreman, *Advancing the Frontier*, 37. *Cherokee Phoenix and Indians' Advocate* (New Echota, Ga.), July 15, 1829, pp. 1–2.
32. Memorial to Congress by the Territorial Assembly [November 21, 1829], in Carter, *Territory of Arkansas*, XXI, 114–15. *Arkansas Gazette*, February 2, 1830, p. 3; February 16, 1830, p. 3.
33. Fulton to Secretary of War, April 19, 1830; Fulton to Clark [April 9, 1830]; Arbuckle to Fulton [April 8, 1830], in Carter, *Territory of Arkansas*, XXI, 213–17. Arbuckle to Butler, April 25, 1830, Office of the Adjutant General, Letters Received, 1822–1860, Roll 49.
34. *Arkansas Gazette*, May 11, 1830, p. 3.
35. C. T. Foreman, "The Cherokee War Path," *Chronicles of Oklahoma*, Vol. IX (September, 1831), 236–59. *Cherokee Phoenix and Indians' Advocate* (New Echota, Ga), September 18, 1830, p. 2. Arbuckle to Jones, July 24, 1830, Office of the Adjutant General, Letters Received, 1822–1860, Roll 49.
36. *Arkansas Gazette*, February 2, 1830, p. 3; February 16, 1830, p. 3. *Missionary Herald* (Boston), XXVI (September, 1830), 287.
37. Arbuckle to Jones, May 8, 1830, Office of the Adjutant General, Letters Received, 1822–1860, Roll 49.

Chapter 7

1. Houston To Jackson, May 11, 1829, Amelia W. Williams and Eugene C. Barker (eds.), *The Writings of Sam Houston, 1813–1863*, I, 132–34. M. K. Wisehart, *Sam Houston: American Giant*, 52. Donald

Day and Harry Herbert Ullon (eds.), *The Autobiography of Sam Houston*, 49. Jack Gregory and Rennard Strickland, *Sam Houston with the Cherokees, 1829–1833*, 126.

2. Marquis James, *The Raven: A Biography of Sam Houston*, 115–16.
3. *Ibid.*, 88. Wisehart, *Sam Houston*, 103. Houston to Jackson, May 11, 1829, Williams and Barker, *The Writings of Sam Houston*, I, 132–34.
4. Houston to Jackson, June 24, 1829 [with subsequent endorsement by Houston dated June 25, 1829], Grant Foreman Collection, Thomas Gilcrease Institute of American History and Art.
5. Houston to Eaton, June 24, 1829, Williams and Barker, *The Writings of Sam Houston*, I, 134–36.
6. Gregory and Strickland, *Sam Houston with the Cherokees*, 92. Houston to Arbuckle, July 8, 1829, Williams and Barker, *The Writings of Sam Houston*, I, 136–39.
7. *Ibid.*
8. [Houston] to Jackson, September 19, 1829, *Ibid.*, 140–43.
9. Wisehart, *Sam Houston*, 58. James, *The Raven*, 127–28. Rogers to Eaton, January 4, 1830, Grant Foreman Collection, Gilcrease Institute.
10. Houston to Van Fossen, April 4, 1830, Williams and Barker, *The Writings of Sam Houston*, I, 147–48. U.S. Congress, House, *Report No. 502*, Twenty-third Congress, first session, 2–3, 24.
11. *Ibid.*, 33. Letter from Tah-Lohn-Tus-Ky [Houston] to *Arkansas Gazette* [June 22, 1830], Williams and Barker, *The Writings of Sam Houston*, I, 155–57.
12. Grant Foreman, *Pioneer Days in the Early Southwest*, 184–85. James, *The Raven*, 109–10, 135. McKenney resisted Houston's efforts to secure the Indian rations contract; DuVal was a brother of William, a partner in a Fort Smith trading house which was a potential rival to the trading post Houston eventually established at Wigwam Neosho; A. P. Chouteau resented the interference of Osage agent Hamtramck. Houston may have been considering a commercial venture with Chouteau. U.S. Congress, House, *Report No. 502*, Twenty-third Congress, first session, 9–10. McClellan to Secretary of War [April 10, 1829]; Arbuckle to Roane, May 13, 1829, in Carter, *Territory of Arkansas*, XXI, 14–16, 33–35. Gregory and Strickland, *Sam Houston with the Cherokees*, 65.
13. McKenney to Secretary of War, January 21, 1830, in Carter, *Territory of Arkansas*, XXI, 177–78. Houston to Jackson, [1830?], Williams and Barker, *The Writings of Sam Houston*, I, 146. Arbuckle to Butler, June 12, 1820, Office of the Adjutant General, Letters Received, 1822–1860, Roll 49.
14. Houston to Eaton, June 13, 1830, Grant Foreman, "Some New

Light on Houston's Life Among the Cherokee Indians," *Chronicles of Oklahoma*, Vol. IX, (June, 1931), 141–42.

15. James, *The Raven*, 150–52. Gregory and Strickland, *Sam Houston with the Cherokees*, 43–44. Wisehart, *Sam Houston*, 60–61.

16. James, *The Raven*, 153–54. Houston to Arbuckle, July 21,1830, Williams and Barker, *The Writings of Sam Houston*, I, 185–86. Randolph to Arbuckle, September 30, 1830, Grant Foreman Collection, Gilcrease Institute.

17. Houston to Van Fossen, August 22, 1830, Williams and Barker, *The Writings of Sam Houston*, I, 187–88. Vashon to Jackson, September 12, 1830, U.S. Congess, Senate, *Document No. 512*, Twenty-third Congress, first session, II, 113. G. Foreman, "Some New Light on Houston's Life Among the Cherokee Indians," *Chronicles of Oklahoma*, Vol. IX (June, 1931), 153–45.

18. Williams and Barker, *The Writings of Sam Houston*, I, 155–85.

19. Gregory and Strickland, *Sam Houston with the Cherokees*, 113. James, *The Raven*, 126.

20. *Cherokee Phoenix and Indians' Advocate* (New Echota, Ga.), May 28, 1831, p. 2. Charles Edward Lester, *The Life of Sam Houston: The Only Authentic Memoir of Him Ever Published*, 260, 55. James, *The Raven*, 160.

21. Thomas B. Williams, *The Soul of the Red Man*, 85. George W. Pierson, *Tocqueville in America*, 388. James, *The Raven*, 122, 128. Vashon to Cass, January 4, 1832, Office of Indian Affairs, Letters Received, 1824–1881, Roll 34.

22. G. Foreman, *Advancing the Frontier*, 109–11, . Arbuckle to Eaton, May 21, 1831; Chouteau to Clark, June 28, 1831, U.S. Congress, Senate, *Document No. 512*, Twenty-third Congress, first session, II, 457–59, 498–500.

23. Wisehart, *Sam Houston*, 63. Houston to Jackson, May 11, 1829, Williams and Barker, *The Writings of Sam Houston*, I, 132–34.

24. Wisehart, *Sam Houston*, 82–85. Robb to Houston, July 16, 1832, Grant Foreman Collection, Gilcrease Institute. Houston's Passport to Texas, 1832, Williams and Barker, *The Writings of Sam Houston*, IV, 11. Although there is no account of discussions between Ellsworth and Houston at Fort Gibson, Houston's subsequent reports to Ellsworth indicate that the two men did confer before Houston went to Texas.

25. Houston to Prentiss, August 18, 1832; Houston to Ellsworth, December 1, 1832; Houston to Ellsworth, February 13, 1833, Williams and Barker, *The Writings of Sam Houston*, I, 263–64, 267–71, 272–74.

26. Robb to Houston, October 4, 1833, Grant Foreman Collection, Gilcrease Institute. Houston to Jackson, February 13, 1833, Williams and Barker, *The Writings of Sam Houston*, I, 274–76.

Chapter 8

1. Annie Heloise Able, "The History of Events Resulting in Indian Con-solidation West of the Mississippi," *Annual Report of the American Historical Association for the Year 1906*, 381–82.
2. Cantonment Gibson Returns for February and July, 1832, Returns from the United States Military Posts, 1800–1916, National Ar-chives, Microcopy 617, Roll 404. *Arkansas Gazette*, October 12, 1831, p. 3; October 26, 1831, p. 3; November 2, 1831, p. 3; November 23, 1831, p. 3; December 7, 1831, p. 3; December 21, 1831, p. 3; January 4, 1832, p. 3; February 22, 1832, p. 3. Jones to Arbuckle, December 3, 1831, Office of the Adjutant General, Letters Received, 1822–1860, Roll 58. Jones to Arbuckle, Sep-tember 17, 1831, Office of the Adjutant General, Letters Sent, 1800–1890, Roll 8. Prucha, *The Sword of the Republic*, 256. Report of the Major General for 1831, U.S. Congress, House, *Document No. 2*, Twenty-second Congress, first session, 54. Actually, this was the second time the posts had been so designated. The com-manding general of the Western Department classified it as a fort in 1827, after the stockade was completed. He was forced to re-scind the order after learning that only the Secretary of War could assign that designation. Arbuckle, who preferred the title "fort," informed the Adjutant General that he hoped it would be con-firmed soon. Five years later the post's name was finally changed to Fort Gibson by an order dated February 8, 1832.
3. Arbuckle to Jones, July 29, 1832; Arbuckle to Jesup, April 29, 1833, Office of the Adjutant General, Letters Received, 1822–1860, Rolls 66, 78.
4. *Arkansas Gazette*, November 24, 1829, p. 2; December 1, 1829, p. 3. Stuart to Adjutant General, October 10, 1833, in Carter, *Terri-tory of Arkansas*, XXI, 799–800.
5. Arbuckle to Jones, October 2, 1830, Office of the Adjutant General, Letters Received, 1822–1860, Roll 49. Grant Foreman (ed.), "An Unpublished Report by Captain Bonneville with Introduction and Footnotes," *Chronicles of Oklahoma*, Vol. X (September, 1932), 330.
6. Kappler, *Indian Affairs*, II, 1035–40, 310–19. U.S. Congress, Senate, *Document No. 512*, Twenty-third Congress, first session, II, 192–96, 419–22. James Henry Gardner, "The Lost Captain: J. L. Dawson of Old Fort Gibson," *Chronicles of Oklahoma*, Vol. XXI (September, 1943), 221, 241–49. Arrell M. Gibson, *The Chicka-saws*, 174. Returns from U. S. Military Posts, 1800–1916, Roll 404.
7. Gardner, "The Lost Captain: J. L. Dawson of Old Fort Gibson," *Chronicles of Oklahoma*, Vol. XXI (September, 1943), 248.

8. Returns from U.S. Military Posts, 1800–1916, Roll 404. Bearss and Gibson, *Fort Smith*, 113. Muriel H. Wright, "The Removal of the Choctaws to the Indian Territory, 1830–1833," *Chronicles of Oklahoma*, Vol. VI (June, 1928), 109.

9. Herring to Armstrong, November 15, 1831, U.S. Congress, Senate, *Document No. 512*, Twenty-third Congress, first session, II, 372–73. Carolyn Thomas Foreman (ed.), "Report of Captain John Stuart on the Construction of the Road from Fort Smith to Horse Prairie on Red River," *Chronicles of Oklahoma*, Vol V (September, 1927), 340–42.

10. *Ibid.*, 340–343.

11. *Ibid.*, 342–47.

12. Eaton to McCoy, April 13, 1831; McCoy to Secretary of War, August 18, 1831, U.S. Congress, Senate, *Document No. 512*, Twenty-third Congress, first session, II, 275–77, 561–66.

13. *Missionary Herald* (Boston), XXVI (September, 1830), pp. 286–87.

14. Arbuckle to Butler, June 3, 1830; Arbuckle to McKee, July 24, 1830, Office of the Adjutant General, Letters Received, 1822–1860, Roll 49.

15. Arbuckle to Secretary of War, February 16, 1830, in Carter, *Territory of Arkansas*, XXI, 186–87. A year later while surveying the Indian country, Isaac McCoy, a zealous advocate of consolidating the Indians into one great nation in the West, suggested that Chickasaw removal would be expedited if the tribe were informed that the government had no intention of purchasing a tract south of Red River from Mexico. President Jackson's intentions concerning Texas were already clear; he had offered Mexico five million dollars for Texas. McCoy to Secretary of War, August 18, 1831, U.S. Congress, Senate, *Document No. 512*, Twenty-third Congress, first session, II, 561–66. Eugene C. Barker, "President Jackson and the Texas Revolution," *American Historical Review*, Vol. XII (July, 1907), 791.

16. Gaines to Arbuckle, July 10, 1831; Arbuckle to Clark, August 10, 1831, Office of the Adjutant General, Letters Received, 1822–1860, Roll 58.

17. James H. Gardner, "One Hundred Years Ago in the Region of Tulsa," *Chronicles of Oklahoma*, Vol. XI (June, 1933), 775–81.

18. Cass to the President, February 16, 1832, U.S. Congress, Senate, *Document No. 512*, Twenty-third Congress, first session, II, 767–81.

19. *Arkansas Gazette*, December 8, 1830, p. 3.

10. *Ibid.*, May 25, 1831, p. 3; July 6, 1831, p. 3. *Missionary Herald* (Boston) XXVII (October, 1831), p. 322.

21. G. Foreman, *Advancing the Frontier*, 113. McCall to Arbuckle, February 16, 1832, Western Division, 1821–1842, Letters Sent.

22. Creek Chiefs to the President, October 29, 1831; Cass to the President, February 16, 1832; Cass to Creek Chiefs, April 14, 1832, U.S. Congress, Senate, *Document No. 512*, Twenty-third Congress, first session, 637, 766–81, 814–15. Almost four years earlier Arbuckle had asked that a portion of his command be mounted to enable them to pursue marauding bands.

23. Cass to Carroll, Stokes, and Vaux, July 14, 1832, *Ibid.*, 870–75. *U.S. Statutes at Large*, IV, 595–96. *American State Papers, Military Affairs*, V, 26–27.

24. William Omer Foster, "The Career of Montfort Stokes in Oklahoma," *Chronicles of Oklahoma*, Vol. XVIII (March, 1940), 36. William H. Ghent, "Montfort Stokes," in *Dictionary of American Biography*, XVIII, 67–68.

25. Otis E. Young, "The United States Mounted Ranger Battalion, 1832–33," *Mississippi Valley Historical Review*, Vol. XLI (December, 1954), 455–57. *Arkansas Gazette*, July 18, 1832, pp. 1 and 3. Captain Boone was the son of Daniel Boone.

26. Jones to Arbuckle, July 7, 1832, Office of the Adjutant General, Letters Sent, 1800–1890, Roll 8. Arbuckle to Jones, August 12, 1832, Office of the Adjutant General, Letters Received, 1822–1860, Roll 66. Vashon to Herring, March 15, 1833, Office of Indian Affairs, Letter Received, 1824–1881, Roll 78.

27. Arbuckle to Jones, September 15, 1832; Arbuckle to Jones, October 6, 1832, Grant Foreman Collection, Gilcrease Institute. Arbuckle to Jones, Office of the Adjutant General, Letters Received, 1822–1860, Roll 6.

28. Charles Joseph Latrobe, *The Rambler in Oklahoma: Latrobe's Tour with Washington Irving* (ed. by Muriel H. Wright and George Shirk), vii–x. Washington Irving, *A Tour on the Prairies* (ed. by John Francis McDermott), xvii. Young, "The United States Mounted Ranger Battalion, 1832–33," *Mississippi Valley Historical Review*, Vol. XLI (December, 1954), 465. Ellsworth to Stillman, December 5, 1832, quoted in Stanley T. Williams and Barbara D. Simison (eds.), "A Journey Through Oklahoma in 1832: A Letter from Henry L. Ellsworth to Professor Benjamin Stillman," *Mississippi Valley Historical Review*, Vol. XXIX (December, 1942), 389.

29. Charles Joseph Latrobe, *The Rambler in North America, 1832–1833*, I, 149. Irving, *A Tour on the Prairies*, xxi. Ellsworth, *Washington Irving on the Prairies*, 25, 101. Young, "The United States Mounted Ranger Battalion, 1832–33," *Mississippi Valley Historical Review*, Vol. XLI (December, 1954), 467.

30. Arbuckle to Clark, October 1, 1832; Clark to Jesup, November 27, 1832, Grant Foreman Collection, Gilcrease Institute. Arbuckle to Jones, December 9, 1832, Office of the Adjutant General, Letters Received, 1822–1860, Roll 66.

31. Gaines to Many, May 10, 1832; McCall to Arbuckle, June 17, 1832, Western Division, 1821–1842, Letters Sent.

32. Arbuckle to Jones, July 29, 1833, Office of the Adjutant General, Letters Received, 1822–1860, Roll 66.

33. *Ibid.*, Jones to Arbuckle, January 23, 1833, Office of the Adjutant General, Letters Sent, 1800–1890, Roll 8. Arbuckle to Jones, March 20, 1833, Office of the Adjutant General, Letters Received, 1822–1860, Roll 66.

34. Vose to Macomb, June 5, 1833, Grant Foreman Collection, Gilcrease Institute. Vashon to Herring, March 15, 1833, Office of Indian Affairs, Letters Received, 1824–1881, Roll 78.

35. *Niles Weekly Register* (Baltimore), March 23, 1833, p. 51. Josiah Gregg, *Commerce of the Prairies* (ed. by Max L. Moorhead (1)), 253–56. *Missionary Herald* (Boston), XXIX (October, 1833), p. 369.

36. James Mooney, "Calendar History of the Kiowa Indians," in *Seventeenth Annual Report*, 255.

37. Jones to Arbuckle, July 7, 1832, Office of the Adjutant General, Letters Sent, 1800–1890, Roll 8. Arbuckle to Jones, April 24, 1833; Arbuckle to Many, May 6, 1833, Office of the Adjutant General, Letters Received, 1822–1860, Roll 78.

38. Young, "The United States Mounted Ranger Battalion, 1832–33," *Mississippi Valley Historical Review*, Vol. XLI (December, 1954), 468–69. Many to Arbuckle, July 4, 1833, Grant Foreman Collection, Gilcrease Institute. Arbuckle to Jones, July 9, 1833, Office of the Adjutant General, Letters Received, 1822–1860, Roll 78.

39. Arbuckle to Macomb, June 6, 1833, *Ibid.*

40. Stambaugh to Secretary of War, January 6, 1833; Stokes, Ellsworth and Schermerhorn to Cass, April 16, 1833, U.S. Congress, Senate, *Document No.* 512, Twenty-third Congress, first session, IV, 10–12 183–84. Stambaugh to Arbuckle, January 2, 1833; Arbuckle to Ross, January 3, 1833; Ross to Cass, May 28, 1833, Office of Indian Affairs, Letters Received, 1824–1881, Roll 78. Kappler, *Indian Affairs*, II, 383–85. Edward E. Hill, *The Office of Indian Affairs. 1824–1880: Historical Sketches*, 33. Frank H. Harris, "Seneca Sub-Agency, 1832–38," *Chronicles of Oklahoma*, Vol. XLII (Summer, 1964), 82–88.

41. Stambaugh to Cass, January 7, 1833; Schermerhorn to Cass, April 3, 1833, U.S. Congress, Senate, *Document No. 512*, Twenty-third Congress, first session, IV, 12–13, 154–55. Kappler, *Indian Affairs*, II, 385–91.

42. *Ibid.*, 394–95. Schermerhorn to Cass, April 3, 1833, U.S. Congress, Senate, *Document No. 512*, Twenty-third Congress, first session, IV, 154–55. Able, "The History of Events Resulting in Indian Consolidation West of the Mississippi," in *Annual Report*, 393. Prucha, *The Sword of the Republic*, 272–73, 301.

43. Stokes to Cass, July 20, 1833, Journal of proceedings of a council held with the Osages commencing February 25, 1833, U.S. Congress, Senate, *Document No. 512*, Twenty-third Congress, first session, IV, 480–43, 207–30. G. Foreman, *Pioneer Days*, 207–12.
44. Wilbur Sturtevant Nye, *Carbine and Lance: The Story of Old Fort Sill*, 6–7. Mooney, "Calendar History of the Kiowa Indians," in *Seventeenth Annual Report*, 257–59. *Missionary Herald* (Boston), XXIX (October, 1833), p. 369. G. Foreman, *Advancing the Frontier, 1830–1860*, 118. G. Foreman, *Pioneer Days in the Early Southwest*, 119.
45. Hannum to Jackson, May 13, 1833, U.S. Congress, Senate, *Document No. 512*, Twenty-third Congress, first session, IV, 232–34. Kappler, *Indian Affairs*, 395–97.
46. Webber, et al. to Arbuckle, July 17, 1833, Office of Indian Affairs, Letters Received, 1824–1881, Roll 78.
47. Arbuckle to Webber, et al., July 18, 1833; Jolly, et al. to Arbuckle, July 19, 1833; Arbuckle to Webber, et al., July 19, 1833; Roane to Cass, October 30, 1833, *Ibid*.
48. Ellsworth to Cass, July 13, 1833; Stokes to Cass, October 27, 1833; Stokes to Cass, November 26, 1833, U.S. Congress, Senate, *Document No. 512*, Twenty-third Congress, first session, IV, 471, 623–26, 734–36.
49. Ellsworth to Herring, December 11, 1833; Stokes to Cass, November 26, 1833, *Ibid.*, 753–55, 734–36.
50. U.S. Congress, House, *Report No. 474*, Twenty-third Congress, first session, 91–105. Stokes to Cass, November 26, 1833, U.S. Congress, Senate, *Document No. 512*, Twenty-third Congress, first session, IV, 734–36.
51. Stuart to Secretary of War, November 10, 1833; Arbuckle to Adjutant General, February 10, 1834, in Carter, *Territory of Arkansas*, XXI, 845–46, 901–904.
52. Schermerhorn to Arbuckle, May 2, 1834; Arbuckle to Schermerhorn, May 5, 1834; Arbuckle to Schermerhorn, May 21, 1834, Office of the Adjutant General, Letters Received, 1822–1860, Roll 91.
53. Leavenworth to Jesup, May 1, 1834; Post Quartermaster, Fort Gibson, Letters Sent, Box 336.

Chapter 9

1. *U.S. Statutes at Large*, IV, 652.
2. Latrobe, *The Rambler in North America, 1832–1833*, II, 231. George Catlin, *Letters and Notes on the Manners, Customs and Condition of the North American Indians*, II, 37. John C. Parish, "Henry Dodge," in *Dictionary of American Biography*, V, 348–49.

3. Louis Pelzer, *Henry Dodge*, 81.
4. [James Hildreth], *The Dragoon Campaigns to the Rocky Mountains*, 37.
5. *Ibid.*, 45.
6. *Ibid.*, 59.
7. *Ibid.*, 86. Pelzer, *Henry Dodge*, 87–88.
8. Nye, *Carbine and Lance*, 8. G. Foreman, *Pioneer Days in the Early Southwest*, 123. Philip St. George Cooke, *Scenes and Adventures in the Army: or Romance of Military Life*, 224. *Niles Weekly Register* (Baltimore), August 2, 1834, p. 389.
9. Arbuckle to Clark, August 10, 1831, Office of the Adjutant General, Letters Received, 1822–1860, Roll 58. Jones to Arbuckle, September 17, 1831, Office of the Adjutant General, Letters Sent, 1800–1890, Roll 8.
10. Arbuckle to Macomb, March 1, 1834, Roll 91. Macomb to Leavenworth, February 19, 1834; Arbuckle to Macomb, March 22, 1834, National Archives, Record Group 393, Records of the United States Army Continental Commands, Letters Received, Fort Gibson, Box 1. Arbuckle to Jones, March 118, 1834, Office of the Adjutant General, Letters Received, 1822–1860, Roll 91. Fort Gibson Returns for April, 1834, Returns from the United States Military Posts, 1800–1916, Roll 404.
11. Leavenworth to Jones, April 29, 1834, Grant Foreman Collection, Thomas Gilcrease Institute of American History and Art. Arbuckle to Leavenworth, May 2, 1834, National Archives Record Group 393, Letters Received, Fort Gibson, Box 1.
12. *Arkansas Gazette*, July 1, 1834, p. 2.
13. [Hildreth], *The Dragoon Campaigns to the Rocky Mountains*, 104–105. W. J. Ghent, "Henry Leavenworth," in *Dictionary of American Biography*, XI, 80.
14. Macomb to Leavenworth, February 19, 1834, National Archives, Record Group 393, Letters Received, Fort Gibson, Box 1, *American State Papers, Military Affairs*, V, 170.
15. Stokes, Ellsworth, and Schermerhorn to Cass, February 3, 1834; Sumner to Dodge, May 24, 1834, National Archives, Record Group 393, Letters Received, Fort Gibson, Box 1. G. Foreman, *Pioneer Days in the Early Southwest*, 119–20. [Hildreth], *The Dragoon Campaigns to the Rocky Mountains*, 118. Stokes to Cass, November 26, 1833, U.S. Congress, Senate, *Document No. 512*, Twenty-third Congress, first session, IV, 734–36. Catlin and Hildreth indicated that the Dragoons returned three Indian women to their tribes. However, the official journal of the expedition mentioned only one Wichita and one Kiowa.
16. Houston and Hughes to Cass, March 12, 1834, cited in Williams and Barker, *The Writings of Sam Houston, 1813–1863*, I, 281–83.
17. Stambaugh to Hawkins, May 24, 1834; Stambaugh to Leavenworth,

May 26, 1834, National Archives, Record Group 393, Letters Received, Fort Gibson, Box 1. Leavenworth to Cass, May 27, 1834; Leavenworth to Almonte, May 25, 1834; Leavenworth to Bean, May 28, 1834, Grant Foreman Collection, Gilcrease Institute.

18. [Hildreth], *The Dragoon Campaigns to the Rocky Mountains*, 103. G. Foreman, *Pioneer Days in the Early Southwest*, 114. Order No. 21, Fort Gibson, June 2, 1834, Grant Foreman Collection, Gilcrease Institute.

19. G. Foreman, *Fort Gibson: A Brief History*, 20. [Hildreth], *The Dragoon Campaigns to the Rocky Mountains*, 119.

20. *Ibid.*, 40–41. Leavenworth to Cass, May 27, 1834, Grant Foreman Collection, Gilcrease Institute.

21. Catlin, *North American Indians*, II, 47. Leavenworth to Adjutant General, May 25, 1834; Leavenworth to Adjutant General, July 3, 1834; Leavenworth to Adjutant General, June 14, 1834, Grant Foreman Collection, Gilcrease Institute.

22. Catlin, *North American Indians*, II, 45. Thompson B. Wheelock, "Peace on the Plains" (ed. by George H. Shirk), *Chronicles of Oklahoma*, Vol. XXVIII (Spring, 1950), 10.

23. Catlin, *North American Indians*, II, 46. Fred S. Perrine and Grant Foreman (eds.), "The Journal of Hugh Evans, Covering the First and Second Campaigns of the United States Dragoon Regiment in 1834 and 1835," *Chronicles of Oklahoma*, Vol III (September, 1925), 182. Louis Pelzer (ed.), "A Journal of Marches by the First United States Dragoons, 1834–1835," *Iowa Journal of History and Politics*, Vol. VII (July, 1909), 342.

24. Wheelock, "Peace on the Plains," *Chronicles of Oklahoma*, Vol. XXVIII (Spring, 1950), 11. Catlin, *North American Indians*, II, 50–51.

25. *Ibid.*

26. Wheelock, "Peace on the Plains," *Chronicles of Oklahoma*, Vol XXVIII (Spring, 1950), 31. Catlin, *North American Indians*, II, 49. This estimate is over twice the number reported ill by Wheelock. Perhaps Catlin included the men who returned to Fort Gibson as well as those who had been temporarily disabled by the fever.

27. Wheelock, "Peace on the Plains," *Chronicles of Oklahoma*, Vol. XXVIII (Spring, 1950), 14. Leavenworth to Dodge, July 5, 1834, Grant Foreman Collection, Gilcrease Institute.

28. Pelzer, "A Journal of Marches by the First United States Dragoons, 1834–1835," *Iowa Journal of History and Politics*, Vol. VII (July, 1909), 344.

29. Catlin, *North American Indians*, II, 54.

30. Pelzer, "A Journal of Marches by the First United States Dragoons, 1834–1835," *Iowa Journal of History and Politics*, Vol VII (July, 1909), 346.

31. Catlin, *North American Indians*, II, 55.
32. *Ibid.*, 56. Pelzer, "A Journal of Marches by the First United States Dragoons, 1834–1835," *Iowa Journal of History and Politics*, Vol. VII (July, 1909), 349. Wheelock, "Peace on the Plains," *Chronicles of Oklahoma*, Vol XXVIII (Spring, 1950), 17.
33. Catlin, *North American Indians*, II, 56.
34. Perrine and Foreman, "The Journal of Hugh Evans," *Chronicles of Oklahoma*, Vol. III (September, 1925), 189. Wheelock, "Peace on the Plains," *Chronicles of Oklahoma*, Vol. XXVIII (Spring, 1950), 18.
35. *Ibid.*, 18–19. Catlin, *North American Indians*, II, 61–62.
36. [Hildreth], *The Dragoon Campaigns to the Rocky Mountains*, 158.
37. Wheelock, "Peace on the Plains," *Chronicles of Oklahoma*, Vol. XXVIII (Spring, 1950), 19.
38. *Ibid.*, 20–21. Pelzer, "A Journal of Marches by the First United States Dragoons, 1834–1835," *Iowa Journal of History and Politics*, Vol. VII (July, 1909), 353.
39. Perrine and Foreman, "The Journal of Hugh Evans," *Chronicles of Oklahoma*, Vol. III (September, 1925), 191.
40. *Ibid.*, 192. Wheelock, in "Peace on the Plains, 22, describes the Indian as the woman's uncle. Pelzer, "A Journal of Marches by the First United States Dragoons, 1834–1835," *Iowa Journal of History and Politics*, Vol. VII (July, 1909), 354.
41. Wheelock, "Peace on the Plains," *Chronicles of Oklahoma*, Vol. XXVIII (Spring, 1950), 22. Perrine and Foreman, "The Journal of Hugh Evans," *Chronicles of Oklahoma*, Vol. III (September, 1925), 193.
42. Wheelock, "Peace on the Plains," *Chronicles of Oklahoma*, Vol. XXVIII (Spring, 1950), 23.
43. *Ibid.*, 23–25. Catlin, *North American Indians*, II, 71.
44. Wheelock, "Peace on the Plains," *Chronicles of Oklahoma*, Vol. XXVIII (Spring, 1950), 27–28.
45. *Ibid.*, 29–30.
46. *Ibid.*, 30–32.
47. [Hildreth], *The Dragoon Campaigns to the Rocky Mountains*, 178.
48. Perrine and Foreman, "The Journal of Hugh Evans," *Chronicles of Oklahoma*, Vol. III (September, 1925), Catlin, *North American Indians*, II, 72. Wheelock, "Peace on the Plains," *Chronicles of Oklahoma*, Vol. XXVIII (Spring, 1950), 34.
49. James D. Morrison (ed.), "Travis G. Wright and the Leavenworth Expedition in Oklahoma," *Chronicles of Oklahoma*, Vol. XXV (Spring, 1947), 11–12. Dodge to Jones, August 24, 1834, Grant Foreman Collection, Gilcrease Institute.
50. Catlin, *North American Indians*, II, 77–79.
51. *Ibid.*, 76. Wheelock, "Peace on the Plains," *Chronicles of Oklahoma*,

Vol. XXVIII (Spring, 1950), 35. Varing Howell Davis, *Jefferson Davis: Ex-President of the Confederate States of America*, I, 155.

52. Wheelock, "Peace on the Plains," *Chronicles of Oklahoma*, Vol. XXVIII (Spring, 1950), 35. Perrine and Foreman, "The Journal

53. Wheelock, "Peace on the Plains," *Chronicles of Oklahoma*, Vol. XXVIII (Spring, 1950), 37. Perrine and Foreman, "The Journal of Hugh Evans," *Chronicles of Oklahoma*, Vol. III (September, 1925), 211–12.

54. Wheelock, "Peace on the Plains," *Chronicles of Oklahoma*, Vol. XXVIII (Spring, 1950), 37–38. *Missionary Herald* (Boston), XXX (December, 1834), 453. Catlin, *North American Indians*, II, 80. Many to Adjutant General, Septermber 25, 1834, Grant Foreman Collection, Gilcrease Institute. Dodge to Jones, October 1, 1834, quoted in Louis Pelzer, *Marches of the Dragoons in the Mississippi Valley*, 47.

55. Leavenworth to Wharton, May 11, 1834, Grant Foreman Collection, Gilcrease Institute. Leo E. Oliva, *Soldiers on the Santa Fe Trail*, 36–41. The best source of information concerning the Wharton expedition is his report reprinted in Fred S. Perrine, "Military Escorts on the Santa Fe Trail," *New Mexico Historical Review*, Vol. II (July, 1927), 269–85.

56. *Ibid.*, 277.

57. *Ibid.*, 284.

58. James D. Richardson (ed.), *A Compilation of the Messages and Papers of the Presidents, 1789–1897*, III, 113.

Chapter 10

1. Cooper to Many, September 20, 1834, Office of the Adjutant General, Letters Sent, 1800–1890, Roll 9. George Catlin, *North American Indians*, II, 82–83.

2. For a biographical sketch of Francis W. Armstrong see Carolyn Thomas Foreman, "The Armstrongs of Indian Territory," *Chronicles of Oklahoma*, Vol. XXX (Autumn, 1952), 293–308. G. Foreman, *Pioneer Days in the Early Southwest*, 154.

3. *Ibid.*, 155. G. Foreman, *Advancing the Frontier*, 137. C. T. Foreman, "The Armstrongs of Indian Territory," *Chronicles of Oklahoma*, Vol. XXX (Autumn, 1952), 303–304. U.S. Congress, House, *Document No. 2*, Twenty-third Congress, second session, 244.

4. Cooper to Arbuckle, September 9, 1834, Office of the Adjutant General, Letters Sent, 1800–1890, Roll 9. Returns from the United States Military Posts, 1800–1916, Roll 404. Seawell to Birch, November 6, 1834; Arbuckle to Jones, November 15, 1834, Fort Gibson Letterbooks. G. Foreman, *Pioneer Days in the Early South-*

west, 115. *Arkansas Gazette,* November 4, 1834, p. 3. For a biographical sketch of Major Mason see Carolyn Thomas Foreman, "General Richard Barnes Mason," *Chronicles of Oklahoma,* Vol. XIX (March, 1941), 14–36.

5. Catlin, *North American Indians,* II, 83. G. Foreman, *Pioneer Days in the Early Southwest,* 157–58. Arbuckle to Many, May 18, 1835, Fort Gibson Letterbooks.

6. *Arkansas Gazette,* January 6, 1835, p. 3. Arbuckle to Jones, January 5, 1835, Fort Gibson Letterbooks.

7. Arbuckle to Armstrong, April 6, 1835; Arbuckle to McCall, January 27, 1835; Miles to Ross, May 18, 1835; Arbuckle to Jones, June 21, 1835, Fort Gibson Letterbooks. McCall to Arbuckle, December 20, 1834, Western Division, 1821–1842, Letters Sent. *Arkansas Gazette,* June 30, 1835, p. 2. Beers, *The Western Military Frontier,* 123–24.

8. Seawell to Bowman, December 27, 1834; Seawell to Britton, January 4, 1835; Seawell to Seaton, February 16, 1835, Fort Gibson Letterbooks. *The Army and Navy Chronicle* (Washington, D.C.), August 27, 1835, p. 279.

9. Arbuckle to Jones, February 1, 1835 and April 3, 1835, Fort Gibson Letterbooks.

10. Arbuckle to Jones, April 15, 1835; Seawell to Raines, April 14, 1835; Arbuckle to Jones, May 4, 1835; Arbuckle to Mason, May 18, 1835; Arbuckle to Macomb, May 18, 1835; Arbuckle to Mason, May 20, 1835, Fort Gibson Letterbooks. Grant Foreman (ed.), "The Journal of the Proceedings at Our First Treaty with the Wild Indians, 1835," *Chronicles of Oklahoma,* Vol. XIV (December, 1936), 398–401.

11. Arbuckle to Many, May 18, 1835, Fort Gibson Letterbooks.

12. The Camp Holmes established in 1835 was not the same as the one established a year earlier by Lieutenant Holmes. The Camp Holmes established in 1834 was located near the present Holdenville, Oklahoma, while the one established by Major Mason was located near the present Lexington, Oklahoma. This site was also referred to as Camp Mason. See William Brown Morrison, *Military Posts and Camps in Oklahoma,* 76–80. Arbuckle to Mason, June 13, 1835; Miles to Seaton, June 15, 1835; Arbuckle to Jones, June 16, 1835, Fort Gibson Letterbooks, Harold W. Jones (ed.), "The Diary of Assistant Surgeon Leonard McPhail on his Journey to the Southwest in 1835," *Chronicles of Oklahoma,* Vol. XVIII (September, 1940), 283.

13. *Ibid.,* 287, 290.

14. Arbuckle to Mason, June 22, 1835; Seawell to Chouteau, July 7, 1835; [Arbuckle to Armstrong], July 7, 1835; Arbuckle to Lee, July 10, 1835; Seawell to Mason, July 8, 1835, Fort Gibson Let-

terbooks. Jones, "The Diary of Assistant Surgeon Leonard McPhail on his Journey to the Southwest in 1835," *Chronicles of Oklahoma*, Vol. XVIII (September, 1940), 285.

15. Seawell to Lee, July 11, 1835; Arbuckle to Armstrong, July 20, 1835, Fort Gibson Letterbooks.

16. Arbuckle to Whistler, September 6, 1835 [This letter is incorrectly dated. It was sent August 6, 1835]; Arbuckle to Vashon, July 15, 1835; Seawell to Jolly, July 15, 1835; Arbuckle to Armstrong, July 20, 1835; Arbuckle to Mason, August 6, 1835, Fort Gibson Letterbooks. Stokes to Cass, July 14, 1835, Lewis Cass Letters, 1835–1839, Regional Manuscript Collections, Division of Manuscripts, University of Oklahoma Library, Box C-32. Armstrong died on August 6, 1835, at his home at the Choctaw agency. C. T. Foreman, "The Armstrongs of Indian Territory," *Chronicles of Oklahoma*, Vol. XXX (Autumn, 1952 and Winter, 1952–53), 306.

17. *Arkansas Gazette*, August 25, 1835, p. 3. Arbuckle to Mason, August 6, 1835, Fort Gibson Letterbooks.

18. George A. Schultz, *An Indian Canaan: Isaac McCoy*, 174–75.

19. G. Foreman, "The Journal of the Proceedings at Our First Treaty with the Wild Indians, 1835," *Chronicles of Oklahoma*, Vol. XIV (December, 1936), 406–407. *Arkansas Gazette*, September 29, 1835, p. 3.

20. G. Foreman, "The Journal of the Proceedings at Our First Treaty with the Wild Indians, 1835," *Chronicles of Oklahoma*, Vol. XIV (December, 1936), 407–408.

21. *Ibid.*, 409–11.

22. *Ibid.*, 406.

23. *Ibid.*, 410–13.

24. *Ibid.*, 413–17. Jones, "The Diary of Assistant Surgeon Leonard McPhail on his Journey to the Southwest in 1835," *Chronicles of Oklahoma*, Vol. XVIII (September, 1940), 289. Returns from the United States Military Posts, 1800–1916, Roll 404. *Arkansas Gazette*, September 29, 1835, p. 3.

25. U.S. Congress, House, *Document No. 2*, Twenty-fourth Congress, first session, 262. Cass to Stokes and Arbuckle, October 14, 1835, The Secretary of War, Letters Sent, 1800–1889, Roll 14. Arbuckle to Cass, September 30, 1835; Arbuckle to Jones, February 16, 1836, Fort Gibson Letterbooks. P. L. Chouteau to Stokes and Arbuckle, April 19 and April 25, 1836, Office of Indian Affairs, Letters Received, 1824–1881, Roll 921.

26. Arbuckle to Gaines, May 17, 1836; Arbuckle to Gaines, May 24, 1836; Arbuckle to McCall, June 7, 1836, Fort Gibson Letterbooks.

27. P. L. Chouteau to Armstrong, February 1, 1837; Armstrong to Harris, February 13, 1837; Stokes to Poinsett, May 20, 1837; Stokes

and A. P. Chouteau to Poinsett, September 8, 1837, Office of
Indian Affairs, Letters Received, 1824–1881, Roll 922.
28. Kappler, *Indian Affairs*, II, 489–90. A. P. Chouteau and Stokes to
Poinsett, September 8, 1837, Office of Indian Affairs, Letters Received, 1824–1881, Roll 922.

Chapter 11

1. Miles to Many, November 24, 1835; Arbuckle to Jones, February 16,
1836, Fort Gibson Letterbooks. One of the best accounts of relations between the United States and Mexico during the period of
the Texas Revolution is Eugene C. Barker, "The United States
and Mexico, 1835–1837," *Mississippi Valley Historical Review*, Vol.
I (June, 1914), 3–30. Another useful summary of the same period
appears in Prucha, *The Sword of the Republic*, 307–11.
2. Arbuckle to Jones, March 8, 1836; Arbuckle to Jones, March 16, 1836;
Arbuckle to Vose, May 26, 1836, Fort Gibson Letterbooks. *Arkansas Gazette*, March 22, 1836, p. 3; April 26, 1836, p. 3.
3. Secretary of War to Gaines, January 23, 1836, in Carter *Territory of
Arkansas*, XXI, 1154–56. *Arkansas Gazette*, February 23, 1836,
p. 3. Jones to Arbuckle, March 10, 1836, Letters Sent, Office of the
Adjutant General, Letters Sent, 1800–1890, Roll 9. Arbuckle to
Whistler, April 20, 1836; Arbuckle to Gaines, April 28, 1836, Fort
Gibson Letterbooks. Gaines' role in the border unrest produced
by the Texas Revolution is traced in James W. Silver, *Edmund
Pendleton Gaines, Frontier General*, 191–215.
4. Gaines to Arbuckle, April 12, 1836, Western Division, 1821–1842,
Letters Sent. Arbuckle to Gaines, May 8, 1836, Fort Gibson Letterbooks.
5. Mather to Emily [last name unknown], May 8, 1836; Mather to Emily
[last name unknown], May 20, 1836, Grant Foreman Collection,
Thomas Gilcrease Institute of American History and Art.
6. Arbuckle to Gaines, May 17, 1836, Fort Gibson Letterbooks. *Arkansas
Gazette*, May 3, 1836, p. 3; May 10, 1836, p. 3.
7. Arbuckle to Vose, June 7, 1836, Fort Gibson Letterbooks. *Arkansas
Gazette*, May 17, 1836, p. 3; June 7, 1836, p. 2; May 31, 1836,
p. 3.
8. *Ibid.*, July 26, 1836, p. 2.
9. Arbuckle to Gaines, June 22, 1836; Arbuckle to Jones, June 28, 1836,
Fort Gibson Letterbooks.
10. Cass to Arbuckle, July 20, 1836, Office of the Adjutant General,
Letters Sent, 1800–1890, Roll 9. Arbuckle to Fulton, July 13,
1836; Arbuckle to Fulton, July 18, 1836, Fort Gibson Letterbooks.

11. Arbuckle to McCall, July 18, 1836, *Ibid. Arkansas Gazette*, December 13, 1836, p. 2.
12. Arbuckle to McCall, July 21, 1836; Arbuckle to Fulton, August 16, 1836, Fort Gibson Letterbooks. *Arkansas Gazette*, August 2, 1836, p. 2.
13. Arbuckle to Fulton, August 16, 1836; Arbuckle to Fulton, September 4, 1836, Fort Gibson Letterbooks. *Arkansas Gazette*, August 23, 1836, p. 2; August 30, 183, p. 2; September 6, 1836, p. 3.
14. *Ibid.*, September 27, 1836, p. 3. Arbuckle to Kearny, October 5, 1836; Arbuckle to Vose, September 8, 1836, Fort Gibson Letterbooks.
15. Arbuckle to McCall, September 12, 1836; Arbuckle to Harris, September 12, 1836, *Ibid. Arkansas Gazette*, October 4, 1836, p. 3.
16. *Ibid.* Arbuckle to McIntosh, September 26, 1836; Arbuckle to Gaines, October 3, 1836; Arbuckle to Jones, October 14, 1836, Fort Gibson Letterbooks.
17. Arbuckle to McCall, October 11, 1836; Arbuckle to McCall, October 15, 1836; Arbuckle to Jones, November 1, 1836; Arbuckle to Jones, November 6, 1836, *Ibid.*
18. *Ibid.*
19. Arbuckle to Conway, November 8, 1836; Arbuckle to Wilson, November 15, 1836, *Ibid.* Returns of the United States Military Posts, 1800–1816, Roll 404.
20. *Arkansas Gazette*, October 18, 1836, p. 2; November 22, 1836, p. 2; November 8, 1836, p. 3.
21. *Ibid.*, November 15, 1836, p. 2; January 17, 1837, pp. 1–2; December 20, 1836, p. 2. C. A. H. [Harris] to Arbuckle, October 10, 1836, The Secretary of War, Letters Sent, 1800–1889, Roll 15. Arbuckle to Whistler, November 30, 1836; Arbuckle to Jones, November 28, 1836, Fort Gibson Letterbooks. Returns from United States Military Posts, 1800–1916, Roll 404.
22. Arbuckle to Secretary of War, December 3, 1836; Arbuckle to Jones, December 12, 1836, Fort Gibson Letterbooks. *Arkansas Gazette*, January 10, 1837, p. 2.
23. Arbuckle to Jones, December 27, 1836; Arbuckle to Jones, December 27, 1836 [Arbuckle wrote two letters to Jones on the same day], Fort Gibson Letterbooks. *Arkansas Gazette*, December 27, 1836, p. 2; January 3, 1837, p. 2.
24. Arbuckle to Deas, January 6, 1837, Fort Gibson Letterbooks. *Arkansas Gazette*, January 3, 1837, p. 2.
25. Arbuckle to Jones, January 15, 1837; Arbuckle to Jones, January 3, 1837; Arbuckle to Vose, January 17, 1837; Arbuckle to Jones, January 24, 1837; Arbuckle to Jones, February 21, 1837, Fort

Gibson Letterbooks. *The Army and Navy Chronicle* (Washington, D.C.), April 13, 1837, p. 238.

26. Arden to Rector, March 8, 1837, Fort Gibson Letterbooks. Returns from United States Military Posts, 1800–1916, Roll 404.

27. Arbuckle to Jones, March 14, 1837, Fort Gibson Letterbooks.

28. Folsom to Vose, December 23, 1836; Armstrong to Harris, February 13, 1837, Office of Indian Affairs, Letters Received, 1824–1881, Roll 922. *Arkansas Gazette*, January 10, 1837, p. 2; February 28, 1837, p. 3. Arbuckle to Jones, January 3, 1837, Fort Gibson Letterbooks.

29. Armstrong to Harris, April 20, 1837, Office of Indian Affairs, Letters Received, 1824–1881, Roll 922. *Arkansas Gazette*, March 21, 1837, p. 2; April 25, 1837, p. 2; May 2, 1837, pp. 2–3. Returns from United States Military Posts, 1800–1916, Roll 404.

30. Arbuckle to Jones, December 18, 1836; Arbuckle to Many, May 5, 1837, Fort Gibson Letterbooks. Returns form United States Military Posts, 1800–1916, Roll 404.

Chapter 12

1. Memorial to Congress by the Territorial Assembly, [October 24, 1835], in Carter, *Territory of Arkansas*, XXI, 1112–13. *Arkansas Gazette*, April 19, 1836, p. 2. *American State Papers: Military Affairs*, VI, 181–82.

2. *Ibid.*, 184. Arbuckle to Jones, May 30, 1836; Arbuckle to Jones, June 28, 1836, Fort Gibson Letterbooks.

3. *American State Papers: Military Affairs*, VI, 182–83.

4. *Ibid.*, 149–55, 366–67. *U.S. Statutes at Large*, V, 30

5. *Arkansas Gazette*, August 23, 1836, p. 3; December 13, 1836, p. 2.

6. *Ibid.*, January 31, 1837, p. 2. Arbuckle to the Secretary of War, December 12, 1836, Fort Gibson Letterbooks.

7. Kearny, Smith, and Boon to Secretary of War, January 12, 1837, U.S. Congress, House, *Document No. 278*, Twenty-fifth Congress, second session, 14–15.

8. *Arkansas Gazette*, March 21, 1837, p. 2. *The Army and Navy Chronicle* (Washington, D.C.), April 13, 1837, p. 238.

9. Bearss and Gibson, *Fort Smith*, 149–50. Prucha, *The Sword of the Republic*, 342–43. G. Foreman, *Advancing the Frontier*, 52. *Arkansas Gazette*, January 10, 1838, p. 2.

10. Whistler and Stuart to Macomb, September 30, 1837, U.S. Congress, Senate, *Report No. 224*, Twenty-fifth Congress, second session, 9–11.

11. Whistler and Stuart to Poinsett, December 15, 1837, *Ibid.*, 14–15.

12. *Ibid.*, 1. Bearss and Gibson, *Fort Smith*, 151–52.
13. G. Foreman, *Advancing the Frontier*, 33, 55, 77.
14. *Annual Report of the Commissioner of Indian Affairs for 1837*, 37–38.
15. Armstrong to C. A. Harris, May 28, 1837; Chouteau to Harris, September 8, 1837; Chouteau to Poinsett, September 18, 1837; Chouteau to Harris, January 3, 1838, Office of Indian Affairs, Letters Received, 1824–1881, Roll 922.
16. Arbuckle to Trenor, October 31, 1837; Arbuckle to Jones, November 5, 1837; Arbuckle to Jones, December 5, 1837, Fort Gibson Letterbooks. Chouteau to Harris, November 25, 1837, Office of Indian Affairs, Letters Received, 1824–1881, Roll 922. *Arkansas Gazette*, December 5, 1837, p. 3.
17. Chouteau to Harris, December 8, 1837; Chouteau to Harris, December 16, 1837, Office of Indian Affairs, Letters Received, 1824–1881, Roll 922. Simmons to Northrop, April 10, 1838, Fort Gibson Letterbooks.
18. Rains to Harris, May 22, 1838; Stokes to Poinsett, June 20, 1838; Chouteau to Harris, June 28, 1838, Office of Indian Affairs, Letters Received, 1824–1881, Roll 922. Arbuckle to Chouteau, June 1, 1838, Fort Gibson Letterbooks.
19. *Annual Report of the Commissioner of Indian Affairs for 1838*, 515. Arbuckle to Gaines, July 17, 1838, Fort Gibson Letterbooks. Armstrong to Crawford, December 31, 1838, Office of Indian Affairs, Letters Received, 1824–1881, Roll 922.
20. Armstrong to Crawford, December 31, 1838; Northrop to Poinsett, February 14, 1839; Rogers to Arbuckle, May 3, 1839, *Ibid.* Simmons to Bowman, May 8, 1839, Fort Gibson Letterbooks.
21. Simmons to Armstrong, May 27, 1839; Arbuckle to Armstrong, June 3, 1839, *Ibid.* Armstrong to Crawford, June 8, 1839, Office of Indian Affairs, Letters Received, 1824–1881, Roll 922.
22. *Arkansas Gazette*, December 5, 1837, p. 3.
23. Arbuckle to the Adjutant and Inspector General, Headquarters, Western Division, November 21, 1837; Simmons to Cooke, December 23, 1837; Arbuckle to Jones, December 24, 1837; Arbuckle to Jones, January 3, 1838, Fort Gibson Letterbooks.
24. Arbuckle to Trenor, March 31, 1838; Arbuckle to Jones, April 1, 1838; Arbuckle to Jones, April 16, 1838; Arbuckle to Tuckbachchi Mico, April 19, 1839; Arbuckle to Darrissau, April 19, 1838; Arbuckle to Harris, August 27, 1838, *Ibid.*
25. [Arbuckle or his aide] to Northrop, November 4, 138; Arbuckle to Armstrong, September 26, 1838; Arbuckle to Armstrong, September 29, 1838; Arbuckle to Armstrong, January 9, 1839; Arbuckle to Crawford, January 11, 1839; Arbuckle to Crawford, January 25, 1839, *Ibid.* Kappler, *Indian Affairs*, II, 525–27.

26. Arbuckle to Ritchie, February 14, 1839; Simmons to Bowman, March 19, 1839, Fort Gibson Letterbooks.

27. Edwin C. McReynolds, *The Seminoles* 173.

28. Arbuckle to Jones, June 13, 1838; Arbuckle to Armstrong, August 14, 1838; Arbuckle to Jones, September 11, 1838, Fort Gibson Letterbooks. Grant Foreman, *Indian Removal: The Emigration of the Five Civilized Tribes of Indians*, 370.

29. Arbuckle to Armstrong, April 15, 1839; Arbuckle to Opoth-le-y-ohole, April 19, 1839, Fort Gibson Letterbooks.

30. Armstrong to Crawford, May 2, 1839, Office of Indian Affairs, Letters Received, 1824–1881, Roll 922. Arbuckle to Armstrong, June 19, 1839, Fort Gibson Letterbooks.

31. Kappler, *Indian Affairs*, II, 550–52. Grant Foreman, *The Five Civilized Tribes*, 223–35.

32. *Arkansas Gazette*, November 21, 1837, p. 2; November 28, 1837, p. 2. Simmons to Vose, February 10, 1838; Arbuckle to Jones, February 11, 1838, Fort Gibson Letterbooks.

33. Vose to Arbuckle, April 12, 1838; Vose to Jones, April 13, 1838, U.S. Congress, Senate, *Report No. 487*, Twenty-fifth Congress, second session, 2–4. *Arkansas Gazette*, April 11, 1838, p. 2.

34. Arbuckle to Jones, May 16, 1838; Arbuckle to Conway, May 16, 1838, Fort Gibson Letterbooks. *Arkansas Gazette*, May 23, 1838, p. 2; May 30, 1838, p. 2.

35. *Ibid.* Arbuckle to Jones, May 23, 1838; Arbuckle to Jones, May 30, 1838; Arbuckle to Jones, June 6, 1838, Fort Gibson Letterbooks.

36. Arbuckle to Jones, May 30, 1838; Simmons to Vose, May 30, 1838, *Ibid.*

37. Arbuckle to the Adjutant and Inspector General, Headquarters, Western Division, June 6, 1838, *Ibid. Arkansas Gazette*, June 20, 1838, p. 2.

38. Arbuckle to Jones, June 19, 1838, Fort Gibson Letterbooks. Cooper to Arbuckle, July 26, 1838, The Secretary of War, Letters Sent, 1800–1889, Roll 19.

39. Arbuckle to Jones, July 17, 1838, Fort Gibson Letterbooks. *Arkansas Gazette*, September 19, 1838, p. 2; September 26, 1838, p. 3.

40. *Ibid.*, October 10, 1838, pp. 2–3.

41. Arbuckle to Mason, July 31, 1838; Arbuckle to Jones, August 3, 1838, Fort Gibson Letterbooks.

42. *Arkansas Gazette*, August 1, 1838, p. 2. Arbuckle to Crawford, January 12, 1839, Fort Gibson Letterbooks. Kappler, *Indian Affairs*, II, 524–25.

43. *Arkansas Gazette*, September 19, 1838, p. 2.

44. *Ibid.* Arbuckle to the Adjutant and Inspector General, Headquarters, Western Division, September 4, 1838; Arbuckle to Vose, Sep-

tember 4, 1838; Arbuckle to Roan, September 5, 1838, Fort Gibson Letterbooks. Wisehart, *Sam Houston: American Giant*, 346.

45. *Arkansas Gazette*, September 5, 1838, p. 2; September 26, 1838, p. 2. Arbuckle to Jones, September 12, 1838; Arbuckle to Ried, September 29, 1838, Fort Gibson Letterbooks.

46. Arbuckle to Jones, September 12, 1838, *Ibid. Arkansas Gazette*, October 10, 1838, p. 2.

47. Arbuckle to the Principal Chief of the Cherokees, September 23, 1838; Arbuckle to Jones, September 25, 1838; Arbuckle to Mason, September 29, 1838; Arbuckle to Reid, September 29, 1838, Fort Gibson Letterbooks.

48. Arbuckle to the Adjutant and Inspector General, Headquarters, Western Division, October 24, 1838; Arbuckle to the Adjutant and Inspector General, Headquarters, Western Division, October 31, 1838; Arbuckle to Jones, January 19, 1839, *Ibid.*

49. Stokes to Crawford, March 20, 1839, Office of Indian Affairs, Letters Received, 1824–1881, Roll 83.

Chapter 13

1. Arbuckle to Gaines, July 17, 1838, Fort Gibson Letterbooks.

2. Morris L. Wardell, *A Political History of the Cherokee Nation, 1838–1907*, 12. Stokes to Poinsett, July 24, 1839, *Annual Report of the Commissioner of Indian Affairs for 1839*, 354–55.

3. Address of John Ross to General Council of the Eastern and Western Cherokees at Takattokah, June 10, 1839; Resolution of the National Committee and Council of the Eastern Cherokees, June 19, 1839, National Archives, Record Group 393, Letters Received, Fort Gibson. Brown, Looney, and Rogers to Stokes, June 19, 1839; Ross et al. to Stokes, June 21, 1839, *Annual Report of the Commissioner of Indian Affairs for 1839*, 356–57. Arbuckle to Opoth-yo-ho-to, July 4, 1839, Fort Gibson Letterbooks. G. Foreman, *The Five Civilized Tribes*, 292.

4. Grant Foreman (ed.), "The Murder of Elias Boudinot," *Chronicles of Oklahoma*, Vol. XII (March, 1934), 23–24. U.S. Congress, House, *Executive Document No. 185*, Twenty-ninth Congress, first session, 55. *Arkansas Gazette*, August 21, 1839, p. 2. Wardell, *A Political History of the Cherokee Nation*, 17.

5. Arbuckle to Ross, June 23, 1839; Arbuckle to Opoth-yo-ho-to, July 4, 1839; Arbuckle to Ross, June 24, 1839, Fort Gibson Letterbooks. Ross to Arbuckle, June 23, 1839; Ross to Arbuckle, June 24, 1839 [two letters, same date]; Lear to Arbuckle, June 25, 1839, *Annual Report of the Commissioner of Indian Affairs for 1839*, 360–63.

6. Brown, Looney, Rogers, and Smith to Ross and other chiefs or prin-

cipal men of the emigrant Cherokees, June 28, 1839; J. Ross, Lowry, Gunter and L. Ross to Arbuckle and Stokes, June 30, 1839, *Ibid.*, 364–68. Arbuckle and Stokes to John Ross and other chiefs or principal men of the emigrant Cherokees, June 29, 1839; Arbuckle to Opoth-yo-ho-to, July 4, 1839, Fort Gibson Letterbooks.

7. Ross, et al. to Brown, Looney, and Rogers, July 5, 1839, *Annual Report of the Commissioner of Indian Affairs for 1839*, 370–71. Arbuckle to Ross and others, July 8, 1839, Fort Gibson Letterbooks.

8. Arbuckle to Jones, July 10, 1839, *Ibid.* Armstrong to Crawford, July 20, 1839; Proclamation of the Cherokee National Convention, July 12, 1839; Proclamation of the Cherokee National Convention, July 13, 1839; Proclamation of the Cherokee National Convention, July 10, 1839, *Annual Report of the Commissioner of Indian Affairs for 1839*, 375–76, 389–93.

9. Lowry, Guess, et al. to Arbuckle, July 12, 1839; Lowery, Guess, et al. to Arbuckle, July 20, 1839, *Ibid.*, 394, 400–402. Arbuckle to Ross and others, July 14, 1839; Arbuckle to Ross and others, July 17, 1839, Fort Gibson Letterbooks.

10. Arbuckle to Ross and others, July 18, 1839; Arbuckle to Ross and others, July 20, 1839, *Ibid.* Lowery, Guess, et al. to Arbuckle, July 20, 1839, *Annual Report of the Commissioner of Indian Affairs for 1839*, 400–402.

11. Lowry, Guess, et al. to Arbuckle, July 24, 1839, *Ibid.*, 376–78. Arbuckle to Brown, Looney and Rogers, July 22, 1839; Arbuckle to Ross and others, July 29, 1839, Fort Gibson Letterbooks.

12. *Ibid.* Lowery, et al. to Arbuckle, August 7, 1839, *Annual Report of the Commissioner of Indian Affairs for 1839*, 382–83.

13. Arbuckle to Brown, Looney, and Rogers, July 22, 1839; Arbuckle to Ross and others, August 4, 1839, Fort Gibson Letterbooks. Brown, Looney and Rogers to Arbuckle, August 3, 1839; Lowry, Guess, et al. to Brown, Looney, and Rogers, August 6, 1839, *Annual Report of the Commissioner of Indian Affairs for 1839*, 380–82.

14. Brown, Looney & Rogers to Armstrong, August 9, 1839; Lowery, Guess, et al. to Armstrong, August 27, 1839; Resolution of the Cherokee National Convention, August 23, 1839, *Ibid.*, 384–87. Arbuckle to Ross and others, August 12, 1839, Fort Gibson Letterbooks.

15. Resolution, treaty party of the Cherokee Indians, August 20, 1839; Resolution of treaty party of the Cherokee Indians to Poinsett, August 20, 1839; Proclamation of the National Convention, August 28, 1839; Adair and Bell to Armstrong, September 2, 1839, *Annual Report of the Commissioner of Indian Affairs for 1839*, 405–409.

16. Arbuckle to Jones, September 4, 1839; Arbuckle to Bell and others, September 2, 1839; Arbuckle to Ross and others, September 4,

1839, Fort Gibson Letterbooks. Armstrong to Adair, Bell and others, September 4, 1839, *Annual Report of the Commissioner of Indian Affairs for 1839*, 410.

17. Lowery, et al. to Arbuckle, September 5, 1839; Cooper to Arbuckle, August 20, 1839, *Ibid.*, 419, 413–14.

18. Arbuckle to Yell, September 24, 1839, Fort Gibson Letterbooks.

19. Armstrong to Crawford, October 10, 1839, *Annual Report of the Commissioner of Indian Affairs for 1839*, 424. Arbuckle and Armstrong to Ross, September 28, 1839, Fort Gibson Letterbooks.

20. Ross to Arbuckle and Armstrong, September 30, 1839, *Annual Report of the Commissioner of Indian Affairs for 1839*, 420–21. Arbuckle to Ross, October 14, 1839, Fort Gibson Letterbooks.

21. Arbuckle to Jones, October 8, 1839, *Ibid.*

22. Coodey, Wolf, Ross, and Vann to Stokes, October 7, 1839; Coodey, Wolf, & Ross to Lynch and Carter, October 12, 1839, U.S. Congress, House, *Document No. 129*, Twenty-sixth Congress, first session, 108–10, 26.

23. Armstrong to Yell, October 15, 1839; Arbuckle to Jones, October 16, 1839; Simmons to Mason, November 3, 1839, Fort Gibson Letterbooks.

24. Arbuckle to Kearny, November 10, 1839; Arbuckle to Kearny, November 12, 1839; Arbuckle to Jones, November 19, 1839, *Ibid.*

25. Crawford to Armstrong, October 8, 1839; Poinsett to Armstrong, October 12, 1839, *Annual Report of the Commission of Indian Affairs for 1839*, 114–17.

26. Stokes to the people composing the Cherokee nation, November 11, 1839; Resolution of the Cherokee National Council, November 5, 1839; Rogers, Smith, and Dutch to Arbuckle, November 7, 1839; [Adair] to [Bell and Watie], November 26, 1839, U.S. Congress, House, *Document No. 188*, Twenty-sixth Congress, first session, 17–21, 41. Arbuckle to John and William Rogers, October 23, 1839; Arbuckle to Rogers, Smith and Dutch, November 10, 1839, Fort Gibson Letterbooks.

27. Arbuckle to Armstrong, October 16, 1839, *Ibid.* Stokes to the people composing the Cherokee nation, November 11, 1839, U.S. Congress, House, *Document No. 188*, Twenty-sixth Congress, first session, 20–21.

28. Rogers, Smith, and Dutch to Wilson, November 16, 1839; Stokes and Arbuckle to [Wilson], November 16, 1839, *Ibid.*, 21–23.

29. Rogers, Smith and Dutch to Stokes, November 22, 1839; Crawford to Armstrong, January 2, 1840, *Ibid.*, 25–26.

30. Arbuckle to Jones, November 24, 1839, Fort Gibson Letterbooks.

31. *Ibid.*

32. Arbuckle to Vann, December 5, 1839; Arbuckle to Poinsett, De-

cember 11, 1839, *Ibid*. Vann to Arbuckle, December 6, 1839, U.S. Congress, House, *Document No. 188*, Twenty-sixth Congress, first session, 29.

33. Poinsett to Arbuckle, November 9, 1839, *Annual Report of the Commissioner of Indian Affairs for 1839*, 425–26. Arbuckle to Vann, December 14, 1839; Arbuckle to Rogers, December 15, 1839, Fort Gibson Letterbooks.

34. Stokes to the chiefs, council, and head men of the Cherokee Nation [undated]; Stokes, Vann, et al. to the Cherokee people, December 20, 1839; Agreement between Stokes and Vann et al., December 20, 1839, U.S. Congress, House, *Document No. 129*, Twenty-sixth Congress, first session, 14–17.

35. Arbuckle to Vann, December 24, 1839; Arbuckle to Poinsett, December 26, 1839, Fort Gibson Letterbooks. Vann to Arbuckle, December 24, 1839, U.S. Congress, House, *Document No. 188*, Twenty-sixth Congress, first session, 34.

36. Arbuckle to Vann, January 3, 1840; Arbuckle to Vann, January 14, 1840, Fort Gibson Letterbooks.

37. Address of Stokes to Cherokee National Convention [no date]; Decrees of Cherokee National Convention, January 16, 1840, U.S. Congress, House, *Document No. 129*, Twenty-sixth Congress, first session, 20–22.

38. Coodey, Wolf, and Carter to Arbuckle, January 17, 1840; Page to Arbuckle, January 20, 1840, U.S. Congress, House, *Document No. 188*, Twenty-sixth Congress, first session, 47–49. Arbuckle to Poinsett, January 22, 1840, Fort Gibson Letterbooks.

39. Arbuckle to Poinsett, January 28, 1840; Arbuckle to Poinsett, February 10, 1840, *Ibid*. Report of the Select Committee of the Cherokees, February 7, 1840, U.S. Congress, House, *Document No. 188*, Twenty-sixth Congress, first session, 64.

40. [unidentified clerk writing in behalf of the Secretary of War], to Lynch, et al., January 2, 1840; Poinsett to Lynch, et al., January 4, 1840, *Ibid.*, 38, 40. Petition and Memorial of Ross, et al., February 28, 1840, U.S. Congress, House, *Document No. 129*, Twenty-sixth Congress, first session, 1–10.

41. Rogers, Bell, and Watie to Poinsett, January 22, 1840, U.S. Congress, House, *Document No. 188*, Twenty-sixth Congress, first session, 42–43.

42. Poinsett to Crawford, March 6, 1840; Poinsett to Arbuckle, March 7, 1840, *Ibid.*, 53–56.

43. Arbuckle to Rogers, April 9, 1840, Fort Gibson Letterbooks. Address of General M. Arbuckle to deputation of Old Settlers, April 21, 1840; Martin, et al. to [Arbuckle], April 22, 1840; Vann to Arbuckle, April 24, 1840; Resolution of the Cherokee National Council, April 24, 1840; Statement of the Cherokee National

Council, April 25, 1840, *Annual Report of the Commissioner of Indian Affairs for 1840*, 262–66.

44. Arbuckle to Vann, May 11, 1840; Arbuckle to Vann, June 2, 1840; Arbuckle to Poinsett, June 9, 1840, Fort Gibson Letterbooks. Bennington, Wolf, and Vann to Arbuckle, June 3, 1840, *Annual Report of the Commissioner of Indian Affairs for 1840*, 270.

45. Arbuckle to Poinsett, June 28, 1840, Fort Gibson Letterbooks. The Act of Union does not contain this provision, which apparently was an unwritten understanding suggested by Arbuckle to break the deadlock in negotiations. Wardell observed, "The Old Settlers, however, had accepted the constitution of September 6, 1839, only on the condition that it be referred to the people for approval. This was never done." Wardell, *A Political History of the Cherokee Nation*, 41–42.

46. Arbuckle to Poinsett, June 28, 1840, Fort Gibson Letterbooks. Agreement by representatives of the Eastern and Western Cherokees, June 26, 1840, *Annual Report of the Commissioner of Indian Affairs for 1840*, 271–72.

47. Arbuckle to Wallace, June 30, 1840; Arbuckle to Jones, June 1, 1841; Arbuckle to Sevier, June 1, 1841, Fort Gibson Letterbooks. *Arkansas Gazette*, July 7, 1841, p. 2.

48. Arbuckle to Jones, June 21, 1841, Fort Gibson Letterbooks.

Chapter 14

1. William T. Hagan, *American Indians*, 86–87. Helen H. H. Jackson, *A Century of Dishonor: A Sketch of the United States Government's Dealings with Some of the Indian Tribes*, 29.
2. G. Foreman, *Indian Removal*, 8–9.
3. Francis Paul Prucha, *The Sword of the Republic*, xvi.

Bibliography

Primary Sources

MANUSCRIPTS

Fort Gibson Letterbooks, Records of the United States Army Continental Commands, 1821–1920, National Archives, Record Group 393.

Fort Gibson, Letters Received, Records of the United States Army Continental Commands, 1821–1890, National Archives, Record Group 393.

Grant Foreman Collection, Thomas Gilcrease Institute of American History and Art, Tulsa, Oklahoma.

Inspection Reports of the Office of the Inspector General, 1814–1842, National Archives, Microcopy 624.

"Journal of Union Mission" (typescript in Cherokee Room) Northeastern Oklahoma State University.

Lewis Cass Letters, 1835–1839, Regional Manuscript Collections, Division of Manuscripts, University of Oklahoma Library.

Office of Indian Affairs, Letters Received, 1824–1881, National Archives, Microcopy 234.

Office of the Adjutant General, Letters Received, 1822–1860, National Archives, Microcopy 567.

Office of the Adjutant General, Letters Sent, 1800–1890, National Archives, Microcopy 565.

Officers' Roster, Fort Gibson, 1824–1857, Compiled by the Adjutant General's Office, War Department, June 11, 1936, Grant Foreman Collection, Oklahoma Historical Society, Oklahoma City.

Post Quartermaster, Fort Gibson, Letters Sent, Records of the Office of the Quartermaster General, National Archives, Record Group 92.

Returns from United States Military Posts, 1800–1916, National Archives, Microcopy 617.

Sam Houston Collection, Thomas Gilcrease Institute of American History and Art, Tulsa, Oklahoma.

The Secretary of War, Letters Sent, 1800–1889, National Archives, Microcopy 6.

Western Division, 1821–1842, Letters Sent, Records of the United States Continental Army Commands, 1821–1920, National Archives, Record Group 393.

GOVERNMENT DOCUMENTS

American State Papers: Indian Affairs, I, II.
American State Papers: Military Affairs, V, VI.
Arkansas Acts: Acts Passed at the Fifth Session of the General Assembly of the Territory of Arkansas, Little Rock, 1828.
Carter, Clarence E., comp. and ed. *Territorial Papers of the United States*. Washington, Government Printing Office, 26 vols., 1949–1962. *The Territory of Louisiana-Missouri, 1806–1821*. Vols. XIV and XV, 1949–1951. *The Territory of Arkansas, 1819–1836*. Vols. XIX, XX, and XXI, 1953–54.
Heitman, Francis B. *Historical Register and Dictionary of the United States Army*. 2 vols. Washington, Government Printing Office, 1903.
Kappler, Charles J., comp. and ed. *Indian Affairs: Laws and Treaties*. 3 vols. Washington, Government Printing Office, 1904.
La Flesche, Francis. "The Osage Tribe," In *Thirty-Sixth Annual Report*. Bureau of American Ethnology. Washington, Government Printing Office, 1921.
Mooney, James. "Calendar History of the Kiowa Indians." In *Seventeenth Annual Report*. Part 1. Washington, Government Printing Office, 1898.
———. "Myths of the Cherokee." In *Nineteenth Annual Report*. Bureau of American Ethnology. 2 parts. Washington, Government Printing Office, 1900.
Report of the Commissioner of Indian Affairs, 1837–1840.
Richardson, James D., ed. *A Compilation of the Messages and Papers of the Presidents, 1789–1897*. 10 vols. Washington, Government Printing Office, 1896.
Royce, Charles C. "The Cherokee Nation of Indians." In *Fifth Annual Report*. Bureau of American Ethnology. Washington, Government Printing Office, 1887.
Thian, Raphael P., comp. *Notes Illustrating the Military Geography of the United States*. Washington, Government Printing Office, 1881.
United States House of Representatives. *Document No. 263*. Twentieth Congress, first session.
———. *Document No. 2*. Twenty-second Congress, first session.
———. *Document No. 172*. Twenty-third Congress, first session.
———. *Report No. 474*. Twenty-third Congress, first session.
———. *Report No. 502*. Twenty-third Congress, first session.
———. *Document No. 2*. Twenty-third Congress, second session.
———. *Document No. 2*. Twenty-fourth Congress, first session.
———. *Document No. 278*. Twenty-fifth Congress, second session.
———. *Document No. 129*. Twenty-sixth Congress, first session.
———. *Document No. 188*. Twenty-sixth Congress, first session.
———. *Executive Document No. 185*. Twenty-ninth Congress, first session.

United States Senate. *Document No. 1.* Twenty-third Congress, first session.
———. *Document No. 512.* Twenty-third Congress, first session.
———. *Report No. 224.* Twenty-fifth Congress, second session.
———. *Report No. 487.* Twenty-fifth Congress, second session.
United States Statutes at Large, III, IV, V.

NEWSPAPERS

Arkansas Gazette (Little Rock).
The Army and Navy Chronicle (Washington, D. C.).
The Cherokee Phoenix and Indians' Advocate (New Echota, Ga.).
Missionary Herald (Boston).
Niles Weekly Register (Baltimore).

BOOKS

Adams, John Quincy. *Memoirs of John Quincy Adams Comprising Portions of His Diary from 1795 to 1848.* Ed. by Charles Francis Adams. 11 vols. Philadelphia, Lippincott, 1874–77.
Catlin, George. *Letters and Notes on the Manners, Customs, and Condition of the North American Indian.* 2 vols. 4th ed. London, David Bogue, 1844.
Cooke, Philip St. George. *Scenes and Adventures in the Army: or Romance of Military Life.* Philadelphia, Lindsey and Blakiston, 1857.
Coues, Elliott, ed. *The Expeditions of Zebulon Montgomery Pike: To Headwaters of the Mississippi River, Through Louisiana Territory, and in New Spain, During the Years 1805-6-7.* 3 vols. New York, Francis P. Harper, 1895.
Davis, Varing Howell. *Jefferson Davis: Ex-President of the Confederate States of America.* 2 vols. New York, Belford Company, Publishers, 1890.
Ellsworth, Henry Leavitt. *Washington Irving on the Prairies or A Narrative of a Tour of the Southwest in the Year 1832.* Ed. by Stanley T. Williams and Barbara D. Simison. New York, American Book Company, 1937.
Gregg, Josiah. *Commerce of the Prairies.* Ed. by Max L. Moorhead. Norman, University of Oklahoma Press, 1954.
[Hildreth, James]. *The Dragoon Campaigns to the Rocky Mountains: Being a History of the Enlistment, Organization, and First Campaigns of the Regiment of United States Dragoons: Together with Incidents of a Soldier's Life, and Sketches of Scenery and Indian Character.* New York, Wiley and Long, 1836.
Houck, Louis, ed. *The Spanish Regime in Missouri.* 2 vols. Chicago, R. R. Donnelley & Sons, 1909.

Irving, Washington. *A Tour on the Prairies.* Ed. by John Francis McDermott. Norman, University of Oklahoma Press, 1956.

James, Edwin. *Account of an Expedition from Pittsburgh to the Rocky Mountains, Performed in the Years, 1819, 1820.* Vols. XIV, XV, XVI, and XVII of *Early Western Travels, 1748–1846.* Ed. by Reuben G. Thwaites. Cleveland, The Arthur H. Clark Company, 1905.

Latrobe, Charles Joseph. *The Rambler in North America, 1832–1833.* 2 vols. New York, Harper & Brothers, 1835.

———. *The Rambler in Oklahoma: Latrobe's Tour with Washington Irving.* Ed. by Muriel H. Wright and George Shirk. Oklahoma City and Chattanooga, Harlow Publishing Corporation, 1955.

Murray, Charles Augustus. *Travels in North America During the Years 1834, 1835, and 1836.* 2 vols. London, Richard Bentley, 1839.

Nuttall, Thomas. *Journel of Travels into the Arkansas Territory during the Year 1819.* Vol. XIII of *Early Western Travels, 1748–1846.* Ed. by Reuben G. Thwaites. Cleveland, The Arthur H. Clark Company, 1905.

Prucha, Francis Paul, ed. *Army Life on the Western Frontier: Selections from the Official Reports Made Between 1826 and 1845 by Colonel George Croghan.* Norman, University of Oklahoma Press, 1958.

Washburn, Cephas. *Reminiscences of the Indians.* Ed. by Hugh Park. Van Buren, Arkansas, Press-Argus, 1955.

Williams, Amelia W. and Eugene C. Barker, eds. *The Writings of Sam Houston, 1813–1863.* 8 vols. Austin, University of Texas Press, 1938.

ARTICLES AND ESSAYS

Archer, Robert L. "Middle West in Pioneer Days," *National Republic: A Magazine of Fundamental Americanism,* Vol. XXIV (May, 1936), 12–13, 23.

Douglas, Walter B., ed. "Documents—Captain Nathaniel Pryor," *The American Historical Review,* Vol. XXIV (January, 1919), 253–65.

Foreman, Carolyn Thomas, ed. "Notes and Documents: Reports from Fort Gibson, 1835 to 1839," *Chronicles of Oklahoma,* Vol. XXXI (Summer, 1953), 205–11.

———. "Report of Captain John Stuart on the Construction of the Road from Fort Smith to Horse Prairie on Red River," *Chronicles of Oklahoma,* Vol. V (September, 1927), 333–47.

Foreman, Grant, ed. "Captain Nathan Boone's Survey Creek-Cherokee Boundary Line," *Chronicles of Oklahoma,* Vol. IV (December, 1926), 356–65.

———. "The Journal of the Proceedings at Our First Treaty with the

Wild Indians, 1835," *Chronicles of Oklahoma*, Vol. XIV (December, 1936), 393–418.

———. "The Murder of Elias Boudinot," *Chronicles of Oklahoma*, Vol. XII (March, 1934), 19–24.

———. "An Unpublished Report by Captain Bonneville with Introduction and Footnotes," *Chronicles of Oklahoma*, Vol. X (September, 1932), 326–30.

Jones, Harold W., ed. "The Diary of Assistant Surgeon Leonard McPhail on His Journey to the Southwest in 1835," *Chronicles of Oklahoma*, Vol. XVIII (September, 1940), 281–92.

McDermott, John F., ed. "Isaac McCoy's Second Exploring Trip in 1828," *Kansas Historical Quarterly*, Vol. XIII (February, 1945), 400–62.

Morrison, James D., ed. "Travis G. Wright and the Leavenworth Expedition in Oklahoma," *Chronicles of Oklahoma*, Vol. XXV (Spring, 1947), 7–14.

Pelzer, Louis, ed. "A Journal of Marches by the First United States Dragoons, 1834–1835," *Iowa Journal of History and Politics*, Vol. VII (July, 1909), 331–78.

Perrine, Fred S. and Grant Foreman, eds. "The Journal of Hugh Evans, Covering the First and Second Campaigns of the United States Dragoon Regiment in 1834 and 1835," *Chronicles of Oklahoma*, Vol. III (December, 1925), 174–215.

Reynolds, John Hugh, ed. "Official Correspondence of Governor Izard," *Publications of the Arkansas Historical Association*, Vol. I (1906), 423–54.

Thoburn, Joseph B., ed. "The Dragoon Campaign to the Rocky Mountains," *Chronicles of Oklahoma*, Vol. VIII (March, 1930), 35–41.

Wheelock, Thompson B. "Colonel Henry Dodge and his Regiment of Dragoons on the Plains in 1834," *Annals of Iowa*, Vol. XVII, Third Series (January, 1930), 173–97.

———. "Peace on the Plains," Ed. by George H. Shirk, *Chronicles of Oklahoma*, Vol. XXVIII (Spring, 1950), 2–41.

Williams, Stanley T. and Barbara D. Simison, eds. "A Journey through Oklahoma in 1832; A Letter from Henry L. Ellsworth to Professor Benjamin Stillman," *The Mississippi Valley Historical Review*, Vol. XXIX (December, 1942), 387–93.

Secondary Sources

BOOKS

Baird, David W. *The Osage People*. Phoenix, Indian Tribal Series, 1972.

Bearss, Ed and Arrell M. Gibson. *Fort Smith: Little Gibralter on the Arkansas*. Norman, University of Oklahoma Press, 1969.

Beers, Henry Putney. *The Western Military Frontier, 1815–1846*. Philadelphia, Times and News Publishing Co., 1935.

Brackett, Albert G. *History of the United States Cavalry from the Formation of the Federal Government to the First of June, 1863*. New York, Harper and Brothers Publishers, 1865.

Clarke, Dwight L. *Stephen Watts Kearny: Soldier of the West*. Norman, University of Oklahoma Press, 1961.

Clarke, Mary Whatley. *Chief Bowles and the Texas Cherokees*. Norman, University of Oklahoma Press, 1971.

Coit, Margaret L. *John C. Calhoun: American Portrait*. Sentry ed. Boston, Houghton Mifflin Company, 1950.

Cullum, George W. *Biographical Register of the Officers and Graduates of the U.S. Military Academy at West Point, N. Y., from its Establishment, March 16, 1802 to the Army Reorganization of 1866–67*. 3 vols. New York, D. Van Nostrand, 1868.

Day, Donald and Harry Herbert Ullom, eds. *The Autobiography of Sam Houston*. Norman, University of Oklahoma Press, 1954.

Dyer, Brainerd. *Zachary Taylor*. New York, Barnes & Noble, Inc., 1967.

Elliott, Charles Winslow. *Winfield Scott: the Soldier and the Man*. New York, Macmillan, 1937.

Foreman, Grant. *Advancing the Frontier, 1830–60*. Norman, University of Oklahoma Press, 1933.

———. *The Five Civilized Tribes*. Norman, University of Oklahoma Press, 1934.

———. *Ft. Gibson: A Brief History*. Norman, University of Oklahoma Press, 1936.

———. *Indian Removal: The Emigration of the Five Civilized Tribes of Indians*. Norman, University of Oklahoma Press, 1932.

———. *Indians and Pioneers: The Story of the American Southwest Before 1830*. Norman, University of Oklahoma Press, 1936.

———. *Pioneer Days in the Early Southwest*. Cleveland, The Arthur H. Clark Company, 1926.

———. *A Traveler in Indian Territory: A Journal of Ethan Allen Hitchcock, Late Major-General in the United States Army*. Cedar Rapids, Iowa, The Torch Press, 1930.

Frazer, Robert W. *Forts of the West: Military Forts and Presidios and Posts Commonly Called Forts West of the Mississippi River to 1898*. Norman, University of Oklahoma Press, 1965.

Ganoe, William Addleman. *The History of the United States Army*. Rev. ed. New York, Appleton Century, 1924.

Gibson, Arrell M. *The Chickasaws*. Norman, University of Oklahoma Press, 1971.

Graves, William W. *The First Protestant Osage Missions.* Oswego, Kansas, The Carpenter Press, 1949.

Gregory, Jack and Rennard Strickland. *Sam Houston with the Cherokees, 1829–1833.* Austin, University of Texas Press, 1967.

Hagan, William T. *American Indians.* Chicago, The University of Chicago Press, 1961.

Hill, Edward E. *The Office of Indian Affairs, 1824–1880: Historical Sketches.* New York, Clearwater Publishing Company, Inc. 1974.

Hunter, Louis C. *Steamboats on the Western Rivers: An Economic and Technological History.* Cambridge, Harvard University Press, 1949.

Hyde, George. *The Pawnee Indians.* Norman, University of Oklahoma Press, 1973.

Jackson, Helen H. H. *A Century of Dishonor: A Sketch of the United States Government's Dealings with Some of the Indian Tribes.* Boston, Roberts Brothers, 1887.

James, Marquis. *The Raven: A Biography of Sam Houston.* Indianapolis, The Bobbs-Merrill Company, 1929.

Lester, Charles Edward. *The Life of Sam Houston: The Only Authentic Memoir of Him Ever Published.* Philadelphia, G. G. Evans, 1860.

McReynolds, Edwin C. *The Seminoles.* Norman, University of Oklahoma Press, 1957.

Malone, Dumas and Allen Johnson, eds. *Dictionary of American Biography.* 22 vols. New York, Charles Scribner's Sons, 1928–1958.

Mathews, John Joseph. *The Osages: Children of the Middle Waters.* Norman, University of Oklahoma Press, 1961.

Mayhall, Mildred P. *The Kiowas.* Norman, University of Oklahoma Press, 1962.

Morrison, William Brown. *Military Posts and Camps in Oklahoma.* Oklahoma City, Harlow Publishing Corporation, 1936.

Nye, Wilbur Sturtevant. *Carbine and Lance: The Story of Old Fort Sill.* Norman, University of Oklahoma Press, 1937.

Oglesby, Richard Edward. *Manuel Lisa and the Opening of the Missouri Fur Trade.* Norman, University of Oklahoma Press, 1963.

Oliva, Leo E. *Soldiers on the Santa Fe Trail.* Norman, University of Oklahoma Press, 1967.

Pelzer, Louis. *Henry Dodge.* Iowa City, The State Historical Society of Iowa, 1911.

————. *Marches of the Dragoons in the Mississippi Valley: An Account of Marches and Activities of the First Regiment United States Dragoons in the Mississippi Valley Between the Years 1833 and 1850.* Iowa City, The State Historical Society of Iowa, 1917.

Pierson, George W. *Tocqueville in America.* Garden City, Anchor Books, 1959.

Prucha, Francis Paul. *American Indian Policy in the Formative Years: The*

Indian Trade and Intercourse Acts, 1790–1834. Cambridge, Harvard University Press, 1962.

————. *Broadax and Bayonet: The Role of the United States Army in the Development of the Northwest, 1815–1860.* Madison, The State Historical Society of Wisconsin, 1953.

————. *A Guide to the Military Posts of the United States, 1789–1895.* Madison, The State Historical Society of Wisconsin, 1964.

————. *The Sword of the Republic: The United States Army on the Frontier, 1783–1846.* New York, The Macmillan Company, 1969.

Rippy, J. Fred. *Joel R. Poinsett, Versatile American.* Durham, Duke University Press, 1935.

Schultz, George A. *An Indian Canaan: Issac McCoy.* Norman, University of Oklahoma Press, 1972.

Silver, James. W. *Edmund Pendleton Gaines: Frontier General.* Baton Rouge, Louisiana State University Press, 1949.

Starr, Emmet. *History of the Cherokee Indians and Their Legends and Folk Lore.* Oklahoma City, The Warden Company, 1921.

Viola, Herman J. *Thomas L. McKenney: Architect of America's Early Indian Policy, 1816–1830.* Chicago, The Swallow Press, Inc., 1974.

Wardell, Morris L. *A Political History of the Cherokee Nation, 1838–1907.* Norman, University of Oklahoma Press, 1938.

Weigley, Russell F. *History of the United States Army.* New York, The Macmillan Company, 1967.

Wesley, Edgar Bruce. *Guarding the Frontier: A Study of Frontier Defense from 1815–1825.* Minneapolis, University of Minnesota Press, 1935.

Williams, Thomas B. *The Soul of the Red Man.* n.p., 1937.

Wisehart, M. K. *Sam Houston: American Giant.* Washington, Robert B. Luce, Inc., 1962.

Woodward, Grace Steele. *The Cherokees.* Norman, University of Oklahoma Press, 1963.

Wright, Muriel H. *A Guide to the Indian Tribes of Oklahoma.* Norman, University of Oklahoma Press, 1951.

Young, Otis E. *The First Military Escort on the Santa Fe Trail 1829.* Glendale, Calif., The Arthur H. Clark Company, 1952.

ARTICLES AND ESSAYS

Able, Annie Heloise. "The History of Events Resulting in Indian Consolidation West of the Mississippi." *In Annual Report of the American Historical Association for the Year 1906,* I. Washington, Government Printing Office, 1908, 233–450.

Ashcraft, Ginger L. "Antoine Barraque and his Involvement in Indian Affairs of Southeast Arkansas. 1816–1832," *Arkansas Historical Quarterly,* Vol. XXXII (Fall, 1973), 226–40.

Barker, Eugene C. "The United States and Mexico, 1835–1837," *Mississippi Valley Historical Review*, Vol. I (June, 1914), 3–30.

———. "President Jackson and the Texas Revolution," *American Historical Review*, Vol. XII (July, 1907), 788–809.

Eaton, Rachel Caroline. "The Legend of the Battle of Claremore Mound," *Chronicles of Oklahoma*, Vol. VIII (December, 1930), 369–77.

Fensten, Joe. "Indian Removal," *Chronicles of Oklahoma*, Vol. XI (December, 1933), 1073–83.

Foreman, Carolyn Thomas. "The Armstrongs of Indian Territory," *Chronicles of Oklahoma*, Vol. XXX (Autumn, 1952 and Winter, 1952–53), 292–308, 420–53.

———. "The Cherokee War Path," *Chronicles of Oklahoma*, Vol. IX (September, 1931), 233–63.

———. "Col. Jesse Henry Leavenworth," *Chronicles of Oklahoma*, Vol. XIII (March, 1935), 14–29.

———. "Colonel James B. Many," *Chronicles of Oklahoma*, Vol. XIX (June, 1941), 119–28.

———. "Colonel William Whistler," *Chronicles of Oklahoma*, Vol. XVIII (December, 1940), 313–27.

———. "General John Nicks and His Wife, Sarah Perkins Nicks," *Chronicles of Oklahoma*, Vol. VIII (December, 1930), 389–406.

———. "General Richard Barnes Mason," *Chronicles of Oklahoma*, Vol. XIX (March, 1941), 14–36.

———. "Lieutenant General Theophilus Hunter Holmes, C. S. A., Founder of Fort Holmes," *Chronicles of Oklahoma*, Vol. XXXV (Winter, 1957–58), 425–34.

———. "Military Discipline in Early Oklahoma," *Chronicles of Oklahoma*, Vol. VI (June, 1928), 140–44.

———. "Nathan Boone," *Chronicles of Oklahoma*, Vol. XIX (December, 1941), 322–47.

———. "Pierce Mason Butler," *Chronicles of Oklahoma*, Vol. XXX (Spring, 1952), 6–28.

Foreman, Grant. "Captain John Stuart's Sketch of the Indians," *Chronicles of Oklahoma*, Vol. XI (March, 1933), 667–72.

———. "River Navigation in the Early Southwest," *Mississippi Valley Historical Review*, Vol. XV (June, 1928), 34–55.

———. "Some New Light on Houston's Life Among the Cherokee Indians." *Chronicles of Oklahoma*, Vol. IX (June, 1931), 139–52.

Foster, William Omer. "The Career of Montfort Stokes in Oklahoma," *Chronicles of Oklahoma*, Vol. XVIII (March, 1940), 35–52.

Gallaher, Ruth A. "The Military-Indian Frontier 1830-1835," *Iowa Journal of History and Politics*, Vol. XV (July, 1917), 393–428.

Gardner, James Henry. "The Lost Captain: J. L. Dawson of Old Fort

Gibson." *Chronicles of Oklahoma*, Vol. XXI (September, 1943), 217-49.

———. "One Hundred Years Ago in the Region of Tulsa," *Chronicles of Oklahoma*, Vol. XI (June, 1933), 765-85.

Harris, Frank H. "Seneca Sub-Agency, 1832-38," *Chronicles of Oklahoma*, Vol. XLII (Summer, 1964), 75-94.

Haskett, James N. "The Final Chapter in the Story of the First Fort Smith," *Arkansas Historical Quarterly*, Vol. XXV (Autumn, 1966), 214-28.

Meserve, John B. "Chief Opothleyahola," *Chronicles of Oklahoma*, Vol. IX (December, 1931), 439-53.

———. "Governor Montfort Stokes," *Chronicles of Oklahoma*, Vol. XIII (September, 1935), 338-40.

———. "The Indian Removal Message of President Jackson," *Chronicles of Oklahoma*, Vol. XIII (March, 1935), 63-67.

Morrison, William B. "Fort Towson," *Chronicles of Oklahoma*, Vol. VIII (March, 1930), 226-32.

Perrine, Fred S. "Military Escorts on the Santa Fe Trail," *New Mexico Historical Review*, Vol. II (April, 1927 and July, 1927), 175-93, 269-304.

Rister, C. C. "A Federal Experiment in Southern Plains Indian Relations, 1835-1845," *Chronicles of Oklahoma*, Vol. XIV (December, 1936), 434-55.

Ryan, Harold W. "Matthew Arbuckle Comes to Fort Smith," *Arkansas Historical Quarterly*, Vol. XIX (Winter, 1960), 287-92.

Van Zandt, Howard F. "The History of Camp Holmes and Chouteau's Trading Post," *Chronicles of Oklahoma*, Vol. XIII (September, 1935), 316-40.

Watson, Richard L. "Congressional Attitudes Toward Military Preparedness, 1829-1835," *Mississippi Valley Historical Review*, Vol. XXXIV (March, 1948), 611-36.

Westbrook, Harriette Johnson. "The Chouteaus," *Chronicles of Oklahoma*, Vol. XI (June and September, 1933), 786-97, 942-66.

White, Lonnie J. "Arkansas Territorial Indian Affairs," *Arkansas Historical Quarterly*, Vol. XXI (Autumn, 1963), 193-212.

———. "James Miller: Arkansas' First Territorial Governor," *Arkansas Historical Quarterly*, Vol. XIX (Spring, 1960), 12-30.

Whitham, Louise Morse. "Early Times Along the Arkansas River," *Chronicles of Oklahoma*, Vol. XXIII (Spring, 1945), 26-29.

Worley, Ted R. "Arkansas and the 'Hostile' Indians 1835-1838," *Arkansas Historical Quarterly*, Vol. VI (Summer, 1947), 155-64.

Wright, Muriel H. "Early Navigation and Commerce Along the Arkansas and Red Rivers in Oklahoma," *Chronicles of Oklahoma*, Vol. VIII (March, 1930), 65-88.

———. "The Removal of the Choctaws to the Indian Territory, 1830–1833," *Chronicles of Oklahoma*, Vol. VI (June, 1928), 103–28.
Young, Otis E. "Military Protection of the Santa Fe Trail and Trade," *Missouri Historical Review*, Vol. XLIX (October, 1954), 19–32.
———. "The United States Mounted Ranger Battalion, 1832-1833," *Mississippi Valley Historical Review*. Vol. XLI (December, 1954), 453–70.

DISSERTATIONS

Gamble, Richard Dalzell. "Garrison Life at Frontier Military Posts, 1830–1860." Unpublished Ph.D. dissertation, University of Oklahoma, 1956.
Moulton, Gary Evan. "John Ross, Cherokee Chief." Unpublished Ph.D. dissertation, Oklahoma State University, 1974.

Index

Abbay, George B.: 106, 121, 133, 138
Act of Union: 200, 203–204, 250 n.45
Adams, John Quincy: 43, 51, 52, 56, 59–61
Adams-Onis Treaty: 69
Alabama: 160
Alamo: 88
Alligator (Seminole Chief): 176
Arapaho: 68, 171
Arbuckle, Matthew: 63, 81, 91–92, 103, 107, 142, 230 n.2, 232 n.22, 250 n.45; establishes post, 6, 29, 30–31, 55; arrives at Fort Smith, 19; role of in Osage-Cherokee rivalry, 20, 22–23, 25, 45–47, 49–54; comments on Osage attack on Barraque-Welborn party, 26–28, 41–42; and road building, 32–33; and post gardens, 35; and Santa Fe trade, 35–36; and whisky trade, 36–40; helps draft Osage constitution, 43–44; assists Creek exploring party, 56; visits immigrant settlements, 57; role of in dispute over Lovely's Purchase, 58–60; and disturbance along Red River, 63–65, 67, 70, 72, 74–75; condones intertribal conflict, 76; relationship of with Houston, 77, 79–81, 83–84; and renovation of Fort Gibson, 89–90; and Plains Indians disturbances 95–98, 100; and Mounted Rangers, 100, 102; and plan for frontier defense, 104, 106; administering justice, 110; and Stokes Commission, 112; leaves Fort Gibson 112–13; and rivalry with Leavenworth, 118–19; relinquishes command, 119–20; resumes command, 141; and Osage depredations, 143; plans council, 144; and meeting with Plains Indians, 145–48; tries to contact Kiowas, 149; responds to events in Texas, 151, 154, 156–57; and Creek immigration, 158–60; disciplines militiamen, 162; health problems of, 163; and instructions to Many, 164; defends location of Fort Gibson, 165–67, 169; and relations with Plains tribes, 170–73; responds to Osages, 174–75; and Seminoles, 176; and immigrant hostility, 177–78, 180–84; and involvement in Cherokee schism, 185–204; final report of, 204; departs, 205, 210; dies, 240 n.16
Arkansas: 36, 66, 70, 104, 109, 181–82; Cherokees accept tract in, 8; first territorial governor of, 13; military frontier of, 25, 63; whisky trade on frontier of, 37–38; and impact of Indian migration, 55–61; turbulence in southwestern part of, 68–69; and memorial of assembly, 74; and